CONTENTS

SUBMITTED MATERIAL

TIMBER SALVAGE SITUATION ON PUBLIC LANDS AFFECTED BY INSECTS, DISEASE AND FIRE

FRIDAY, FEBRUARY 10, 1995

HOUSE OF REPRESENTATIVES,
SUBCOMMITTEE ON RESOURCE CONSERVATION,
RESEARCH, AND FORESTRY,
COMMITTEE ON AGRICULTURE,
Washington, DC.

The subcommittee met, pursuant to call, at 10:05 a.m., in room 1324, Longworth House Office Building, Hon. Wayne Allard (chairman of the subcommittee) presiding.

STATEMENT OF HON. WAYNE ALLARD, A REPRESENTATIVE IN CONGRESS FROM THE STATE OF COLORADO

Mr. ALLARD. I am going to call the Agriculture Subcommittee on Resource Conservation, Research, and Forestry to order, and without objection, we will go ahead and proceed with the agricultural hearing. And we will allow the members of the Subcommittee from Resources to sit in and join us in the hearing process.

It is my hope that we can go ahead and move along with this hearing rather rapidly. We have a number of people who are here who have traveled all the way from the west coast, and you probably will find in visiting with them that it costs quite a bit to get here. Originally, we had an objection that was raised on the floor of having this with the Interior Committee so we are going to go ahead under an Agriculture Committee hearing.

I am glad to hear that because those individuals, like I mentioned earlier, did spend a lot of time to get here. I think it would really be a poor showing on our part if after they traveled all the way to get here that they couldn't be heard. So I am going to go ahead and make an opening statement, and then I will call on my colleague from the Resource Committee to make a comment for his subcommittee. Again, I would like to thank all of you for being here. I will make my remarks brief because I know we have a long hearing ahead of us. However, I want to state clearly that the forest's health is one of the top priorities of my subcommittee because of the devastation of last year's fires on local communities. The monetary costs these fires placed on Federal and local governments, the cost of the scenic value of our Federal lands, and, most importantly, the cost to the firefighters who lost their lives last year fighting these fires adds an element of urgency to act and act now.

Both the Resources Committee, the Agriculture Committee, and the Administration have an obligation to address this issue to avoid the reoccurrence of last year's devastation. To put in perspective how devastating these fires were last year, all we need to do is look at how much we spent on fire suppression in 1994. During last summer alone, we spent almost $1 billion, that is billion with a B, to fight these fires. During last August alone, we were spending $7.8 million a day. Certainly, the collective wisdom of our committees and the Administration can reach a solution that will stop this from ever happening again.

What truly disturbs me is the almost unanimous conclusion of forestry experts that the intensity of these fires are unparalleled. The report of the National Commission on Wildfire Disaster stated the problem clearly when they wrote, "Compared to historic fires, these wildfires attain intensities and impact levels that cause unnaturally altered soil, watershed, and plant conditions, adverse wildlife impacts, high levels of soil erosion, and runoff, and globally significant emissions of carbon and other greenhouse gases."

I think everyone involved in this issue agrees on the large scope of the problem. Now, we need to come to agreement on the solution. It seems to me that our first priority should be to remove as much dead timber from last year's fires in order to remove fuel loads that could make this year's fires more intense. Removing dead timber caused by last year's fires would not only decrease the intensity of last year's fires but would also provide jobs for beleaguered timber communities and provide revenues for the Treasury.

The Forest Service and the Bureau of Land Management now need to aggressively assess where salvage timber is located. After that is taken care of, all of us then need to determine a better way to manage Federal lands to preserve them for the future, prevent future forest fire disasters, and maintain a healthy economy for timber-reliant communities.

I would now like to recognize the ranking member of my subcommittee, Tim Johnson of South Dakota, for an opening statement, and then I will recognize the Chairman of the subcommittee.

Mr. JOHNSON. Thank you, Mr. Chairman. I welcome this opportunity to continue the issue of salvage sales and forest health review. I commend the actions of the Administration that have been taken to react to the tremendous number of fires that occurred in 1994 and the lingering effects of the previous year's fires as well. The issue of what to do with areas that have been affected by fire is not a simple one, and as I am certain we will hear from witnesses today, there are a great many issues involved in the salvage of the timber in those areas.

I am certain that Mr. Thomas will continue to do all that he can within the law to help ensure the economic viability of the communities affected and the health of the forests. I am sure that the cooperation of the other agencies involved will also be a topic of discussion today.

It is my hope that we will not see another fire season like we did last year, one of the most deadly and costly on record, so the debate surrounding the success or necessity of salvage sales will be reasoned and muted. If we are fortunate enough to see that happen, we can focus continuing shrinking funds in the Forest Service budget towards proactive forest health initiatives. And with that, I yield back my time, Mr. Chairman.

Mr. ALLARD. I would now like to go ahead and recognize the Chairman of the Subcommittee on National Parks, Forests & Lands from the Committee on Resources. Congressman Hansen.

Mr. HANSEN. Thank you, Mr. Chairman, and I want to especially thank you for allowing members of our committee to sit with you at your hearing today, and I thank you for allowing us to do that. I appreciate the hard work that has gone into getting this subject before your committee in such a rapid manner, and we certainly hope to have more lead time in the future with these type of hearings.

The reason we are having such a large and important hearing only six weeks into this session is because this is an emergency situation that requires this body to act in a swift and effective manner. Our national forest lands are in a crisis. Our current management practices are leading to the destruction of millions of acres of timber that will not be reclaimed for years.

During the 1994 fire season, this nation lost over four million acres of timberland to fire. Not only did we lose millions of dollars of economic opportunity to the dying timber communities throughout the west, we experienced the loss of 33 lives fighting these fires. Trees can be replaced, and lives cannot. At the rate we are headed, we will not replace our dying national forests during most of our lifetimes.

In many of our forests, we are experiencing negative growth rates. Yes, some forests are dying faster than they are growing. This means fire. No one knows when, but Mother Nature has a way of cleaning up her forests and that is through fire. Fire is but evidence of the more global problem of forest health. This hearing is about the condition of our forests, how they got this way, and, more importantly, what we are going to do about it.

Man has the ability to manage these forests, and we must do it in a proactive way. These forests have been managed for hundreds of years even before Europeans came to this land, and there is no going back to a natural state. It is irresponsible for the agencies and this body to sit back in paralysis while our forests die and go up in flames. We must act responsibly and swiftly, and this hearing is the first step in the process. I look forward to the testimony and thank the witnesses for being here, and thank you, Mr. Chairman, for allowing me to give an opening remark.

Mr. ALLARD. I would also now like to recognize the ranking member on the Subcommittee on National Parks, Forests & Lands, Congressman Richardson.

Mr. RICHARDSON. Thank you very much, Mr. Chairman. Mr. Chairman, I must question why with barely a week's notice the subcommittee felt it necessary to rush to hold this oversight hearing today. While the committee rules provide that only one week's notice has to be given on a hearing, I hope and expect that this will not be the normal practice.

Unfortunately, like the recent full committee Wolf Reintroduction hearing, today's hearing was announced on short notice. This compressed time frame has made it extremely difficult for members and the public to adequately prepare and participate in the hearing. Members on our side of the aisle recognize the importance of this issue, of fire, forest health and salvage issues. Committees on Natural Resources and Agriculture held a joint hearing last fall on these very issues, and this rush to act today is both unnecessary and, in my judgment, counterproductive. I note that the subcommittee is not scheduled to meet next week. Why this hearing could not have been next week instead of being rushed forward today escapes me.

Mr. Chairman, in addition, this hearing has been irregular from the start. When first announced, it was listed as an oversight hearing on forest health and emergency salvage sales. Two days later, without a word to us, it was announced it is now a joint oversight hearing on the timber salvage situation in national forest and BLM lands. Because of the shortened time frame, witnesses found it impossible to comply with committee rules on the submittal of testimony. Most testimony arrived only last night.

I must especially express my concern about the witness list. After repeated inquiries, Democrats were only able to get a witness list at 5 p.m. last night. It was only then that we learned that the subcommittee had scheduled 24 witnesses, an extraordinary number that combined with a large membership of the two committees and the House floor schedule today will make it difficult to have any meaningful questioning of witnesses.

Further, of the 24 witnesses today, only four are here at the request of members from our side of the aisle. You might say that is all we asked for. In a normal hearing, that would likely be true. However, if we had known that the majority was going to stack the witness list, we would have sought a more equitable distribution of witnesses.

In addition, Mr. Chairman, I am concerned that even though the committee rules provide that after the announcement of a hearing to the extent practicable, the committee shall make available immediately to all members of the committee a concise summary of the subject matter under consideration. That was not done here. In fact, the longstanding subcommittee practice of providing background information at a hearing for all members has been abandoned.

Mr. Chairman, Democrats want to meaningfully participate in subcommittee hearings. However, the problems I have outlined have hindered such participation and compromise this hearing. This shouldn't need be the case. With adequate notice and preparation, we can hold substantive hearings, and I particularly regret making this statement because I have two friends that will be testifying shortly, Senator Burns and Congressman Herger.

And I will say to Chairman Hansen, up to now, your conduct has been one of cooperation, one of working with us, and I must say that many on our side, certainly on the natural resources side, feel very strongly about this, that this cannot continue if we are going to engage in a cooperative, bipartisan fashion to deal with a problem that is bipartisan. And if the gentleman would like, I will yield to either Chair or——

Mr. ALLARD. Well, let me just respond to the gentleman from New Mexico. It is unfortunate that the circumstances that evolved did evolve up to this point. We have a very congenial relationship as far as the Agriculture Committee, and we try and work together, and I just felt it was imperative that we move ahead with this hearing since we have had people that have spent their time and resources to be here all the way from the West Coast. And, as you know, that is not an inexpensive trip to be made.

We are doing everything we can to cater to those who are being impacted. For far too many years, this operation has catered to people within the beltway, and I think we need to reach out into grassroots America. I appreciate your being here on the Agriculture Committee as a guest, and I understand, some of the problems that you may have. But I would hope that we could work together in a much more bipartisan way that recognizes the fact that we do have some real problems in managing our country's forests, and we need to get to those problems instead of bickering among our committees here in the Congress. Since you yielded some of your time to Congressman Hansen, let me give him just a moment or two, and then we will proceed with the hearing.

Mr. HANSEN. Like Chairman Allard pointed out, we do want to work in a cooperative way. We do feel there is an emergency situation, and we do feel the witnesses are here. They are prepared. It is like we only received the information from the minority side last night which could have come much sooner because this was aware to everyone, but it is water under the bridge. I think the issue overpowers the parliamentary games or procedure, and so as far as I am concerned, this issue is extremely important to all of us. And I think it is very important that we move ahead on this, and if we have offended the minority side, it wasn't intentional, and we surely don't intend to do that. We want to work with you in harmony as we have thus far, and we want to in the future. So I think this hearing though is overpowering and extremely important to us so I hope we could go ahead and all of us gain the benefits which we expect to gain from the witnesses we have today.

Mr. RICHARDSON. Mr. Chairman, if I could just——

Mr. ALLARD. We do need to get on with the hearing, but I will give you one minute.

Mr. RICHARDSON. Mr. Chairman, again, I want to stress that we are not talking about the substance of this issue. We are talking about procedures; the fact that background memos, notice, witness lists should be given with adequate time. I think that is only fair to ask. This is a rule adopted by this committee. The committee is controlled by the majority, and I appreciate Chairman Hansen's words because I know he is working hard to work with us.

But you have many members of the minority staff and minority membership on our subcommittee very upset. We recognize these people have come from a long distance, and I respect that too. But we could have held this hearing next week with adequate preparation, and, again, Mr. Chairman, I hope that this does not happen again.

Mr. ALLARD. Is there anybody else on the committee that feels compelled to make a comment or two? Okay. Let us go ahead and proceed with our witnesses. We have on the first panel Senator Burns from Montana, and we had slated on there to have Senator Gorton, but I guess he is not with us. And we have got Congressman Wally Herger from California, and Congressman Riggs was slated to be on, but I guess he is not with us. So let me start with Senator Conrad Burns from Montana, and, Senator, it is great to have you with us this morning and please share some of your thoughts with us, if you would.

STATEMENT OF SENATOR CONRAD BURNS, A SENATOR FROM THE STATE OF MONTANA

Senator BURNS. I want to first of all thank you, both Chairmen of these very important subcommittees here on the House side, for holding what I think are very important time-sensitive hearings about this forest help and timber salvage. I would ask unanimous consent that my full statement be in the record as given.

Mr. ALLARD. Without objection.

Senator BURNS. And I will try to pull this thing together a little bit. Salvage is of great importance to my state of Montana, but not only to us but I think to the West and to all the people who receive benefits of the resources of the forest system. Forest health management and the resolution of timber salvage question is a top priority to all the people in this land who use and enjoy the forest, not only for the resources but also for the pleasure.

In recent years, the health of the forests have declined dramatically due to the action and inaction of some of the managing agencies. Our forests have reached a point in time where there are now more trees per acre than even in presettlement times. The degree of overpopulation in the forests have created overaged, insect, and disease-infected forests, the perfect conditions for disaster. And, once again, that disaster points to the heart of our problem and what we are talking about in this committee.

This past summer, the western forests of our country went through a historic period. Throughout the entire region fires burned at a rate that has never been seen in prior times, maybe with the exception in Montana to 1988. From the early spring fire seasons in the southwest to the late summer and fall fire seasons in the Northwest, we saw those fires ravage our national forest lands; fires, which in any other year would have been normal, grew way beyond the imagination due in part to the neglect of Federal land management agencies and some of that caused by the laws that are in place now; fires that destroyed countless acres of prime timber and threatened the very lives and, of course, did take lives as was noted by the Chairman of the Subcommittee on Natural Resources. Property and livelihoods of our fellow citizens were at risk.

Under the current laws of this nation, the Federal land managers must complete an exhaustive and complicated process to thin and salvage the residue of the damaged areas. Although many of these laws were written to protect the environment, they have been used and abused way beyond the scope of intent. It has reached a point where the people most affected by the impact of the diminished forest health are at the mercy of people thousands of miles away from that neighborhood with no vested interest in the land or the forest.

Last year, I called upon the managers of the U.S. Forest Service to answer some questions about the condition of the forests in northern Idaho and northwestern Montana. Severe and dangerous undergrowth had infested the forests, and a disaster of major proportions was on the horizon. Yellow and orange trees had overwhelmed the natural green forest, the results of disease and insect infestation. That disaster did occur, and today the forest in that area is black, the result of tragic fires this summer.

There continues to be thousands of board feet of salvage timber waiting to be removed. Again, Federal agencies and the constraints of technical reviews have jeopardized the future of salvage material. Using the current standards, it will be halfway through 1996 before the forest managers will be able to open these lands for the salvage sale process. By that time, the timber for salvage will be unacceptable.

I am committed to the future health of the American forests. Late in January, I placed in the Congressional Record a report requested by the Forest Service regarding the plans to deal with the western forest health. Phase one of the report was completed and offered specific suggestions for solutions to the problem that was found in western forests. However, after the review within the Department, phase two was instituted which does nothing to answer the questions of forest health and denies that problem even exists. I personally wonder why actions of this nature occur. When the field personnel name and prepare a course of action to address the problem of forest health, why does the staff, miles away from the problem, completely rewrite a document to portray a healthy and vital environment on the public lands of this country. I have worked with Senator Craig of Idaho. We have introduced legislation just yesterday to declare certain areas designated as emergency and high-risk areas so that we can get on with the reforestation and restoration of our forests.

And I will now just go from here, but, Mr. Chairman, thank you for this opportunity. I feel very strongly about this. We have a situation and we were told and it didn't take a rocket scientist, it didn't take a biologist, it didn't take a botanist, it didn't take anybody to walk through the Yak—I wish I would have had my big pictures with me today—and see the disease and dying trees allowed to accumulate and the biomass that accumulated on the floor of those forests. And it only took one lightning strike—one. And we had the warnings of that over two or three years. Last year dry conditions; drought conditions; it happened and we burnt.

Now, it doesn't take very smart people to try to remedy that situation, and I go back to the old story about the preacher who came out and called on the rancher, and the old preacher says, "It is a nice looking ranch you and the Lord has got here," and the old rancher said, "Yep. You should have seen it when the Lord had it by himself."

And I go right back that sometimes we have to help Mother Nature just a little bit for the prevention of some of these very disastrous things that can happen to our communities. The social and the economic fiber of those communities depend on the resources of those forests, and letting them burn is just absolutely a sin to this land, and it is a sin to people who have spent their whole life in resource development, resource management, and resource conservation.

And I thank the Chairman. Thank you very much for considering this, and thanks for the joint meeting because I don't think even as in your body as in our body the committees talk to each other as much as they should. Thank you very much.

[Statement of Senator Burns follows:]

REMARKS OF SENATOR CONRAD BURNS
JOINT HOUSE SUBCOMMITTEE HEARING ON
FOREST HEALTH AND TIMBER SALVAGE SALES
FEBRUARY 10, 1995

I would like to thank the chairmen of the Subcommittee on Resource Conservation, Research and Forestry, and the Subcommittee on National Parks, Forests and Lands, for holding this very important and time sensitive hearing on the issues of Forest Health and timber salvage. This is an issue of great importance not only to my state of Montana, but to the west and the citizens of the United States. Proper forest health management and the resolution of the timber salvage question are a top priority to the all the people of this land that use and enjoy the forests, not only for the resources, but also pleasure.

In recent years the health of forests have declined dramatically due to action and inaction of the managing agencies. Our forests have reached a point in time where there are now more trees per acre, than even in pre—settlement times. The degree of overpopulation in the the forests have created over—aged, insect and disease infected forests. The perfect conditions for disaster to once again strike at the heart of our public lands.

This past summer the western forests of our country went through a historic period, throughout the entire region fires burned at a rate which had never been seen in prior times, with the exception of 1988. From the early spring fire season in the southwest to the late summer and fall fire seasons in the northwest, we saw fires ravage our national forest lands. Fires, which in any other year, would have been normal grew beyond imagination due in part, to the neglect of the federal land management agencies. Fires that destroyed countless acres of prime timber and threatened the very lives, property and livelihoods of our fellow citizens.

Under the current laws of this nation, the federal land managers must complete an exhaustive and complicated process to thin and salvage the residue of the damaged areas. Although many of these laws were written to protect the environment, they have been used and abused way beyond the scope of intent. It has reached a point where the people most effected by the impact of the diminished forest health are at the mercy of people thousands of miles away with no vested interested in the land or forest.

Last year I called upon the managers of the U.S. Forest Service to answer questions about the condition of forests in northern Idaho and Northwestern Montana.

Severe and dangerous undergrowth had infested forests, and a disaster of major proportions was on the horizon. Yellow, and orange trees had overwhelmed the natural green of the forest, the results of disease and insect infestation. That disaster did occur and today the forest in that area is black, the result of the tragic fires of the summer. There continues to be thousands of board feet of salvage timber waiting to be removed. Again federal agencies and the constraints of technical reviews have jeopardized the future of salvage material. Using the current standards it will be half way into 1996, before the forest managers will be able to open these lands to the salvage sale process. By that time the timber for salvage will be unacceptable.

I am committed to the future health of the American forests. Late in January, I placed into the Congressional Record a report requested by the Forest

Service regarding the plans to deal with the Western Forest Health. Phase one of the report was completed and offered specific suggestions for solutions to the problems found in western forests. However after review within the department, phase two was instituted which does nothing to answer the questions of forest health, and denies that the problem exists. I personally wonder, why actions of this nature occur. When the field personnel, name and prepare a course of action to address the problem of forest health, why does the staff miles away from the problem completely rewrite a document to portray a healthy and vital environment on the public lands of this country.

In addition I have worked with Senator Craig of Idaho, to introduce legislation in the Senate to declare certain areas for designation as 'emergency' and 'high risk' for the purpose of forest health protection and restoration. I will continue to work with Senator Craig and members of both the Agriculture Committee and as a member of the Energy and Natural Resources Committee to pass this legislation and move it over here for your approval. It is my hope that a bill of this importance could be passed out of Congress this year and become law before it is too late.

As I stated in my introduction, this is an issue of extreme importance to the forests and citizens of this land. Forest health and salvage is a time sensitive matter, for if this issue is not addressed soon, the small window of opportunity we have to heal our land and our forests will close, and we will miss the chance to provide healthy and productive lands for future generations.

I would like to thank the members of this committee for the opportunity to share my outlook on forest health and timber salvage with you. This is an issue important enough for us to work together on and I look forward to working with you to work for the health of our national forests and public lands.

Thank you for allowing me to testify this morning.

Mr. ALLARD. Thank you for your comments, and while I think about it, I am going to request unanimous consent that members be allowed to submit their statements into the record and the same with the witnesses if you have an additional extension of remarks, and then call on Congressman Wally Herger, the gentleman from California.

STATEMENT OF HON. WALLY HERGER, A REPRESENTATIVE IN CONGRESS FROM THE STATE OF CALIFORNIA

Mr. HERGER. Thank you very much, Chairman Allard, Chairman Hansen, members of the respective committees for this opportunity to testify before you on this dire emergency within our western states.

Last year, fires consumed over 2 million acres of forests in the northwest United States. Over 375,000 acres were in my own home state of California. The economic cost of fighting these fires was staggering. Last year, U.S. taxpayers paid nearly $1 billion to fight wildfires. Added to this tremendous cost were the losses suffered by hundreds of fire victims, many of whom helplessly watched fire destroy their homes, property, and livelihood.

Even more devastating, however, was the loss of human life. In Colorado, 14 brave firefighters lost their lives battling wildfires in that state. These tragedies will occur again in 1995 unless immediately emergency measures are taken by this Congress to remove the danger of wildfire. The single greatest contributor to wildfire is the epidemic of dead and dying trees in our forests. I have forests in my district with as much as 60 to 70 percent dead and dying timber. Dead and dying timber in the Lassen National Forest totaled over 1/2 billion board feet. These trees turn the forest into a tinder box ready to ignite.

In order to avoid repeated catastrophe in coming years, we must immediately pass emergency timber salvage legislation that will provide for the removal of these dead and dying trees. Such legislation would have at least three positive effects. First, it would preserve our forests by calling for the immediate removal of natural fuels.

Second, it would provide much needed economic relief to our beleaguered timber-dependent communities. In my district alone, 27 mills have closed in recent years. Third, it would return revenue to the Federal treasury. At present, we have enough salvageable timber in our country to generate hundreds of millions of dollars in net revenues to the United States Government.

Yet, in order to have the desired effect, to remove the dangerous levels of natural fuels in our forests, any piece of legislation we pass must meet a number of essential criteria. I suggest four. First, the legislation must be passed quickly. Due to the severe Federal restrictions on timber harvests, the number of timber purchasers in our country is dwindling. In the Klamath province of my district, the number of purchasers with outstanding harvest contracts has been reduced from 30 in the mid-1980's to only four in 1995. If legislation is not passed quickly, there is a good chance there will not be enough contractors around to harvest the timber.

Second, it must cover a specific time period. Dead timber in my district begins to significantly lose its economic value after only one year. At the end of two years, it is worthless. This rate is accelerated in the southern states with more humid climates. The legislation must provide a timber harvest plan that will be completed within two years.

Third, specific timber harvest levels must be targeted to ensure that a significant amount of dead and dying timber is removed from our forests. Fourth, it must contain mechanisms for streamlining the environmental documentation process and eliminating protracted litigation. Presently, environmental analyses and litigation can take years to complete. We don't have years. We have months. Our legislation must accommodate this fact.

In conclusion, I thank this committee again for its attention to the crisis in our national forests. I respectfully urge each member of either committee represented here today to seriously consider these suggestions and then pursue the emergency measures necessary to save our forests and our timber-dependent communities from annihilation. Thank you.

[Statement of Mr. Herger follows:]

TESTIMONY BEFORE JOINT COMMITTEE HEARING ON TIMBER SALVAGE

STATEMENT OF CONGRESSMAN WALLY HERGER

* Thank you, Mr. Chairman Hansen and Mr. Chairman Allard and members of your respective committees for this opportunity to testify.

* I wish to commend this body for recognizing the state of emergency that exists in our U.S. forests.

* Last year fires consumed over 2 million acres of forest in the northwest United States. Over 375,000 of these acres were in my state of California.

* The economic cost of fighting these fires was staggering. Last year U.S. taxpayers paid nearly $1 billion to fight wildfires. Added to this tremendous cost were the losses suffered by hundreds of fire victims, many of whom helplessly watched fire destroy their homes, property and livelihoods.

* Even more devastating, however, was the loss of human life. In Colorado, 14 brave fire fighters lost their lives battling wildfires in that state.

* These tragedies will occur again in 1995 unless immediate emergency measures are taken by this Congress to remove the danger of wildfire.

* The single greatest contributor to wildfire is the epidemic of dead and dying trees in our forests. I have forests in my district with as much as 60% - 70% dead and dying timber. Dead and dying timber in the Lassen National Forest totals over 1/2 billion board feet. These trees turn the forest into a tinder box ready to ignite.

* In order to avoid repeated catastrophe in the coming year, we must immediately pass emergency timber salvage legislation that will provide for the removal of these dead and dying trees.

* Such legislation would have at least three positive effects.

* First, it would preserve our forests by calling for the immediate removal of natural fuels.

* Second, it would provide much needed economic relief to our beleaguered timber-dependent communities. In my district alone 27 mills have closed in recent years.

* Third, it would return revenue to the federal treasury. At present, we have enough salvageable timber in our country to generate hundreds of millions of dollars in net revenues for the United States government.

* Yet, in order to have the desired effect - to remove the dangerous levels of natural fuels in our forests, any piece of legislation we pass must meet a number of

essential criteria. I suggest four:

* First, the legislation must be passed quickly. Due to severe federal restrictions on timber harvests, the number of timber purchasers in our country is dwindling. In the Klamath province of my district the number of purchasers with outstanding harvest contracts has been reduced from 30 in the mid 1980's to 4 in 1995. If legislation is not passed quickly, there is a good chance that there will not be enough contractors around to harvest the timber.

* Second, it must cover a specific time period. Dead timber in my district begins to significantly lose its economic value after one year. At the end of two years, it is worthless. This rate is accelerated in southern states with more humid climates. The legislation must provide a timber harvest plan that will be completed within two years.

* Third, specific timber harvest levels must be targeted

to ensure that a sufficient amount of dead and dying timber is removed from our forests.

* Fourth, it must contain mechanisms for streamlining the environmental documentation process and eliminating protracted litigation. Presently environmental analyses and litigation can take years to complete. We don't have years. We have months. Our legislation must accommodate this fact.

* In conclusion, I thank this body again for its attention to the crisis in our national forests. I respectfully urge each member of either committee represented hear today to seriously consider my suggestions and then pursue the emergency measures necessary to save our forests and our timber-dependent communities from annihilation. Thank you.

TIMBSALV.PTS

Mr. ALLARD. I thank the gentleman from California for his testimony. I don't have any questions. Does the ranking member on Agriculture have any questions? The Chairman from Resources have any questions?

Mr. HANSEN. I have no questions.

Mr. ALLARD. Okay. Any questions from committee members?

Mrs. CHENOWETH. Mr. Chairman, I have some questions.

Mr. ALLARD. Congresswoman Chenoweth.

Mrs. CHENOWETH. Congressman Herger, I really appreciate your testimony. And being a representative from California and having served in the last term of Congress, isn't it true that we lost 33 lives fighting fire last year? According to my figures, that is a fact, that we lost 33 lives in fighting fire last year.

Mr. HERGER. That is correct, and in one fire alone one emergency situation where the fires came over the hill we lost 14 firefighters just in one instance. And, of course, this is something that can happen at anytime; it is very hazardous fighting fires.

And the tragedy, as you know so well, is that we can do something about it. We can identify these areas that are most susceptible to burn. We can go in and remove those dead and dying trees before they create the fire. And I might mention as you know, the bark beetles that move into these dead trees not only are eating up these dead trees but are going out and killing otherwise healthy trees that would have survived.

Mrs. CHENOWETH. Mr. Chairman and Mr. Herger, is it not true that there were a number of homes that were lost to fire in your state last year? Now, they were not on public land. They were on private land. Right?

Mr. HERGER. That is correct. Several hundred homes burned as well.

Mrs. CHENOWETH. And is it not true that like the management of the understory and the brush growth down there in California due to the Endangered Species Act we are also seeing a paralysis of management on our public lands as well? Is that not true?

Mr. HERGER. That is absolutely correct. As a matter of fact, we even have government agencies at odds with each other. We have fire departments that are saying we need to go in and clear out brush behind people's homes, and yet in one instance in my state, we had a supposedly endangered kangaroo rat that the environmentalists would not allow them to clear out this brush, and we did have a fire that did go through and destroyed several hundred homes just in this last year.

Mrs. CHENOWETH. So, Mr. Chairman and Mr. Herger, one of the reasons that we are seeing the lack of management and good sustainable resource management on our public lands is because of the Endangered Species Act?

Mr. HERGER. There isn't any doubt about that, and I certainly feel, and many of us do, that preserving our environment and preserving our endangered species and yet protecting property and protecting our forests are not mutually exclusive, but yet the way the Endangered Species Act is being interpreted, it would appear that way. We are losing property. We are losing lives because of an Endangered Species Act that has gone amuck, and it needs some common sense instilled into it.

Mrs. CHENOWETH. Mr. Chairman and Mr. Herger, last year this Congress responded to the California earthquake disaster very quickly, didn't it?

Mr. HERGER. Yes, it did.

Mrs. CHENOWETH. Mr. Herger, how many lives were lost in the California earthquake?

Mr. HERGER. I don't have the number, but there were several lives that were lost—in the dozens.

Mrs. CHENOWETH. So was it close to, say, 33 or around that number? A life is a life. I just have to say that I really appreciate your testimony, and I just have to say in response to Mr. Richardson that his is an emergency not unlike other natural emergencies that have occurred. And I appreciate you for bringing that out in your testimony, and I appreciate these committee Chairmen for allowing us to have this committee hearing at this time. Thank you, Mr. Herger.

[Statement of Mrs. Chenoweth follows:]

HELEN CHENOWETH
1ST DISTRICT, IDAHO

Congress of the United States
House of Representatives
Washington, DC 20515-1201

STATEMENT OF THE HONORABLE HELEN CHENOWETH BEFORE THE HOUSE RESOURCES SUBCOMMITTEE ON PARKS, FORESTS AND LANDS
FEBRUARY 10, 1995

MR. CHAIRMAN, IDAHO IS IN A STATE OF CRISIS. NINE YEARS OF DROUGHT AND CATASTROPHIC WILDFIRES HAVE LEFT IDAHO FORESTS GASPING FOR LIFE. THE NATIONAL FOREST SERVICE AND BUREAU OF LAND MANAGEMENT HAVE FAILED TO MEET THEIR RESPONSIBILITY OF MAINTAINING THE HEALTH OF THESE FORESTS AND APPLYING MEASURES THAT WOULD LESSENED THE INTENSITY OF DAMAGE FROM NATURAL DISASTERS.

I INTEND TO DO EVERYTHING IN MY POWER TO HELP SPEED THE REMOVAL OF DEAD AND DYING TREES FROM THE RAVAGED FORESTS. IF THIS HARVEST DOES NOT BEGIN BY THIS SUMMER, THE LANDSCAPE WILL CONTINUE TO ERODE TOP SOIL INTO MOUNTAIN STREAMS TO THE POINT THAT CRITICAL SPAWNING GROUNDS FOR SALMON, STEELHEAD AND TROUT WILL BE SEVERELY DAMAGED.

MY GREATEST CONCERN, HOWEVER, IS THE SAFETY AND LIVELIHOOD OF THE RURAL COMMUNITIES NEAR THE WILDFIRE SITES. IF THE DEAD AND DYING TIMBER IS NOT REMOVED IMMEDIATELY, IT WILL BECOME THE FUEL TO FEED THE NEXT ROUND OF WILDFIRES. IN ADDITION, THE PROHIBITION OF HARVESTING OF DECAYING FOREST HAS COST THOUSANDS OF JOBS, AS WELL AS MILLIONS OF DOLLARS IN LOST REVENUE TO THE COMMUNITIES AND FEDERAL TREASURY -- THE COMMERCIAL VALUE OF THE BURNED PINE DETERIORATES EVERY DAY THAT IT IS LEFT TO ERODE UNHARVESTED.

AT THIS POINT, MILLIONS OF ACRES OF RENEWABLE RESOURCES HAVE BEEN DESTROYED. WHILE THESE FIRES WERE CAUSED BY FORCES OF NATURE, PROPER MANAGEMENT OF OUR FORESTS COULD HAVE PREVENTED THE FIRES FROM CAUSING AS MUCH DEVASTATION AS THEY DID. UNUSUALLY HEAVY STANDS OF DEAD AND DYING, DISEASE AND INSECT-INFESTED TIMBER THAT SHOULD HAVE BEEN REMOVED FROM THESE FORESTS WAS LEFT TO FEED THE FIRES.

I IMPLORE THE COMMITTEE TODAY TO WORK WITH ME ON EMERGENCY LEGISLATION THAT WILL ALLOW FOR IMMEDIATE SALVAGE OF THIS TIMBER AND HELP RESTORE THE HEALTH OF OUR FORESTS. THE FEDERAL AGENCIES WHICH SHOULD HAVE USED PREVENTATIVE MAINTENANCE TO CONTROL FOR SUCH SITUATIONS HAVE ABANDONED THE PRINCIPLES ON WHICH PRESIDENT THEODORE ROOSEVELT ESTABLISHED THE NATIONAL FOREST SYSTEM. WE NEED NOW TO PLACE THE MANAGEMENT OF OUR NATURAL RESOURCES BACK ON THEIR INTENDED COURSE.

Mr. HERGER. Well, thank you, Mrs. Chenoweth. Thank you for your question. Again, I thank the committee.

Mr. ALLARD. I will now recognize the gentleman from California, Mr. Doolittle.

Mr. DOOLITTLE. Thank you. Mr. Herger, you testified in your district alone 27 mills have closed in recent years?

Mr. HERGER. That is correct.

Mr. DOOLITTLE. Would you venture a guess as to how many mills are still functioning in your district? I am just curious. Twenty-seven out of roughly how many do you think it might be?

Mr. HERGER. Over half of the mills in our district have closed, and the other half are in danger of closing because of lack of supply. And this is at a time when we are growing more timber. Actually, if we could just harvest the dead and dying trees that we have in our forests, we would have enough to keep our mills open. We are not even allowed to do that because, again, of the extreme policies, not common sense policies, of environmentalists.

And I like to include myself as an environmentalist, a third generation rancher, one living on the land, but because of extreme measures we were unable to manage well and be able to keep our mills open and provide ourselves with the paper products that our nation needs.

Mr. DOOLITTLE. You, no doubt, have looked at Option 9 advanced by the Clinton Administration as the solution to our problems in the forests. I wonder if you have an opinion as to how that, were it to be fully implemented, would impact your district?

Mr. HERGER. Well, it would be disastrous and is disastrous for our district. It does virtually nothing to, again, either eliminate the dead and dying trees that will eventually destroy our forests completely or supply even the minimum amount of timber that we need to keep our forests going. But even Option 9 is not being enforced. We are not even seeing the very minimal amounts that were set up in Option 9 being implemented at this time.

Mr. DOOLITTLE. Thank you.

Mr. HERGER. You are welcome.

Mr. ALLARD. I recognize the gentlelady from Washington.

Mrs. SMITH. Thank you. I sat here for a while and listened to some of the discussion about the hearing and why it is so quick, and I was watching your eyes, Wally, because I think you have the same thing happening that I do. I am going to go home and drive through an area that is burnt, but you used the word consumed. Our burned-out area around Wenatchee is not consumed. In fact, it is singed.

And it is an emergency for us to get those trees down to be able to use those to fuel our mills, and I can tell you that since 1989, the Pacific Northwest has lost over 51 mills that I can see. And I have lost some mills in Vancouver, Longview, Centralia, Olympia, and I can just keep going—in my area. And we are in the thousands and thousands of jobs lost.

But I have something else that I was thinking as I was looking at how to get the timber supply up, and, by the way, five percent is not very much, and that is what it looks to me like we are at. Do you have blown-down timber in your area? I have got areas that have blow-downs. I mean, we are going to talk about millions of board feet, but it is enough to keep some of my smaller mills alive and my people eating. Is that an issue that you have had in your area and that you have looked to address?

Mr. HERGER. Well, it has particularly lately. With the flooding and the storms that we have had just in the last month or two in California, six of my ten counties have been declared disaster counties because of flooding. But part of the winds that were associated with this flooding in our timber areas, there are areas that have as much as 20 percent of the trees blown down.

So, yes, this is, particularly with this last storm, a concern and is one of the natural processes that takes place within the forests, and it is one other way that we have dead and dying trees that, again, if this is not taken out—and as the gentlelady from Washington is aware of, through history we would have occasional fires that would come through.

Since for the last 60 years Smoky the Bear, we have eliminated fires, and now we have this tremendous, unnatural buildup of fire material there that if it is not removed, we do go in and not only have fires, but, as you mentioned, we completely destroy the land where we cannot even grow trees again. And in the area just north of Lake Tahoe, just north of Truckee in my district, a fire we had just this last summer charred the land so intensely that we will not be able to grow trees there for some years to come. So this is a severe situation, an emergency.

It is too bad the gentleman from New Mexico left who had the complaints of this hearing, but I want to thank this committee. We have not been able to have these hearings in the prior eight years I have been here, and I thank you for having them today to bring out just how serious an emergency this is. It affects not just those of us who live in our timber areas, but the entire nation that is dependent on wood products.

Mrs. SMITH. Thank you, Mr. Chairman. I just wanted to make a comment. It appears to me that blow-down is an issue. I mean, it would help me, and I don't see any way to deal with this so I would be interested in finding a way to deal with that so that we don't get sued every time we have to go in and clean out something after a storm or a flood.

Mr. ALLARD. I thank the gentlelady for her remarks. I would like to proceed on to the first panel. Do we have anybody here that really feels that they need to ask any further questions of Congressman Herger? Congressman Lewis.

Mr. LEWIS. Yes. Mr. Herger, it seems to me that the regulations that are intended to protect the species that are considered to be endangered are actually causing more harm because these forests are being burned and the habitat that they survive in is being eliminated because of the regulations that are in place. Is that a fair assumption?

Mr. HERGER. Well, that is absolutely correct. And these forests that, again, if you fly over, there isn't anything left because they have burned so completely. It is very difficult for the northern spotted owl to live where there isn't anything. So what you are saying is exactly the case and would become even more so the case as time goes on unless we get in and in an intelligent way using modern science begin to eliminate these problems that are taking place.

Mr. LEWIS. Thank you.

Mr. ALLARD. Mr. Cooley.

Mr. COOLEY. Thank you, Mr. Chairman. Congressman Herger, in your area, this is not the first time you have had a fire in your district. Is that correct?

Mr. HERGER. That is correct. We had 475,000 acres burned in 1987. Each year, we have at least several hundred thousand acres burning over the last eight years.

Mr. COOLEY. Could you give this committee sort of a summary of what has occurred since 1987 when you had the fire as far as what work has been done by the Forest Service or any government agencies to reenergize those past burns?

Mr. HERGER. Well, the goal is that they go in when there is a burn; they go in and replant.

Mr. COOLEY. Has that been accomplished?

Mr. HERGER. That has not been accomplished.

Mr. COOLEY. Do you have any idea, even though we have a burn and we are not doing anything about salvage, why we are not going back on this potential production land that belongs to all of us and not replanting it so we can have a sustainable yield? Do you have any idea of why that is not occurring?

Mr. HERGER. Well, there are several reasons. One is funding. Even though our forests have historically produced a net of several hundred million dollars per year for the revenues of the Federal Government, there have not been adequate dollars put into the budget to be able to carry this out. People that are able to do this are being laid off. They are the ones that are being eliminated first, the ones who are doing work in this area. And, again, we are seeing this tragedy taking place of mismanagement, I feel, both on the part of the prior Congresses and that of the Forest Service.

Mr. COOLEY. So we can assume that we have a public asset here that has burned, we are not properly managing it by removing it, and we are not properly managing it because we are not replanting?

Mr. HERGER. That is exactly correct.

Mr. COOLEY. And we have literally thousands of acres in your district since 1987 which we could have now looked at a possibility of an eight-year growth or five years of growth of new plants that are not being planted?

Mr. HERGER. That is correct.

Mr. COOLEY. I guess we are talking about forest health and the necessity to manage our forests properly. I think we also should weigh out the factor that we are talking about economics, and by not salvaging what is salvageable, we lose the income from that so, therefore, we are not able to replant.

It looks to me like we could assume from this that there is sort of an effort underway not to do anything and allow this land to become sterile and nonproductive which is part of the assets of the American public. It looks like a little bit of a bad management situation using excuses of everything in the world not to do anything.

Economically, could you give us kind of an idea of how much you think since 1987, the first big fire that we can recall back, that we might have lost an income to the United States Treasury by not adequately going in and salvaging those trees that could be salvaged—some kind of a ballpark figure on how much income we have lost?

Mr. HERGER. I have heard estimates that could be in the vicinity of $1 billion or more that we have lost just in salvage. Now, this is nationally that we are losing by not being able to salvage. I have heard them as high as $3 billion.

Mr. COOLEY. Thank you, congressman. I really appreciate your input. Thank you, Mr. Chairman.

Mr. ALLARD. Thank you, members, and thank you, Congressman Herger, for being with us. And now I would like to go ahead and call the first panel made up of timberworkers. We have on that panel Mr. Mark Simmons, Western Council of Carpenters. We have Mr. Don Besaw from the United Paperworkers. And then also I would like unanimous consent to move Jim Carlson up from the fifth panel to join these members at this table.

Gentlemen, your comments will be inserted in the record with the full text. I would like to limit each one of your testimony to five minutes.

We will also ask members of the committee to follow the five-minute rule and follow the same signals so that we can get through this hearing in a timely fashion. With that, we will go ahead and proceed with the testimony, and I am going to call on Mr. Mark Simmons of the Western Council of Carpenters to give his testimony first.

STATEMENT OF MARK SIMMONS, WESTERN COUNCIL OF CARPENTERS; ACCOMPANIED BY RANDY BESAW, MEMBER, UNITED PAPERWORKERS INTERNATIONAL UNION; JAMES CARLSON, PRESIDENT, CEO, J & J FOREST PRODUCTS, INC.

Mr. SIMMONS. Thank you very much. I do have some pictures to submit. The first picture is a picture of some private land in eastern Oregon that has been managed carefully. The others are pictures of blow-down that hasn't burned; blow-down and dead and diseased timber that has fallen over. Some of them are places that have burned; salvageable material. I would like to submit those and have them passed around.

I also have some examples of some of the stuff that we are running through the mills today. I had a friend of mine pull these out of the chipper just Wednesday. This side of the log shows where the faller in the woods has cut it off, and you see a lot of rot in here. This is what we are running. Everything above this went into the mill, and as long as the rot persists, it goes into the chipper, and everything else is then sold as 2 × 4's and 2 × 6's there at the mill in Elgin.

I want to thank the Chairpersons and the members of the committees for allowing us this opportunity to testify. I want to recognize my representative, Mr. Cooley. I appear before you today on behalf of the 30,000 members of the Western Council of Industrial Workers including the 325 men and women who are represented there by Locals 2780 and 2910 in Elgin, Oregon. I serve as president of Local 2910. I have worked there for about 18 years as a heavy equipment mechanic.

During the past several years, actions to protect the northern spotted owl and other endangered species have all but stopped timber harvesting on public lands in the Pacific Northwest, and more than 17,930 of our members have lost their jobs. I am here today because these jobs aren't just numbers to me. These are personal friends and acquaintances who are now struggling to make ends meet and are relying upon unemployment insurance to cover the expenses of the family.

I have seen how the timber supply problems in the West affect workers across the United States. I had the opportunity to travel to Des Moines, Iowa, last year and met with some of the carpenters there. And they told us how our government's unwillingness to deal with the problem in the Pacific Northwest has caused restrictions in the market and the prices of the raw materials to skyrocket to where it is affecting the economy there in Des Moines, Iowa.

Timber workers like myself were raised to believe that economic opportunity lay in our forests that surround our homes, and we believed that mills could remain there forever as long as we managed the forest intelligently. And we have, by and large for the most part, managed our forests very carefully. Our forests are still there, but our jobs are vanishing.

Some say that we should be relocated or be retrained as these mills shut down. We lost over 100 members here recently in two mill shutdowns in Joseph, Oregon. Those people are now on the unemployment line and trying to figure out what to do with their severance pay.

The jobs and the land are our heritage. People in my community are frustrated, they are bitter, and they are angry. Their faith in the Federal Government has been seriously undermined by the inability of the government to find a balanced solution to this timber supply crisis.

I have to say that people in the west, small-town communities, are very disgusted about the salvage situation. We walk through our forests and see millions and millions of board feet of salvageable timber just laying on the ground. We have had a lot of detractors in the environmental community telling us, "Well, the forest has to have a lot of dead and dying material to be a healthy forest." Well, when I walk out there, I see all this dead and dying as in the pictures I submitted to you. I wonder, "Well, how many dead trees does it take to make a healthy forest?" And I submit to you that we have got more than enough.

We are angry, we are betrayed, and we are heartbroken about the condition of our forests, and we need something to be done about it. Recognition of the problem is not adequate. We have to have action. Please give us some action. Give it some implementation on the ground. Thank you.

[The statement of Mr. Simmons appears at the conclusion of the hearing.]

Mr. ALLARD. I would now like to call on Randy Besaw. Go ahead and give us your testimony please.

STATEMENT OF RANDY BESAW

Mr. BESAW. Good morning. I thank the Chairman and the committee for allowing me to testify today on such an important topic to pulp and paperworkers like myself. My name is Randy Besaw, and I am a dryer operator at the Pope and Talbot mill in Halsey,

Oregon. I also am a member of the United Paperworkers International Union, Local 1189, and my congressman, Peter DeFazio, is also on this committee. I appear here today in support of the salvage logging on behalf of my union brothers and sisters and pulp and paperworkers throughout the United States.

I would like to mention respectfully to the gentleman from New Mexico at the top of the meeting asking why this meeting has to be rushed, and why could it not be put off until next week. Each week we put off hearings and meetings, more jobs like mine are being lost. These meetings needed to be taking place yesterday.

I first became involved in natural resource issues when I saw the effect the northern spotted owl issue and the resulting timber supply crisis is having on working people in Oregon, Washington, and northern California. I have seen mills close and good people lose their jobs. And it is not just timberworkers. The truth is, pulp and paperworkers in our region also are suffering from the timber supply crisis. The less timber processed by saw mills, the fewer good chips available for our mills to turn into pulp and paper products.

As harvest levels go down to zero and have been zero, the price of chips escalate and continue to escalate. I have seen the problem firsthand. Workers at our mill in Halsey were laid off last summer because of a lack of chip supply. I have close friends who didn't know how they were going to feed their families. That is a terrible fear. All of us at the facility now live in fear that our mill will shut down next. We see these mills closing all around us. We see our neighbors on the unemployment line.

We know that wood chips are increasingly difficult to come by, and those you can get are extremely expensive. Although pulp prices have soared in the last four quarters—in some cases prices are at record levels—the Douglas fir chips used by many mills in our area are so expensive that the high cost of the end products barely covers our production costs. We know that our employees will soon have to make some tough choices, and we know we may lose our jobs as a result.

While we haven't been hit as hard as our friends in the timber industry, and the number has been thrown around here today, all you have to do is look at the lumber and plywood industry. I have got 131 mill closures in the last five years in Oregon and Washington so you see what is in store for the pulp and paper industry. We have had three pulp mills shut down in the last two years. Two of the mills are scrap. The other mill is being disassembled and sent to China.

More pulp and paper mills will close in the next three years if something doesn't happen soon. Good paying family wage jobs are lost and why? I don't think people back here in the East fully realize what is going on in our communities. Many seem to think we are about to cut the last tree. That is crazy. We love the forests. We work in the forests, and we hunt and fish in the forests. The forests provide our livelihoods. That is why we care so much about the forest health. That is why I have traveled across the country to appear before you today.

For the pulp and paperworkers in the West, our interest in forest health is two-fold. First, the forests of the western United States have been desperately dry during the past several summers and falls. Meanwhile, foresters have been prevented by Federal restrictions and judicial injunctions from removing damaged, dead, and diseased timber from national forests. The buildup of this material threatens forest health and, when combined with the dry conditions, increases the likelihood of wildfire. Wildfires endanger animals, forest ecosystems, and surrounding communities where many of our members and families live.

[The statement of Mr. Besaw appears at the conclusion of the hearing.]

Mr. ALLARD. I thank the gentleman for his comment. We will get the rest of your comments put in the record. We have a vote that is running right now so I am going to go ahead and ask Congressman Hansen to run the committee hearing while we go ahead and vote. I am going to run over now and get back shortly and then we will continue. So any of the members that want to vote, you can kind of filter in and out gradually, and we will keep the hearing going. Chairman Hansen.

Mr. HANSEN [presiding]. Thank you, Mr. Besaw. We appreciate your comments. As Chairman Allard said, I think probably it would be wise for the members to go back and forth as rapidly as they can. We wouldn't want to miss out on this in the interim period because we have a large group here. We want to continue the hearing going on. Mr. Jim Carlson, could we call upon you at this particular time?

STATEMENT OF JIM CARLSON

Mr. CARLSON. My name is Jim Carlson. I am from J & J Forest Products on the Olympic Peninsula in western Washington. I want to thank you folks for allowing me the opportunity to testify under these rather intimidating circumstances.

Photos that I brought here reflect how our national forests are being run under current science.

Mr. HANSEN. Mr. Carlson, could I ask you to suspend? There is a question on the parliamentary procedure we are following here. There has been a point of order raised that the Interior Committee could not respond to this because of an objection yesterday. That is fine with me. What we are going to do is we are going to just turn that light off, and you are going to have your whole five minutes as soon as the committee reconvenes, and this meeting stands adjourned until they come back.

[Whereupon, the subcommittees recessed, to reconvene the same day.]

Mr. ALLARD. I am going to go ahead and call the committee back to order. And, Senator Gorton, I understand you have arrived.

Senator GORTON. Yes.

Mr. ALLARD. If you would join the panel there, we will give you an opportunity. Jim Carlson was testifying. I think there was a point of order raised at that point. Jim, do you want to finish your testimony, and then we will call on Senator Gorton to give his testimony. Go ahead, Jim.

Mr. CARLSON. Yes. My name is Jim Carlson. I am from J & J Forest Products on the Olympic Peninsula in western Washington. And I am here to tell the story of one tree in my five minutes that I am allotted.

This is the story of a tree that blew down on the Olympic Peninsula several years ago, and we tried to get the Forest Service to put this tree up for sale for a competitive bid for lumber production, and we were denied. Subsequent to that, we made a request to the Forest Service to purchase this on what is called a personal use permit, and we were going to use this tree to build an interpretive building for a tourism project that we were working on. We had been mandated—these rural communities—to diversify our economies, and so we thought we would saw this tree up and use it in a building on our ranch that we were working on, this tourism project. This particular tree has 21,000 feet gross scale in it, about 18,500 net scribner. Converted in our sawmill, this would have produced over $60,000 worth of lumber. It would have provided employment for the mill and woods crew, generated revenue for the U.S. Government, return money to our schools and community. And there are thousands of others, but I only have time to tell the story of one tree.

This tree was ultimately sold for $5 a cord for a firewood permit. It is incredible to us that are unemployed—we used to have 100 employees and subcontractors working for us. I am the only person left at the company right now, and I am not employed. In fact, this is my first trip to Washington, and I am here in a final, desperate effort to save my company. And it is hard for us to understand how this New Age science can produce outcomes like this.

There is a final irony to this story. This tree was sold to an unemployed timberworker for this firewood permit, and on January 13 on the Courthouse steps in Montesano, Washington, they sold this timberworker's home for $931.91 because he could not pay his property taxes. It is hard for us in these communities to understand how we can treat these extremely valuable and renewable resources in this fashion.

I come to Washington looking for justice and consideration and common sense in forest policy. The people that I left at home are depending on me to eloquently deliver this message, and I hope I am up to the task. I have produced a photo album that I am going to submit for the record, an executive summary, that will depict what is going on throughout the Olympic Peninsula.

There are literally tens of thousands of these trees, and one of the things that is happening in this forest health debate is we have heard a lot about fire-damaged timber. On the Olympic Peninsula in Washington, we have a continuing, ongoing blow-down situation where literally millions of feet of timber blow down on an ongoing basis. The reason for this is because of high winds associated with high moisture contents in the soils, and we have a tremendous amount of volume on the ground that is just going to waste.

One Federal forester told me about the nutrient value in these trees and how important they were to forest health. I contacted the University of Washington because I was skeptical, and I found out that they had indeed did a survey on this. And they concluded that 90 percent or better of the nutrients that were returned to the forest ecosystem came from the crown of this tree, the foliage, and the stem, which is the part of this tree that drives the economies in our community, returns very little to the forest ecosystem. Thank you very much for this opportunity.

[The statement of Mr. Carlson appears at the conclusion of the hearing.]

Mr. ALLARD. I would like to thank you, Jim, for taking your time to be here. I know that you are here with considerable personal sacrifice and cost. Let me call on Senator Slade Gorton for his comments, and then hopefully we will have some more committee members here, and we can ask some questions of the panel. Senator Gorton, thank you.

STATEMENT OF SENATOR SLADE GORTON, A SENATOR FROM THE STATE OF WASHINGTON

Senator GORTON. Thank you, Mr. Chairman, for holding this hearing. I have two fundamental reasons for joining you here this morning. First, to get people in my state back to work and, second, to help restore and to maintain the health of our forests.

The subject the subcommittees are studying here today is very important to me and of obvious importance, as you have heard from Jim Carlson, to people in my state of Oregon and, for that matter, by extension all across the country. Action will truly represent the difference between a mill shutting down and more people being unemployed or staying open and staying employed. It is the difference between one unemployed timberworker and one employed. In my mind, we are talking here about jobs. People in Washington State and in Oregon—you have two witnesses from Washington State in Jim Carlson, who has just testified, and Chad Oliver—do bring a unique perspective to this issue.

Last summer, wildfires raged across the western United States. The fire season started early, and by the time the smoke had cleared, nearly 3 million acres of land in the western part of the United States had burned, double the amount that burned in 1993. In the States of Washington and Oregon alone, almost 1.4 billion board feet of Federal timber burned.

Last summer, after listening closely to the concerns of residents of the Olympic Peninsula and of other parts of rural Washington, I offered an amendment during a House-Senate Interior Appropriations conference to provide the Forest Service with the authority to expedite salvage sales. I emphasize we didn't tell the Forest Service what it had to do. We just wanted to allow any sales that it wished to undertake to be expedited.

Salvage, as you know, represents not only burned timber but dead and dying, blow-down and bug-infested trees too. Unfortunately, I could not convince the members of the conference committee to include that amendment in the final bill, and so salvage timber is still sitting on the ground.

Today, most, if not quite all, of that 1.4 billion board feet remains on the ground in Oregon and Washington deteriorating with each passing day. Obviously, not all of it is eligible for harvest, but Forest Service calculations indicate that about 50 percent of total volume burned in a wildfire normally can be salvaged. As a result, perhaps 700 million board feet is eligible for some kind of salvage activity. But so far the Forest Service has made only token efforts to prepare the sales necessary to harvest this valuable timber. And as you all well know, the need to expedite these sales is overwhelming because the quality of that timber declines each day. Regrettably, inaction is principally what we have gotten from the Forest Service.

In response to the wildfires last summer, the Forest Service began to study forest health. Last December, the Service issued a report on its study entitled, "The Western Forest Health Initiative." The report highlighted 330 forest health-related projects in the western United States, but the majority of these projects were not developed in response to the summer wildfires.

In Washington and Oregon, for instance, only 40 projects were identified in response to summer fires. Of the 40 projects, only a few were actual salvage operations. So while it was a good idea to have the Forest Service identify forest health-related projects, it is clear, absolutely clear, that the Forest Service needs to do more and needs to do it more quickly.

Mr. Chairman, the people in Washington State constantly ask themselves and us why. Why isn't the Forest Service going into the burned-out areas and allowing the timber to be taken out? Why isn't the Forest Service restoring the health of our forests? Why isn't the Forest Service helping us put people back to work? Now, I think we know the answer. The answer is largely driven by the fact that the Forest Service will certainly have to go to Court if it begins even a modest effort to conduct salvage operations. It is the threat of legal action in large measure which causes the Forest Service to figure that if it does something, it will be sued. If it does nothing, it is at least all right as far as the lawyers are concerned, if not the people affected.

The people in Washington and many other western states are terribly frustrated. They are frustrated with a Federal Government that is so petrified at the potential filing of lawsuits, that it will not undertake even the most limited of management activities in our nation's forests. We can't and we should not, Mr. Chairman, stop managing our forests simply because of the obstructionist tactics of a few groups and individuals.

For these reasons, I can report to you that I have begun to work with my colleagues in the Pacific Northwest and especially in the State of Washington to craft legislation that will provide the Administration with the legal protection it needs to prepare salvage sales without the threat of frivolous lawsuits. I want to work with my colleagues in both Houses and in both parties to construct a provision that will expedite salvage operations, limit the ability to file endless appeals, and provide for a limited and reasonable environmental assessment of the sales.

I would like to thank you, Mr. Chairman, for holding this hearing. In the five short months since last year's fire season, I have not forgotten about the timber lying on the forest floor setting the stage for another round of devastating forest fires this summer.

More importantly, I have not forgotten about the people who live and work in these timber communities. We must not forget how important this issue is to these communities and to these people because truly it will make the difference between a mill being able to keep its doors open or watching another close its doors with additional unemployment. I want to work as hard as I possibly can in the next few weeks to put together an amendment to restore the health of our forests and get timber flowing back to our mills. And

I am sure, Mr. Chairman, that you and your committee share that goal completely.

Mr. ALLARD. Thank you for your testimony, Senator Gorton. I know you have a very busy schedule. If you want to hang around for a few questions, you are certainly welcome to. If you feel like you need to get moving——

Senator GORTON. We have a vote at 11:30 so I have got about 12 more minutes, and I would be happy to answer any questions any of you have in that period of time.

Mr. ALLARD. Let me call on Congressman Doolittle. I think he has got a question or two.

Mr. DOOLITTLE. Senator, I appreciate your concern. I was pleased to read your comments in one of the newspapers that were handed out up here. You have a lot of friends beyond Washington and Oregon. In California you have a lot. I represent a district that is heavily forested. I wondered if you had heard—I intend to ask the head of the Forest Service when he comes up here—but I understand that in this latest round of reinventing government, they have targeted foresters and engineers for layoffs, it is my understanding, they have been given the early retirement or whatever the program is that allows people to voluntarily opt out. Have you heard anything like that?

Senator GORTON. I have heard exactly the same thing, and, you know, we seem to be faced with a situation in which if we wait much longer, we won't have the technical expertise necessary in the Forest Service to do even what we in Congress may direct or authorize the Forest Service to do. It seems to be systematically, you know, abandoning the idea that a significant part of its duties are to see to it that a steady and regular and reasonable harvest is available.

Mr. DOOLITTLE. And then we have a very interesting and insidious report known as the, "Green Scissors Report," which purports to be taxpayer advocates. And in this report they have called for not the partial but the total elimination of funding for the maintenance and the construction of timber roads. That, of course, would prevent any effective salvage effort from going forward.

When you take all these things in tandem, all of these lawsuits, the purlieu of the experience, people preparing the timber sales, this unholy alliance producing this monstrosity, it seems as much a coincidence as it would be to be walking in the sands of the Sahara and to find a Rolex watch in perfect condition running. Do you have any feelings, Senator, about what we might do to move things along here and to get—we are just concentrating on dead trees. What is the matter with harvesting green trees?

Senator GORTON. That seems to me to be our obvious goal even in the midterm much less the long term. And I know that these two committees here today have one or the other under their jurisdiction, the National Forest Management Act and the Endangered Species Act, two of the Acts which alone or in tandem have so totally frustrated and brought to a halt orderly, reasonable, and regular timber harvests and the planning for those harvests.

When we speak here today and the proposal to which I speak is a temporary proposal. I hope that for this season perhaps we can get the Congress at least to end the lawsuits with respect to what the Forest Service in at least some aspects of its bureaucracy wants to do; what the President has said that he wants to do with respect to Option 9; with sales that have already been authorized under laws previously passed by this Congress. But if we do that, we will be doing something for people, you know, for this summer and perhaps for a little bit longer period of time than that.

In my view, we have got to take a look at all of the statutes which relate to the management of our forests and see to it that we do return to an appropriate and balanced multiple use. And at the heart of even the longterm solution as well as the shortterm solution will be the restriction on the absolutely unlimited nature of legal challenges which have so plagued everything we have tried to do in the last several years.

Mr. DOOLITTLE. I think we have got a genuine emergency. I support you 100 percent in your efforts. I would encourage you to be bolder even than you are talking. I mean, Option 9 is a disaster for northern California. If this is help from the Clinton Administration, I would hate to see what they would do if they were going to hurt us. It is just pathetic, and I would hope that we would—and I encourage you, and I will support you on this end, be doing things over here, but I would sure like to get beyond Option 9. I would like to get back to the 1980s. It was a good decade in a number of respects and certainly in the area of harvesting trees.

Senator GORTON. Well, my goal is certainly a sustained harvest but considerably in excess of Option 9. I think you are right. The President and his people when they come up with Option 9 told us their hands were tied, that this was the best they could do given the law in its present form.

Mr. DOOLITTLE. Well, they were tied by their left-wing, extreme environmentalist friends. Maybe we need to get some new friends.

Senator GORTON. If I can go on a little bit, I think, you know, they were probably accurate in their assessment, at least as the Courts have said it, with the present law. What I found overwhelmingly frustrating with the President and with his people was their unwillingness to recommend any change in the law which would put people into the equation. When the President says, “My hands are tied,” tells us, in effect, what laws tie his hands and then doesn’t recommend our untying them, it is time for us to do that untying without any leadership from the Administration.

Mr. DOOLITTLE. Well, I thank you for your efforts and look forward to working together with you.

Mr. ALLARD. I would like to go ahead and proceed with the hearing. I would just thank Senator Gorton.

Senator GORTON. Thank you for your courtesy, Mr. Chairman.

Mr. ALLARD. Thank you, Senator Gorton. I would like to ask a question that pertains to some of the testimony that we heard from Jim Carlson where we had, obviously, a large tree fall down; something that could be processed for high quality lumber actually being used for firewood because of some of the rules and regulations that we are dealing with from the Forest Service. Would the members of the panel comment as to whether this is a common occurrence or just an isolated incident? Jim, is this just an isolated incident, or is this something that has been occurring fairly regularly in your part of the country?

Mr. CARLSON. This is not an isolated incident. I can speak with accuracy and experience on the Quinault Ranger District and the Olympic National Forest. This has been a conscious decision. In fact, there was a decision memo signed in June of 1994 that laid out the parameters of this woodcutting deal. And the decision memo said that the Quinault District would be opened in its entirety for harvesting of firewood with the exception of a small area that was called a national scientific study area, and if there were any timber harvest sales going on, those areas would be excluded also.

Also, there was a timber salvage strategy that the Forest Service goes through. It is called a five-year timber salvage strategy plan that is updated annually. And if that is the case, I guess that further documents that this is a conscious decision.

And I just selected this tree because there was a lot of ironic twists to it. I was very conservative when I valued this tree at $60,000. There was a very similar tree to this that has been cut up for decking for the U.S.S. Constitution. That lumber has been selling for $7,000 to $10,000 per thousand board feet. I thought if I extrapolated with those numbers, Congress would not believe me. And so I am here to tell you that I was very conservative in those numbers, and it is ironic because they had great difficulty finding the lumber to restore the U.S.S. Constitution. And I understand they have even been trying to procure some of it in Canada.

Mr. ALLARD. Thank you. Similar situations, Mr. Simmons or Mr. Besaw?

Mr. SIMMONS. Yes, sir. In eastern Oregon and the interior forests, we do have a lot of timber that has just been blown over or killed by insects and disease and fallen over that could be salvaged, could be used, not unlike this junk that we passed around, even as it ages, that is just being left in the woods that could be used.

Mr. ALLARD. How many trees like that, Mr. Carlson, would it take to keep your mill going?

Mr. CARLSON. I would probably require about 150 trees like that on an annual basis to keep our sawmill operating. I have a small, custom-cut mill, and if I had 150 trees like that, I would probably send the U.S. Government, as I did historically, $250,000 to $300,000 in income taxes.

This Congress has been debating a lot on health care and the previous one. We would solve part of the health care system in our company. We had Hillary's ultimate health care plan at our company. All 60 employees had their insurance paid in full by the company including their families. One hundred and fifty trees takes care of a lot of social and economic problems.

Mr. ALLARD. Thank you, gentlemen. I now will call on members of the committee. We will start with the first minority member that I saw when we were called to order. Mr. Minge, do you have any questions?

Mr. MINGE. I will pass in the interest of letting other members and the witnesses proceed.

Mr. ALLARD. Congressman Doolittle.

Mr. DOOLITTLE. Sir, was it your testimony that the tree we are looking at in the picture there was going to be a $60,000 tree?

Mr. CARLSON. That tree would produce in excess of $60,000 worth of lumber. It was sold for firewood and stovewood. And it is very difficult when people are out of work to see these kinds of transactions taking place. They have no job, and yet we are selling this Nation's treasures and resources for stovewood, and it is almost insidious, is it is like Chinese water torture—I think someone in these halls was referring to that the other day—to sit here and watch this kind of activity go on when you have no job.

Mr. DOOLITTLE. Well, just so I understand, why was it sold for stovewood as opposed to for lumber?

Mr. CARLSON. I am as confused as you are, and that is why I entitled my presentation the realities of Option 9 and the current science that we are managing under. This is the outcomes from the science that is driving forest management today.

Mr. DOOLITTLE. So you mean, just so I understand it, it is okay to cut them down for firewood but not for commercial purposes?

Mr. CARLSON. On our district, we was unable to buy this tree and literally thousands of other trees, but, yes, they were available for stovewood permits, and they sold those permits on a personal use basis for $5 a cord, and commercial woodcutting, which was allowed as well, I believe was $15 a cord.

Mr. DOOLITTLE. I know there is a broad range, but does that fit within the broad range of what they would commercially take?

Mr. CARLSON. These are the kind of trees they were cutting. Because of the woodcutter's story and them selling his house as he was cutting this tree, I selected this tree. This is a beautiful tree. There is no question about it.

Mr. DOOLITTLE. And this would be considered a real good tree for commercial purposes, wouldn't it?

Mr. CARLSON. Absolutely. It would provide the decking for the restoration of the U.S.S. Constitution. I have an album here full of beautiful timber that I could have bankrupted myself developing film, and so I brought a selection for you to look at.

Mr. DOOLITTLE. Did you say how old that tree was? If you did, I missed it.

Mr. CARLSON. That is about a 450 or 500-year-old tree.

Mr. DOOLITTLE. So we are roped off from cutting most stuff like that now. Right?

Mr. CARLSON. Well, this tree was felled by God. We have lots of blow-down.

Mr. DOOLITTLE. Okay. But that was a blow-down type situation.

Mr. CARLSON. Millions of feet of blow-down in our district. We are on the coast of Washington. And this is a very common occurrence. This happens every year where we have a lot of high winds associated with this moisture content and the soils, and so we have a lot of timber that blows down. The forest is continually rotating.

Mr. ALLARD. Would the gentleman yield?

Mr. DOOLITTLE. Sure.

Mr. ALLARD. How long would that stay as a viable piece of lumber that could be harvested in a downed condition like that?

Mr. CARLSON. It is dependent on species. This particular tree, which is a Douglas fir tree, has a lot of longevity to it. This tree could stay out there for years, and there would still be commercial value in it. We are in a white wood forest. We have a lot of Hemlock and White Fir. That type of wood goes through a transition from when it is freshly blown down. It will make fine lumber products such as doors, window casings, cabinets and stuff.

As it deteriorates and the ambrosia beetles get into it, the ambrosia beetles come from the outside of the log and bore inward, and they consume and ruin the best portions of the log, the clearer yielding portions of the log first. As the ambrosia beetles work on the log, it takes that high grade, high value lumber and turns it into a construction grade lumber like 2 × 4's for framing houses.

And as this process continues, ultimately, it turns into a chip log which even a chip log has a lot of value now. A load of pulp wood right now they are talking as high as $60 a ton, you know, 1,000—$1,500 a load just for chip wood. And then it goes to chip wood, and then it goes to bug manure. That is the last step.

Mr. ALLARD. I will yield back to the gentleman. Do you have any more questions?

Mr. DOOLITTLE. One last question.

Mr. CARLSON. Yes.

Mr. DOOLITTLE. What did he pay for the permit to get that tree?

Mr. CARLSON. I believe he paid $5 a cord so there is about 800 board feet to a cord; somewhere in the neighborhood of $150 I am going to guess. But there is a little more to that story. When you purchase a firewood permit, understand that you have got desperate people out there that are buying a permit. They will go in and say, "I want a permit for four cords of wood," and they will hand over $20. It is hard to say how many cords are really being cut. There is no way to monitor this, and this is a classic case of a deficit timber sale if I have ever seen one.

Mr. DOOLITTLE. Yes. $150 for $60,000 worth of wood.

Mr. CARLSON. It is stranger than fiction.

Mr. DOOLITTLE. Thank you.

Mr. ALLARD. Let me call on somebody from the minority side. Mr. DeFazio, you are welcome to ask questions if you would like.

Mr. DEFAZIO. I thank the Chairman. Although I am not a member of the committee or subcommittee, I have a vital interest representing what was formerly the most public timber-dependent district in the United States. I can say it is still dependent, but it is not giving the public timber.

I really at this point don't have questions. I guess what I am going to wait for is I am intrigued by the testimony here and will look forward to asking the Chief of the Forest Service to respond to the gentleman's testimony regarding this. I am not that familiar with the Quinault District, but it seems odd to me that, you know, if the ultimate theory were to allow the logs to deteriorate, then I don't know why they would give firewood permits as opposed to any other permit, let alone a commercial sale, for something as valuable as the gentleman states this tree would be. So you might be able to respond to that. If not, I am certainly going to look forward to having the chief address that question.

Mr. CARLSON. I think I can respond a little, and it will be a little bit of conjecture. But there is a great effort to destroy the infrastructure of this industry. We have had over 200 sawmills close in the West affecting over 20,000 workers. The Forest Service recently is embarking on a road obliteration project; this kind of timber going for stovewood in lieu of lumber products.

You can see that there are a series of events happening here that are beyond a coincidence, and it is the destruction of the industry, the infrastructure, and if they are successful in doing that, we don't have to come back and revisit this. There will be no industry. These rural communities will disappear, and it is an economic warfare. That is how you fight wars in these times. You fight them with money. And, quite frankly, I come to Washington the same way that Sam Adams come to Washington. People in my community put up money to send me here, and we are at the end of our rope.

Mr. DEFAZIO. I thank the gentleman. I will be interested in the response of the chief. I have a lot of Forest Service employees in my district, and I talk to them as much as I talk to the mill workers and other folks in the industry and the environmentalists, and I guess I am going to look for another explanation. I don't believe there is that degree of cynicism or conspiracy in the Forest Service, but I am puzzled as to how it could be okay to chop this up into firewood but not bid it out commercially. I would like to welcome Mr. Besaw here. I know it is a long trip, and I appreciate his coming all the way back to talk.

Just one question because there is one thing I can never quite keep straight from conversation to conversation with you, Randy. You talked about the cost of Douglas fir chips and that the predominant amount of the salvage in Oregon is east side mostly. Some of it is fir but a lot of it is lodgepole and other sorts of pine. How much of your mix these days is from those species that are most predominant in a potential salvage program on the east side, and how much would it help your particular mill or other mills that you are aware of?

Mr. BESAW. Congressman, it would help us very much. One thing the committee might note, after they get the value out of this log, if they could get it, we are basically a by-product of it. We can run our mill on sawdust, the waste that the sawmills provide, and take that sawdust and make pulp and paper products out of it. Our mill in Halsey was at one time primarily a Douglas fir mill, and because of the Douglas fir limitations, we are trying to retool and shift to more of a sawdust mill because it is cheaper, and it is a little bit more available.

But if something isn't done through the salvage and as Congressman Doolittle mentioned through green trees, my mill and many more mills will end up having to close, not because they want to. Unlike the baseball strike, we have got a good contract with our company. We get along with our company. We work hand in hand to try to provide good jobs and provide good workers, but we have no resources. We have got many millions of dollars worth of mills sitting there with no resources.

Mr. DEFAZIO. I guess the question is more on the pine versus the fir. I assume this is a fir log, but are you using pine?

Mr. BESAW. We are using a very little bit of pine. My point is, as the Douglas fir is not available, depending on if there is much cost involved, we will try and shift to other fibers to try and keep the mill open. But sawdust and Douglas fir is the main species.

Mr. DEFAZIO. I thank the gentleman, and I thank the Chair.

Mr. ALLARD. I hope the members of the minority party who tried to kill this hearing were listening when this gentleman said that his community even chipped in for his cost to be here for this hearing. With that, I will go ahead and call on the congressman from California, Mr. Pombo.

Mr. POMBO. Thank you, Mr. Chairman. Mr. Besaw, you said something in your opening statement that kind of hit close to home a little bit, and you talked about this being your livelihood. And I guess the point is that you guys depend on the forest for your livelihood, for your heritage, for your kids, and would you do anything as individuals or as people that depend on the forest for your livelihood that would permanently destroy those forests?

Mr. BESAW. Absolutely not. We want to be stewards of the forest, and we fish and hunt in the forest, and we care for the forest probably as much as anybody. I am an environmentalist, and I am not a preservationist. I am not radical. We need a good balance, and that has been being said for how many years. And I said it in my opening statement, that the gentleman from New Mexico, why couldn't this have been put off till next week. Well, as we speak, and yesterday and last week, we are losing jobs.

And we are getting letters from our company. I brought one with me. We are getting these. The employees in the mill are getting these and saying, "Look, guys. If this situation don't turn around, fiber supply doesn't come more readily available, unfortunately, you know, you guys better be watching your car payments, and you better be watching your mortgages, and don't buy much because, unfortunately, the mills are going to be closing." And that is what us workers are living with daily.

My son goes to bed at night and includes his prayers that I hope my dad don't lose his job, and that really hurts me, and we shouldn't have to live in that type of a lifestyle daily.

Mr. POMBO. Some people don't understand what it is like to be brought up in that kind of a heritage and that kind of a background where you do feel that you are part of the land that your whole life depends upon, your clean air, clean water, and the trees growing. Some people don't understand that so maybe we will take about the cold, hard economics a little bit. And for you and the people that you work with and the company that you work for, if we just talk about cold, hard cash, the blunt economics of this, is it not in your best interests to have a sustainable yield to take care of the forests so that they are there next year and the year after that and 30 years from now so that your son can have the same job that you have?

Mr. BESAW. That is a very true statement. It is certainly in the best interests of me, my colleagues, my union, my company, the industry to have a sustainable forest, a health forest so that we can continue to have good family wage jobs in this industry.

Mr. POMBO. What about the city that you live in? Is it not in the best interests of the city that you live in and the county that you live in for there to be a continuing, ongoing sustainable yield coming off those forests and for you guys to be able to continue to produce jobs so that they can pave their roads and pay for their schools?

Mr. BESAW. Absolutely. And Congressman DeFazio probably could reference better than I could how much money our schools in our area have lost from timber sales. And my son last night before I got on the airplane yesterday, he told me that in his third grade class they are going to vote on which teachers should be and which subjects they should be continuing to have in their curriculum. Should physical education be part of it? Should music? Should strings? Some of these support curriculums, should they be part of the schools, and they are bringing it down to the kids making choices because we are losing so much money from timber revenue in our communities.

Mr. POMBO. I just want to say that I represent a district that is in the central valley in California. I do not have trees in my district. My district is primarily an agriculture, farming, ranching district. I have in the center of my district a company that employs over 1,000 people that when you close down, they are going to close down. So this does not just affect you even though it is directly right in your face every day and every night, but it also affects the rest of the economy of the West. And I think that it is an extremely urgent, crisis situation that this Congress needs to act on.

And I just want to thank you and the rest of the members of this panel for coming back here and sharing your story with us. I know it was not easy for you to do this. It was not an easy situation, and hopefully this Congress can act to help alleviate some of the problems that we have created in the past. Thank you very much for being here.

Mr. ALLARD. Mr. Williams.

Mr. WILLIAMS. Thank you, Mr. Chairman. A former member of this committee made a good jump-start on this very problem. Former Democratic member from Idaho named Larry LaRocco represented a district now ably represented by Mrs. Chenoweth. He did about three years of work on salvage timber sales legislation, and I would encourage all the members of the committee to adopt much of the work and much of the language that Mr. LaRocco moved through subcommittee level, a former Democratic member. He worked with both Republicans and Democrats in doing that, and that is my point here.

We might solve the problem if we work together, but some of what I heard at today's hearing makes pretty good politics. But I don't think it is going to solve the solution and keep you fellows and maybe your sons and daughters working in these mills or your profit rolling and maybe your son able to take over your mill. I don't think there are a lot of people skulking around in the Forest Service trying to put you all out of business. I just don't believe it.

I know that there are some people including some of your members, fellows, in my state of Montana, both carpenters and paperworkers—by the way, Mr. Simmons, I used to belong to your union—who take much of the same approach you do with regard to trying to get out dead, damaged, dying, and downed timber. I want you to know when I say I take that approach that I passed the only piece of legislation to become law to skirt a Court injunction and legislate a salvage sale; did that several years ago and gratefully it was signed by former President Bush.

So, generally, I am on your side, but let me find out from the two members of these unions if you agree with your brothers and sisters over our way in Montana. They are outraged that the industry would cut timber and continue to avoid your mills and send it to foreign countries to be milled. Are you as outraged as your brothers and sisters in Montana are about the bosses' action in that regard?

Mr. SIMMONS. We have never supported the export of timber. Our position is that that is something third world countries do in exporting their natural resources, and we have never supported that. We do very much believe that a lot of the pressure that is being put on private land today is due to our government's unwillingness and inability or for whatever reason to address the real crisis we have at hand. And what it amounts to is an irresponsible squandering of our heritage.

Mr. BESAW. And I sit here today and tell you I don't agree with exporting. My union has taken resolutions to stop and lobby or do whatever they can to help pass legislation to stop——

Mr. WILLIAMS. And I, along with some of my colleagues here today, had a hand in passing legislation to not allow it on the public land. The companies still do it, as you know, on their own land, and your brothers and sisters in Montana as well as, obviously, yourselves wish the companies would stop that practice on their land because that would secure your jobs in a very major way.

Mr. BESAW. Yes, that would but like you said private lands, and that goes into private rights, but it still doesn't solve the solution on public and Federal land.

Mr. WILLIAMS. I know it doesn't, but they have the same obligation to try to help your jobs as this Congress has, don't you think, whether it is on their land or your land? Let me ask you this. Your leadership in Montana and many of the members out there recognize the inevitability of some mill closings, and I believe the vast bulk of them have come to believe that it is due to overpromising by both the industry and the government, primarily the Forest Service, in the early days of this country when the laws were such that if you could see it, you could cut it, and so we put mills in almost every small town out west. Do you agree there is some inevitability to reduction in the number of mills because of carrying capacity and the lack of supply?

Mr. SIMMONS. Sir, with this new implementation of ecosystem management, it is our position that if we could actually implement ecosystem management on a broad scale, we would have to install more mill capacity to handle all the dead and dying timber that would be available that could be made into merchantable products to build and provide housing for America.

Mr. ALLARD. I would like to now call on the Chairman of National Parks, Forests & Lands, Chairman Hansen.

Mr. HANSEN. I thank you very much, Mr. Chairman. Gentlemen, I appreciate your testimony. Maybe I missed a point my friend from Montana brought up. Isn't it true it is against the law to export logs off Federal ground to another country? Isn't that right?

Mr. SIMMONS. Yes, sir.

Mr. HANSEN. So it is private and state that could be exported. Is that correct?

Mr. SIMMONS. Correct.

Mr. HANSEN. Okay. Just so I clear that up. How many jobs do you think your industry has lost in your area, say, in the last five years? Has someone got an idea? Maybe you have already answered that. I apologize. I was over on the floor.

Mr. SIMMONS. Over 17,000.

Mr. HANSEN. 17,000 jobs. This is out of the industry? This would be industry-wide; management, labor, truck drivers, the whole nine yards?

Mr. BESAW. It would be higher than that.

Mr. HANSEN. What would you say it is, Mr. Besaw?

Mr. BESAW. There has been so many numbers, sir. I have got 131 mills closed in the last five years, and we have heard several different numbers here today. I don't have those numbers in front of me, but I believe they are well over 20,000 and closer to 30,000 jobs in the wood product industry that have lost jobs out in the Northwest.

Mr. HANSEN. Now, they are direct jobs we are talking. These are in the industry. I am sure someone in your state has come up with a periphery figure. You know, if they say, "Hey, if we lose so many out of the Anchor store, that means so many lawyers, doctors, insurance people, grocers, et cetera, have also lost their jobs." Do you have a wild idea or actual information on that?

Mr. SIMMONS. There are several figures being bantered around, and I am sure there are people here who are more expert on that than what we are, but the indirect jobs calculated in is, I believe, somewhere in the neighborhood of 80,000.

Mr. HANSEN. Where do they all go?

Mr. SIMMONS. I have no idea. I know there are people who are living in their cars in some communities.

Mr. HANSEN. How about retraining? You know, we have come up with a few ideas of retraining these people. Is that working at all?

Mr. SIMMONS. Retraining by and large is a failure.

Mr. HANSEN. So you think that is just a waste of Federal money?

Mr. SIMMONS. I do.

Mr. HANSEN. Do you feel the same way, Mr. Besaw?

Mr. BESAW. Yes.

Mr. HANSEN. Mr. Carlson?

Mr. CARLSON. Absolutely.

Mr. BESAW. The jobs aren't there to be retrained for, and they are not family wage jobs, and they are not good benefits like we have today.

Mr. HANSEN. You folks are probably the premier group when it comes to talking lumber, but in my home state of Utah, we have had a couple of little sawmills, and I see one of the gentlemen is going to respond on this before long—Kaibab Industries, Escalanti—they have really had big trouble in that area.

As I talked to the management of this group, and I hope I am not unfairly portraying their position, I find that a lot of this they feel is a direct result of Federal action and extreme environmental laws. If I threw that question to you, how would you respond to it? Do you feel that some of the problems that you are experiencing are a result of Federal action and extreme environmental laws?

Mr. SIMMONS. Absolutely. It is Federal inaction and by default Federal action and extreme environmental laws. We believe very much that we have the land base out there, that we really can have it all, and that there is so much room in the middle of this debate for all sides to win. We can have a sustainable, predictable timber supply into the mill so we can provide housing for America and paper products, and we can have habitat for all the furry little creatures and bugs and microzoa and fungi that depend upon that forest also. And that is what makes this thing so maddening and so absolutely frustrating and causes the anger in the pit of your stomach and the distrust in our government's ability to do this for us.

Mr. HANSEN. So the three of you feel that you can cut timber and take care of the industry in an environmentally sound way. Is that correct?

Mr. BESAW. That is correct.

Mr. SIMMONS. Absolutely.

Mr. HANSEN. And so you take exception to those people who feel that you are desecrating the forest and all that type of thing?

Mr. SIMMONS. Very much so.

Mr. HANSEN. You mentioned an interesting point, Mr. Simmons. What about the price of homes now? I remember 30 years ago I built my wife's dream house, and a 2 x 4 was 80 something cents as I recall. What is a 2 x 4 now?

Mr. SIMMONS. Loaded on the truck at the mill, the prices vary, and I don't keep track of that. The people who own the mill do, but it has been as high as around $3.50 apiece just loaded on the truck at the mill.

Mr. HANSEN. Do you think some of this is a direct result of inflation going up, a direct result of all the problems we are seeing on the economy?

Mr. SIMMONS. This is a result of our Federal Government's inability and unwillingness to address the root problem which is timber availability on public lands and comprehensive balanced management on public lands.

Mr. HANSEN. The steel manufacturers tell me you can build a house cheaper out of steel now than you can out of wood. Are they being facetious, or do you agree with that?

Mr. SIMMONS. Steel studs are very competitive now, my understanding, with wood, but steel is not renewable. It is not as energy efficient, and there are a lot of downsides to steel. Wood is the best.

Mr. HANSEN. You can also have a shocking experience in a steel home I have noticed. Thank you, Mr. Chairman.

Mr. ALLARD. Let me call on the congresswoman from Idaho now, Congresswoman Chenoweth.

Mrs. CHENOWETH. Thank you, Mr. Chairman. I just have a couple of very short questions. I wasn't here for what I understand was very interesting testimony from Mr. Carlson. I am not sure about the species. Did you say that was a Douglas fir or a red fir?

Mr. CARLSON. Yes. This is a Douglas fir.

Mrs. CHENOWETH. That is a Douglas fir. What I did hear you say was that your figures were probably conservative that you quoted, but I also want to say that in my mills in northern Idaho my mill owners were paying $700 per 1,000 board feet on the stump. So your figures indeed were very conservative. And I just want to thank you very much, all three of you, for being here. It is very good testimony.

And I want to thank the gentleman, Mr. Williams, for his comments. I want you to know I worked with labor to circulate petitions that were put forth by labor to support Mr. LaRocco's forest health bill, and I commend Mr. Williams for his ability to get a bill through the Congress and the Senate and have it signed by a Republican president.

And although Mr. LaRocco in two terms of a Democrat-dominated House and Senate and last year with a Democrat president was not able to get his bill through, I would like to call upon Mr. Williams to help us in the bipartisan manner that he was able to enjoy because it means an awful lot of jobs and ultimately a healthier forest. Thank you, Mr. Chairman.

Mr. ALLARD. Mr. Hostettler.

Mr. HOSTETTLER. Thank you, Mr. Chairman, and thank you, gentlemen, for coming this long distance to be here before us. Mr. Simmons and Mr. Besaw, in your testimony, you referred to earlier the spotted owl, and there has been a lot of controversy surrounding that. And quite a few months ago, I noticed a photograph in one of the periodical magazines of a spotted owl nesting in a billboard or a K–Mart sign or something like that. You all don't cut down and harvest billboards or store signs or anything like that, do you?

Mr. BESAW. No. We try to provide the billboards.

Mr. HOSTETTLER. So it seems that this argument that we have heard doesn't follow a good part of the scientific method and that is observation, that we can observe that this owl will survive—if you cut down this tree, it will go to the next tree or it will find somewhere to live.

Mr. SIMMONS. I think the spotted owl is much more adaptable than it has been given credit for, and I think a lot of the science—my own personal opinion—that that stuff it was based on was pretty bogus.

Mr. HOSTETTLER. And I don't mean to make light of the situation where there has been thousands of jobs that have been lost as a result of this poor science in my opinion, and we talked about those jobs. And then we heard about some beetles that—we have lost thousands of jobs—70 to 80,000, possibly close to 100,000 jobs as a result of what I consider to be bad science, environmental extremism in many cases. How do you think the beetles are faring with this——

Mr. SIMMONS. Quite well.

Mr. HOSTETTLER [continuing]. Compared to the tens of thousands of people that are losing their jobs?

Mr. SIMMONS. They have got an excess of suitable habitat.

Mr. HOSTETTLER. Okay. Mr. Chairman, I just want to make the comment that as we have an Administration that portends to be desirous of creating jobs, that we are losing tens of thousands of jobs because of the desire to save habitat, whereas we have heard earlier that these gentlemen, as do I, hunt on public lands. And we are the best stewards, and these folks count on it as their livelihood—best stewards of the land, the greatest environmentalists because your children are going to probably make their livings off of it someday, and I just commend you and the fact that your communities are so behind this. And I hope you realize that this trend is going to stop, I believe. Thank you very much, Mr. Chair.

Mr. ALLARD. Mr. Cooley.

Mr. COOLEY. Thank you, Mr. Chairman. Just a brief comment before I ask a couple of questions. We have heard earlier in testimony and discussion here about not downsizing the Forest Service. We all know that the Forest Service is being downsized. Everybody is aware of that. The thing that I find from our people in the field that have called us back has said the GS14's and 15's, actual workers that are able to grant contracts and do work to issue permits to cut, are being let go early because of the buyouts. And I don't think it is particularly maybe the Forest Service's fault, but it is the pressure put on maybe by Congress to make that happen.

I am saying and I think everybody should be aware that let us say we do get some legislation passed and we work it through the situation, and then we turn to the Forest Service and demand that they comply with a cut or certain regulations, I can see the future where the Forest Service, no matter how well they are managed, is going to say, "We do not have the personnel available to do this." I think we ought to entertain the idea if they don't, that we go to private industry and have private industry be contracted to do this as well.

I think it should be brought out because I think we are going to put—if we are able to pass some legislation here, therefore, get a timber salvage bill through this Congress, I think we are going to see the Forest Service not able to comply with that bill because of the lack of personnel.

So I think we should go on record to the Forest Service, which their director is here, that we should look at the opportunities of getting private foresters in in order to help them do this work because I think that is going to be very critical. We are putting a tremendous amount of mass, I think, on them to do, and they won't be able to do it. I don't want to use that as an excuse not to comply with some legislation we might put through.

Mark, in our area because I am your representative and I know what devastation the lack of being able to cut damaged, burnt, and dying timber has done in our communities, can you give me a little breakdown because you are closer to it out at La Grande, what is happening up in the little communities like Joseph that has shut down two or three of their mills?

What is happening not only to the millworkers but what is happening to the communities and all of the support; the guy that runs the local service station and the market, dry cleaners, et cetera? Are those still viable today because I know this has happened over several months? Are we seeing these slow businesses of the town being boarded up? Can you give me some feeling of what is happening?

Mr. SIMMONS. As you are aware, congressman, there have been two mills shut down in Joseph, Oregon, just recently. People are very frustrated when they go out in the woods and see all this dead and dying timber, the canal fire just over the hill there from Joseph. Some of the pictures here that we have passed around were taken just outside of Joseph a little ways. It is maddening that they are having to lose their jobs and have all this dead and dying, wasting fiber logs available just wasting in the woods that should be available to bring to the mill.

As you may be aware, there is a bronze foundry there. The bronze foundry there is also laying off now due to concerns. Jerry's Main Street Market is just in a panic to figure out what he is going to do. He is the grocer there in Joseph. People are just really stressed. Some have tried to open little businesses of their own, and things are not working out very well at all. And the fabric of the community—the school is deteriorating and needs some major renovation, and there is just going to be no money to provide that now that we don't have any timber receipt money coming in.

Mr. COOLEY. So we can assume here as members of Congress from our lack of ability to solve some problems that we could solve that we are actually destroying a whole community?

Mr. SIMMONS. Absolutely. I think it is tragic.

Mr. COOLEY. Thank you. Randy, in your area, and I know this is really important to you, since I know you have a good relationship with management there, do you have any projections—have they been telling you how many projections of how long they think they can survive under the present yields that you are enjoying or what little you are enjoying?

Mr. BESAW. Wednesday night before I flew here on Thursday the company had the vice president of the corporation come down and have open meetings with the employees and told us that we are looking at three years. Because the price of pulp right now is at real high levels, even though we are paying extreme amount of prices for chips, we are able to just stay even.

And the last three years, we lost over $40 million in our mill, and he told us that three years from now their projections are that the pulp prices will stay even enough to stay at a break-even point. Even though we are paying this much for chips and the price is at a break-even point, he is saying that three years from now that if they have to go through the same thing they did in the last three years, that they would just go ahead and shut the mill down until fiber costs would come down and make it cost effective for the mill to run. So we are hoping it is at least three years. Whether the market stays three years from now is everybody else's guess.

Mr. ALLARD. The gentleman's time is up.

Mr. COOLEY. Thank you very much, gentlemen, for coming. I appreciate it.

Mr. ALLARD. Mr. Baldacci.

Mr. BALDACCI. Pass.

Mr. ALLARD. Mr. Radanovich.

Mr. RADANOVICH. Thank you, Mr. Chairman. You know, everybody loses their job, and it is a fact of life. It happens. But, you know, maybe if it was because you were a poor businessman, it would be one thing, but to lose it to a foolish notion, to me that is what makes it unbearable. I am new here, and we went through some seminars and some discussions. One bright nuclear physicist gave us one rule and that was never legislate something you don't understand.

I think it is a real good point to make because for two reasons. Number 1, this world is a little bit too big for us to presume that we know how explicitly it operates. I think due to evidence recently of poor science backing up environmental legislation, we should not be presuming to know more of this world than we really do. The second point is I am a grape grower. I don't understand logging, but if you were a grape grower, you and I could talk pretty good about what needs to be done out in the vineyard.

Based on those two reasons, this top-down management system of Washington dictating to you what you should be doing out in the forest is wrong, and I think we have to depend here in Washington on your ability to be good stewards of the land. I mean, we don't have any other choice but to do that. And I would be willing to go so far as privatizing all Federal land in order to prove that. That is just the way this world has to operate.

Now, I come from a district that has two national forests, and it is Sierra National Forest and Sequoia. In the Sierra National Forest, it used to be that sustainable yield was judged at 125 million board feet. The new law rationed that down to 25 million board feet.

Now, there is some discrepancy there, and you can't tell me that we have been operating those forests for over 100 years at 125 million board feet, and then somehow having to say that sustainable yield is 25 million board feet. I used to have three mills in my district. They are all closed now. The last one operated by importing eucalyptus logs to survive to keep the doors open a little bit longer and make the payroll.

So I am glad you guys are here, but the whole point of this thing is you can't have Washington dictating nonreal policy to you people who are the actual stewards of the land, and we have to look to you to be proper stewards. We have to count on you to be that. Otherwise, you get ridiculous stuff like what is going on now.

Mr. SIMMONS. Absolutely.

Mr. RADANOVICH. Thank you, Mr. Chairman.

Mr. DOOLITTLE [presiding]. The Chair recognizes the lady from Wyoming. Let me just make this announcement. Following her questions, we are going then to go vote, all of us, and then we will come back, and we will have the next panel come forward. Mrs. Cubin.

Mrs. CUBIN. Thank you, Mr. Chairman. I don't have a question. I just wanted to make a brief statement. I thank you for coming. I am from Wyoming, and although we don't produce the amount of timber that you do, the policy of the Forest Service is just as devastating to some of our small communities. And so I am really hopeful that we will be able to work with the Forest Service and do something to save jobs and to save our communities. Thank you.

Mr. DOOLITTLE. The Chair would like to thank this panel; the great efforts you have made to be here. The testimony that you shared has been very important, and we will resume following the vote.

[Recess.]

Mr. ALLARD. I will call the Subcommittee on Resource Conservation, Research, and Forestry back to order and continue with our oversight hearing on the timber salvage situation on public lands affected by insects, disease, and fire and the economic and ecological implications of the current salvage harvest schedule.

We have just finished taking testimony on the first panel, and I will move to the second panel which is the agencies. I would like to thank the members of that panel for taking time from their schedule to be here with us today. We have on the second panel Dr. Jack Ward Thomas, Chief of the U.S. Forest Service. We have Ms. Denise Meridith, Deputy Director, Bureau of Land Management, and Mr. Stan Hamilton, State Forester, State of Idaho. Welcome, ladies and gentlemen, and we will start with your testimony, Mr. Thomas.

STATEMENT OF JACK WARD THOMAS, CHIEF, U.S. FOREST SERVICE, DEPARTMENT OF AGRICULTURE; ACCOMPANIED BY GRAY REYNOLDS, DEPUTY CHIEF, NATIONAL FOREST SYSTEM, AND DAVID HESSEL, DIRECTOR OF TIMBER MANAGEMENT; DENISE MERIDITH, DEPUTY DIRECTOR, BUREAU OF LAND MANAGEMENT, DEPARTMENT OF THE INTERIOR; ACCOMPANIED BY WILLIAM TORGENSON, PROFESSIONAL FORESTER, DEPARTMENT OF THE INTERIOR

Mr. THOMAS. Thank you, Mr. Chairman. I will give an abbreviated version to save time for questions. I am accompanied by Gray Reynolds who is Deputy Chief of National Forest System and David Hessel who is our Director of Timber Management.

Last summer, some 56,000 fires burned over 1.3 million acres of state and private lands, 14,000 fires on National Forest System lands burned over 1.5 million acres, and 8,000 fires burned 1.3 million acres of Department of Interior lands. Our policy emphasizes quick removal of dead and dying timber where it is consistent with local forest plan standards and guidelines. However, we are required to follow the same laws for salvage as for logging activities associated with our regular timber sale program. Our actions will help meet public demand for timber, reduce fuels in areas susceptible to wildfire in the future, and assist in reforestation.

Since the major fires in 1987, the Forest Service has maintained a 5-year salvage strategy that is updated annually and funded by the salvage sale fund. The best known part of the program is dead timber harvested after wildfire. This fire salvage will be a significant part of the salvage program strategy for the next 2 years. Historically, about 50 percent of timber burned is not salvageable.

For example, in 1994, we had an estimated 3.7 billion board feet damaged by fires on national forest lands in the West. Much of this wood was in small diameter trees or the defect was so severe that the trees had little commercial value. Isolated trees on steep slopes were not reasonably accessible, and some aspects of fire rehabilitation also cost volume. In other words, these factors reduced the salvageable timber volume from an estimated 3.7 billion to about 1.8 billion board feet, a reduction of about 50 percent.

However, other factors such as compliance with environmental laws, such as the National Environmental Policy Act, the Endangered Species Act, the National Historic Preservation Act, the National Forest Management Act (that is the standards and guides in forest plans), the Clean Water Act, the Wilderness Act, the Wild and Scenic Rivers Act, will reduce the estimated volume even further.

This reduces the available fire salvage volume from the original estimated 1.8 billion board feet to a range somewhere between 656 million to about 1.5 billion. That doesn't include volume loss that might yet occur because of lawsuits. In some burned areas, there may be roadless areas we can access only by using alternative methods such as helicopter.

Over the past 5 years, the salvage program in the western regions has averaged about 1.8 billion board feet per year. In 1995, the Forest Service plans to salvage 1.6 billion board feet, and our projection at this time for 1996 is 1.5 billion. These volume figures may change as we complete analysis of the 1994 fires.

However, ongoing litigation involving salmon in Oregon and Idaho and bull trout in western Montana, Idaho, Oregon, and Washington may further affect our ability to salvage timber. In response to these suits, we are working continuously with the National Marine Fisheries Service to complete the required consultation for the listed salmon in the Columbia River Basin before the Court stay on those cases runs out.

The forest health problem and associated high intensity wildfires are indicators of an ecosystem that is outside the expected range of natural variation. The Forest Health Initiative, which would include salvaging timber from fire areas and areas impacted by disease, insects, and drought, highlights the need to correct short-term, high-risk areas as well as actions on long term forest health.

We have a current ecosystem management assessment going on in the Columbia River Basin that is aimed at determining the long-term effects of our actions in terms of future stand conditions and management actions. We will need to assess the advantages and disadvantages of harvesting versus other management options such as prescribed fire or thinning. Salvage logging is certainly one of the several methods that we will use to reduce fuel loading.

In conclusion, we will make progress toward harvesting salvage timber in addressing forest health. The Under Secretary for Natural Resources and Environment and the Forest Service have committed to convene an interagency team at the highest level. It begins meeting next Monday, February the 13th, to develop a strategy to expedite preparation of salvage sales and other attacks on forest health problems.

The Forest Service then is moving aggressively to assess timber salvage opportunities from areas burned by wildfire in 1994; is following the law in preparing salvage sales; and is continuing its efforts to improve coordination between other State and Federal regulatory agencies and will continue efforts to facilitate consultation.

The Forest Service will act on the key recommendations of the Western Forest Health Initiative report and ensure forest health factors are included. The Forest Service will refine, validate, and expand the database on forest health problems nationally to direct further policy and budget action.

In the long term, we have to consider the economic and ecological results of management actions we take today on the condition and resource capacity in the future. That completes my testimony. I will be happy to answer any questions. Thank you, sir.

[The statement of Mr. Thomas appears at the conclusion of the hearing.]

Mr. ALLARD. I thank the gentleman for his testimony. Would you please introduce to the committees the people that you have with you? I guess one gentleman that I mentioned, Mr. Stan Hamilton, didn't make it, the forester from Idaho, but you have other people that are up there at the table. If you would please introduce them to the committees?

Mr. THOMAS. This is Gray Reynolds to my immediate left who is our Deputy Chief for the National Forest System. And to his left is David Hessel who is the Forest Service Director of Timber Management.

Ms. MERIDITH. And this is Bill Torgenson with me. He is a professional forester on my Washington, DC, staff.

Mr. ALLARD. Go ahead, Denise, if you would and give us your testimony please.

STATEMENT OF DENISE MERIDITH

Ms. MERIDITH. I really appreciate the opportunity to be here as well. The timber salvage issue involves BLM forested lands throughout the entire intermountain and Rocky Mountain west, as well as the State of Alaska.

BLM is not on the same scope as the Forest Service. We manage approximately 50 million acres of forested land, 28 million of which are in the lower 48 states. Approximately 4 million acres are commercial sawlog species, half of which are in western Oregon, and the remainder is woodlands.

Of the 2 million acres outside western Oregon, about half is withdrawn from harvesting because of the restrictions Jack discussed, wilderness study areas, wildlife habitat needs, as well as some things that make them inoperative such as topographic restrictions, fragile sites, and reforestation difficulties. These forests are often very close adjacent to national forests in the transition area between rangeland and higher elevations, and they are very important for providing wood fiber, important fish and wildlife habitat, and recreational opportunities.

I will skip a large part of my testimony here. It will be included in the record so that we can move on to the questions. It is BLM's policy to place a very high priority on timber salvage efforts. This policy recognizes the value of salvaging portions of merchantable tree volume killed by drought, insects, disease, and wildfire. All of our manuals and handbooks direct our field people to put the highest priority on the salvage operation.

In many cases, the salvage of dead and dying timber has a short-term benefit to overall economic health by reducing the potential intensity of wildfire, which you have heard a lot about earlier, and providing long-term benefits for the area. So we put a priority on salvaging appropriate quantities of dead and dying timber ahead of the sale of green timber. At the same time, we recognize that there are some benefits to some amounts of dead wood. These include providing shade and habitat for wildlife as well as other things.

In the last 10 years, I just want to cite a few examples of which we are very proud of our efforts to salvage timber, what we do is use specialists from throughout the country and send them into high priority areas. We have sent a crew from Roseburg, Oregon, for example, to Alaska to help in timber sales there. We have sent crews from Montana to California to lay out and cruise over 17 million board feet of salvage that we have already sold this year.

We have offered a sale of 13 million board feet of salvage beetle-killed fir in southeast Idaho in 1991 and 1992. That also required personal sharing. And we have been salvaging over 50 million board feet in California since 1988. One really good example we had recently was reducing the fire intensity and severity near Klamath, Oregon, by thinning out pine stands there.

I want to mention in 1992, Congress was very helpful to us by establishing the Forest Ecosystem Health and Recovery Fund. This has made a very big difference to BLM in its ability to deal with timber salvage. So far, we have been able to meet our timber salvage goals and objectives through the teamwork of our foresters and making use of this fund that Congress allowed us to set up.

I think the only recommendation we would have in improving this fund which we currently use for administration, site preparation, reforestation is to possibly expand the fund's authority to include practices such as prescribed burns, fuels treatment, and thinning which we feel would only increase our capacity to deal with timber salvage. We are subject to the same laws and restrictions that Jack mentioned; Clean Air Act, Clean Water Act, et cetera. That has in some way hindered our ability to deal with this problem.

Each salvage sale is very unique. It depends on things such as the slope, what wildlife species are present, how severe the burn was, whether land use plans have been done, whether it is economical to harvest. We have attached our best estimate of what we can do in the future in the submission that we made to Committee Chairman Don Young.

We are planning to offer approximately 64 million board feet in fiscal year 1995, and that would equate to about $6.7 million in revenue. And this is based on the states' requests. These requests have come from the local people to us in Washington, and we have honored all requests that we have had for money to donate to timber salvage.

There have been some questions about Alaska, and I will answer more specific questions if they come up. There are several hindrances to our making much use of timber salvage operations in Alaska. One is that most of the land that we have that is affected has been identified by the state as something that they would like to have, and also we have marketability problems on our Alaska timber, and, finally, we have a shortage of people working up in Alaska that would be able to do that. But I will defer right now the rest of my testimony, and we can move on to questions.

[The statement of Ms. Meridith appears at the conclusion of the hearing.]

Mr. ALLARD. Thank you. Your time is up. I have got several questions I would like to ask before we call members of the committee. Dr. Thomas, currently how much salvageable timber volume exists on the National Forest System land?

Mr. THOMAS. We estimate for 1995 that we have a salvage volume of about 1 billion 574 million board feet. That is out of a total volume that includes salvage of about 4 billion. The 1996 planned estimate is about 1 billion 499 million.

Mr. ALLARD. Now, can you elaborate on how you came up with those numbers?

Mr. THOMAS. Yes, sir. We went out to every region into every forest. They looked at the salvageable volume in several different categories, whether it was salvaged after fire or salvage related to forest health or blow-down. Each forest came back with their estimates; not only the total amount that was dead or dying but also that we could reach with existing road systems. They were in areas that were in the timber base, et cetera, and they added it up for us by forest.

Mr. ALLARD. How do you identify a dying tree?

Mr. THOMAS. Well, there are several different ways. I probably should refer to the Chief of Timber Management, but you can do it by changing needles. There are ways that you can do it by testing a cambium layer in bark. If you are looking at pine beetle damage, usually if you have pitch tubes on the tree, you can assume a very high risk of mortality.

Mr. ALLARD. It is relatively easy to identify?

Mr. THOMAS. Within limits. Sometimes you identify trees that are damaged that don't die or are drought stressed that don't die, but the record is pretty good. I would say we could probably hit 80 percent accuracy. Of course, if you are getting needle brown, you know they are dead.

Mr. ALLARD. Yes. Okay. How much do you think would be available under existing law?

Mr. THOMAS. We anticipate about 1 billion 574 million board feet in 1995.

Mr. ALLARD. In the 1996 budget request, the capability figures for salvage is basically the same as your request in 1995 which is about the 1.5 billion feet. Now, this is after the agency spent three months developing a Western Forest Health Initiative. Could you explain to this committee what additional benefits the taxpayers derived from the initiative?

Mr. THOMAS. The salvage you identify was an initial estimate that we had that was put together just after we got the fires out. I have submitted to Chairman Young and will submit to you, updated figures on what we might do, but that was the only thing we could put together that fast. Better estimates of salvage are in my testimony. The salvage is identified, we know where it is, and there is a high probability that we can get that done.

Mr. ALLARD. Given the present and projected future climate conditions, do your fire experts see a potential for catastrophic fire seasons equal to or greater than the one we just experienced this last year?

Mr. THOMAS. Any year right now for the next several that we have weather conditions and drought conditions—the drought continues and the weather conditions are similar to this summer, we should anticipate additional catastrophic fire.

Mr. ALLARD. And in what way does that have an impact on maybe the available salvageable timber? Is it a negligible amount or a significant amount?

Mr. THOMAS. Congressman, I would like to come around or send somebody to visit each one of you. I have a series of overlays with me. If I could show it to you, it would very quickly take the place of about two hours of testimony. If you were looking at this particular forest which is the Payette and you start out with a base map and then you outline the fires that we had this last year, then over that base map you lay down the damage classes—you know, heavy damage, all dead, half dead, partially dead, and salvageable—lay that down and lay over the top of that another.

Now, these overlays that I started to lay down are black. You lay down wilderness classification, and you lay down the next map which is wilderness study areas, and you lay down the next map which is roadless areas subject to consultation on anadromous fish. You lay down the next map which is the wild and scenic river corridors, and you lay down the next map which is the initial riparian protection areas. There is not much left.

So the point of it is there is not a direct relationship between saying I have 100 units burned; therefore, that is how much could be salvaged. Given that sort of a situation, you are looking at well less than half.

Mr. ALLARD. Thank you. Let me go ahead and call on the ranking member on Ag, Mr. Baldacci. Go ahead.

Mr. BALDACCI. Thank you. Dr. Thomas, in your testimony, you noted a number of environmental laws that you must comply with to carry out timber sales. Do you believe that those acts constitute unreasonable constraints, or would good forest management practices suggest that you follow some of those procedures even if the laws did not require it?

Mr. THOMAS. I would agree that I believe in the purpose of every one of those laws. I pledged to obey the law, and we will do that. However, I think we are beginning to understand that the interactions of all those laws that were passed independently are beginning to create an interaction that makes it very difficult. Yes, a great number of the requirements in those laws we would follow as a matter of standard forest practice.

Mr. BALDACCI. So you believe that there is actually a bigger problem with the coordination problem rather than an overlap problem?

Mr. THOMAS. No, sir, I don't know that I would agree with that. I think what the problem is, particularly if you are dealing with salvage, is the amount of time required to come on line with exact compliance to the law. Let us use your original hypothesis that those are things that we would do anyway. Yes, that is true except that it could be done much faster. Also we have the interactions and intersections of those laws that provide a number of avenues for appeal and the amount of time to take it out. Then if it is litigated, it goes on even further.

Mr. BALDACCI. Thank you.

Mr. ALLARD. Let me now call on the Chairman of the Resources Committee, Mr. Young, the gentleman from Alaska.

Mr. YOUNG. Thank you, Mr. Chairman. It is unfortunate that there was a protest of our sitting on the five-minute rule of the Interior Committee, and I hope Mr. Williams would voice that to Mr. Miller which I am going to also do. I think that is very inappropriate. This is a hearing on a very vital issue of salvaged timber in his state and other western states, and these dilatory tactics I think are unheard of. When I was the ranking member, we never used this against any hearing; maybe in a markup but not a hearing.

Mr. Thomas, I think the gentleman alluded to it; both you and the lady from BLM suggested that there was problems with other Acts, and you just answered part of it. Have either one of you, either Departments, came up with suggestions how to expedite this process of salvage?

That is important to me because we can sit here and do it for you, or we would like to have your expertise from you on how we can solve this problem. You just stated we will have other fires in the future equally as bad as we had in the past. The loss of this timber is wrong for the resource base so are you planning on coming to us and saying how we can solve some of these problems?

Mr. THOMAS. Well, I can tell you what my instructions are. First, I will give you some good news. When we got the second lawsuit in Idaho with the immediate order of shutdown of all actions that may affect salmon, we asked for a 45-day stay. We got it. Mr. Schmitten, of National Marine Fisheries, and I have gotten together, and we will complete those consultations at least 15 days before the deadline. We think earlier than that. That is some progress.

On Monday, there is a two-day meeting by the agency directors of the Forest Service, the Fish and Wildlife Service, the National Marine Fisheries Service, and EPA to see what we can do at the top level to expedite, salvage timber sales.

Mr. YOUNG. Jack, in all due respects, that is well and good, and I congratulate you. But I want suggestions from both agencies on how we can solve the problems from your expertise so we can make sure that the interest groups outside that do not want to salvage can't use the Courts to stop what we think is correct and you think is correct. And if you don't come forth, and I have suggested it to you both before, we will write it the way we think it should be done, and we are not necessarily the experts in the field.

So I am asking you because both of you said that these agencies are causing a myriad of problems so either you come forward with the information—I will request if formally if that is what you wish; I guess you do so we will do that. Mr. Chairman and I want to know how we can get beyond this constant delay where the trees stand and rot, and I think it is a terrible loss to mankind. So please do that.

Denise, what do you mean you don't have the people in Alaska to carry forth the sales?

Ms. MERIDITH. We don't have professional foresters in Alaska.

Mr. YOUNG. Why not?

Ms. MERIDITH. Because outside of this issue with the salvage, there hasn't been a need to do much forestry in Alaska.

Mr. YOUNG. Do you want to be directed to have people in Alaska to have forest sales? I mean, we need the forestry. You know, we have shut down mills because we have billions of board feet around us, and we can't cut it because it has been put in the wilderness. So is that in the budget this year?

Ms. MERIDITH. The 60 million board feet that I referred to a few minutes ago has been selected by the state. I think the situation in Alaska, as far as BLM is concerned, are prime habitat regarding forestry—has been selected by the state as, you know, things that they would like to have and keep. Therefore, we have not invested a lot of money or people or personnel in those lands.

Mr. YOUNG. Outside of the state-selected lands, how much board feet do you have?

Mr. TORGENSON. On the figures we got from the state, most of that volume is in the Tiekel Block near Glenallen, and that has recently been selected by the state for retention.

Mr. YOUNG. But before the committee here, I am going to suggest we get the figures out on this because if the state selected it, let us get it to the state because then they can put it up for sale. This is the old check-in-the-mail routine. If they have selected it, what is holding up the transfer of title so they can put it up for sale as timberland? If they have selected it and you are holding up the transfer of title and you are not putting up the sales, that means the timber is not available. So we will do that. Mr. Chairman, I know we are about out of time and——

Mr. WILLIAMS. Would the full committee Chairman yield to me?

Mr. YOUNG. Yes, gladly yield.

Mr. WILLIAMS. I would be pleased to follow the full committee Chairman's recommendation and talk to Mr. Miller as long as the Chairman brings up process though. Let me air this. Perhaps one of the reasons Mr. Miller has invoked the five-minute rule is because of the way some of us were treated. I don't think the Chairman understands this.

I have been in the Congress 17 years. This is the first time a constituent of mine has been invited to a hearing, and I wasn't informed. I have been Chairman for 10 years around here, and I always informed Democrats and Republicans when one of their constituents—the way I knew my good constituent was in town was he was kind enough to drop by my office this morning and inform me. Now, I know it is early, Don, but we really ought to have more courtesy than that.

Mr. YOUNG. Well, I will say this, that we have been more than fair. You haven't sat on this side as long as I have, my friend. Now, if you want to get in an argument we will. But I am just going to tell you right now——

Mr. WILLIAMS. Well, if you are telling me you are trying to get even, you are not getting even with me because I never did that to you.

Mr. ALLARD. I am going to go ahead and just recess the committee until we get back from the votes, and then I will call it back to order when we get some members here.

[Recess.]

Mr. ALLARD. I call the committee back to order. In the process of questioning the panel, Mr. Williams, you are next I guess.

Mr. WILLIAMS. Thanks, Mr. Chairman. Chief, I am not sure I have come to grips with sort of the heart of the reason that we can't get more salvageable material out. Let me use 1994 as the base year referring to your testimony. More than 3.5 billion board feet were damaged by fires.

As I understand your testimony, and please correct me as I go through this if I am wrong, approximately half of all that damaged or downed timber was not salvaged because it was either so defective from the fire that it would have been of no commercial use, it was small timber that had no commercial value, or it was isolated parcels on, say, steep slopes where the access wasn't reasonable. So that is the reason half of the '94 volume didn't come out. Now, as I understand it further, and so that is what—about 1 billion 700 million board feet that didn't come out because of those reasons. Then there was 665 million board feet that you probably couldn't have gotten out because of the various laws such as the Wild Rivers Act or the Clean Water Act. Is that right?

Mr. THOMAS. Yes, sir.

Mr. WILLIAMS. So there is three times as much timber that doesn't come out because it is either inaccessible or it is too badly burned to have commercial value or it is too small. There is three times as much timber lost that way or that is not salvageable as there is because of America's environmental laws?

Mr. THOMAS. I would have to run through that with a pencil, but there is more of it that is not salvageable because of points that you bring forward than there is because of these other actions. That is true.

Mr. WILLIAMS. Well, I think what we are hearing is that there is less than 700 million board feet of all of that burned, and there is 3 billion 700 million board feet burned. There is less than 700 million of that that you can't get out because of Federal law. All of the rest of it, fully half of it, you can't get out because it has no commercial value or because it is not accessible. Is that——

Mr. THOMAS. That was true in 1994. I suspect——

Mr. WILLIAMS. Yes. I am using 1994 as the——

Mr. THOMAS. I suspect in 1995 that nonmerchantable number would be somewhat less than that due to increased stumpage prices and demand for chips.

Mr. WILLIAMS. Were these percentages in 1994 do you think usual or——

Mr. THOMAS. Well, it is usually about 50 percent of damaged material that is actually available for salvage. That runs in a ballpark across years.

Mr. WILLIAMS. Okay. Now, why doesn't the rest of it come out? Because we still have what—a billion board feet left here. Why doesn't that come out?

Mr. THOMAS. It was not accessible because it was in areas that we could not enter or it took us too long to get to it or it was——

Mr. WILLIAMS. But not because of Federal law?

Mr. THOMAS. Let me defer to my experts here.

Mr. REYNOLDS. Yes. Let me just add that some of these areas we talk about aren't accessible. We talked about the salvage material and how it deteriorates after the fire. When you add the time it takes to complete the NEPA processes for project approval, and the addition of time if you have to build roads into some of this country, the timber value is dropping all that time. From a salvage standpoint in unroaded areas, our preference is to use helicopters for logging, assuming that there is a market for the timber.

Mr. WILLIAMS. Because my time has expired, let me just make the point about roads. I have been one who has supported what I think is a reasonable road budget; in fact, more money than some of my environmental friends in Montana like. But there is enormous objection in Montana to build expensive roads to go get fire-damaged timber. The taxpayers are up in arms about that one out there, conservative or liberal.

Mr. THOMAS. Congressman, that is why I think to the extent within the anadromous fish range that we get roadless areas through consultation, I suspect that most of them that are proposed will be proposed for helicopter logging.

Mr. ALLARD. You know, I wasn't clear on your answer there on inaccessible. Is this inaccessible because of rules and regulations or inaccessible because of the topography of the land?

Mr. THOMAS. I think what we meant in that first instance that Mr. Williams referred to would be single trees high up on a steep slope. It would not pay to build a road to get to them or it would not pay to have a helicopter come in and take them; canyons were too steep, the ground was too steep, it was too far away, those sorts of things.

Mr. ALLARD. Okay. Let me call on my Chairman on the Parks and Forest and Lands Subcommittee, Mr. Hansen.

Mr. HANSEN. I thank you, Mr. Chairman. Chief Thomas, prior to the Clinton Administration, if I recall correctly, the Forest Service could exempt salvage sales from administrative appeals. Why can't the Forest Service exempt these sales from administrative appeals now?

Mr. THOMAS. Let me defer to somebody who knows more about that than I.

Mr. REYNOLDS. Yes. Prior to, as I remember, 1991, our appeal regulations gave us the authority to exempt salvage sales from appeal. And then I think it was in the 1991 Appropriation Act we got legislation to go back and revise our appeal regulations. The current regulations that we have in place now do not provide us that opportunity to exempt salvage sales from appeal.

Mr. HANSEN. The thing that bothers me on that, and I am kind of hazy on that changing the legislation, but I can't remember it specifically stating that you couldn't do that. I was under the impression that the Forest Service did that by regulations in and of themselves. Am I wrong on that, Gray?

Mr. REYNOLDS. Yes. Congress did not tell us we couldn't do that. In the hearing, the dialogue back and forth, they did not give us direction. What we went back and did in developing the rules is we have a stay provision that is related to emergency situations. We have utilized that in about eight instances.

I could read you what that portion of the appeal regulation says, but basically if we get one of these salvage sales comes in from a regional forester requesting the chief to use his emergency control, we would look at that as a way to stay. But that is only a very short period in the overall time it takes to get a salvage sale out. All salvage sales we will complete the NEPA process on.

Mr. HANSEN. Yes. But prior to that, you didn't? Prior to this regulation, and you hang that——

Mr. REYNOLDS. Well, we did the NEPA process, but we didn't do the appeal process.

Mr. HANSEN. Surely. Following this up, you did, by those regulations, implement the NEPA process, and that is what you are following now so every salvage sale does go through the NEPA process now. Is that a correct statement?

Mr. REYNOLDS. That is correct.

Mr. HANSEN. And you take that back to the change that you had. So if we change that back, you could very likely change that also?

Mr. REYNOLDS. If that was changed, we could exempt most sales and salvage.

Mr. HANSEN. Especially if Mr. Young here determined he wanted to put it in black and white; thus sayeth the Chairman type of thing. You would go along with that?

Mr. REYNOLDS. Yes.

Mr. HANSEN. Good show. I appreciate that. Let me ask you this. I was interested in the comments that the chief made regarding the amount of timber that you had out there, and I wonder how much of that timber would come under a question of whether or not you wanted to have it harvested because of environmental questions. Have you ever put a percentage on that? You came up with this awesome amount of board feet, but I notice there was some hesitation on both of your part and the BLM part because of some environmental problems. What percentage of that would you say you would not want to get involved in because of an environmental situation?

Mr. REYNOLDS. Well, let me just caution you that this varies by forest. Some forests have a lot more of those problems than others do, but I would estimate that it is in the neighborhood of about 35 or 40 percent.

Mr. HANSEN. You would go that high, 40 percent of it. So really the figure that was brought up that was harvestable timber, we got to reduce that by 40 percent. Is that right?

Mr. REYNOLDS. Yes. And my example is the situation we are dealing with right now in the Columbia Basin.

Mr. HANSEN. And, of course, some of those would run higher per whatever that particular forest was that was experiencing some of those problems. Is that right?

Mr. REYNOLDS. Yes. In some cases, it would probably be down around 20 percent, but in other cases it is high like I mentioned in the Columbia Basin where we have a number of listed species.

Mr. HANSEN. What would you say the Dixie is?

Mr. REYNOLDS. The Dixie has had about 15 to 20 percent.

Mr. HANSEN. So basically you have got 80 percent of that is harvestable in the Dixie?

Mr. REYNOLDS. That is right.

Mr. HANSEN. They keep talking about helicopters to take it in. I can't imagine anything more expensive being an old pilot than having to fly a helicopter in and then take it out one log at a time.

Mr. REYNOLDS. They take more than one log at a time. The capability of helicopters has increased significantly. It depends on the——

Mr. HANSEN. Significantly means about like 10 times? Something like that?

Mr. REYNOLDS. Oh, I would think so.

Mr. HANSEN. At least, yes. Okay. Excuse me. My time is up. I saw the red light go on. Thank you, Mr. Chairman. I appreciate your indulgence.

89-215 O - 95 - 3

Mr. ALLARD. Mr. DeFazio, do you have any questions?

Mr. DEFAZIO. I do, Mr. Chairman, and I think I can hopefully get it in, and we can get to the vote.

Mr. ALLARD. Proceed if you would please.

Mr. DEFAZIO. Thank you, Mr. Chairman. Chief, I guess the issue for me is, you know, whether or not we are getting ahead with the salvage program that even falls outside some of these areas of concern as expeditiously as possible. And I am sure you won't have the numbers right at your fingertips here, but, I mean, I would be curious, you know, what the amount of standing dead or dying timber is in the east side of Oregon, you know, fire and bug kill, and of that how much of it is outside roadless areas, and then how much of it is available this year for salvage.

And while you are thinking about that, I guess while he is working on those numbers, I was very involved in a salvage in my district in my first term which was controversial, and the gentleman will come later who represents the industry who was very concerned that they get a reduced amount of salvage because of my efforts.

And I was also criticized from the other end of the spectrum for getting any salvage out, but it was the Silver Fire salvage. We did it without a new road. We did it with helicopters. Helicopters, in fact—this was before stumpage ran way up—were very economic. We did it without taking out any green trees. We did it on very steep slopes. We found there was no additional siltation. There was no rise in water temperature beyond that which would have happened consequent to the fire. And it worked really well, and we got quite a substantial amount of timber out. So I am wondering why we aren't doing something, you know, like that all across eastern Oregon before it all burns up?

Mr. THOMAS. One of the reasons we are not doing anything in eastern Oregon is we have been shut down for most of it under injunctions, and we still are, until we can clear the consultation process on Forest Plans. We hope to complete all consultations on Forest Plans by the 15th of the month.

Mr. DEFAZIO. Consultation over what issue? It is not owl forest. What is the issue?

Mr. THOMAS. No. It is a salmon issue.

Mr. DEFAZIO. Well, in the John Day Ranger District, Malheur Forest, you don't have salmon issues. I mean, I am curious. You know, there is quite a bit of forest land out there that is not anadromous.

Mr. THOMAS. We are looking at 387 million board feet in Oregon east of the Cascades this year.

Mr. DEFAZIO. You will do 387 you believe?

Mr. THOMAS. That is the number they just handed me. I hope they are right.

Mr. DEFAZIO. Okay. And how much is there total, I mean, if we——

Mr. THOMAS. Go on to your next question. It will allow them to come up with a number.

Mr. DEFAZIO. Okay. All right. Well, you know, that is just my observation. The 387—I think that is substantially more than was done last year, and it sounds like you are moving ahead. But, I mean, as I said, last year when we were considering the LaRocco bill, it seems to me that the Forest Service would prioritize areas that already roaded, areas that are not otherwise sensitive and get in there and expedite a salvage program.

And I know there is always someone who is going to file an appeal on anything, but, you know, when appeals have no merit, you can reject them. And I would hope that the Forest Service moves ahead with that 387, you know, and I think you could under the existing processes. Do you have the total figure there?

Mr. REYNOLDS. Let me just respond to that. On the Wenatchee, they will have completed all their watershed assessments by July of this year. That was an important part in the President's plan, and from then on, they expect to have an EA out each month for the next 9 months to deal with the salvage.

Mr. DEFAZIO. Okay. And then I guess hearing that earlier panel, I guess I don't know if you will be able to answer this because now we are getting down to the ranger district, but, I mean, the testimony about the Quinault Ranger District, I was puzzled that something that would be extremely valuable, merchantable timber as salvage was not just being left for some concern, slopes, whatever, but was being let out on firewood permits but couldn't be sold commercially otherwise. That seemed very curious to me.

Mr. HESSEL. I was a little curious about that too, but I got thinking about why would a ranger not go ahead and sell those blowdown trees. Generally, he showed one tree, but it is pretty hard to get industry in just for one tree.

Mr. DEFAZIO. Well, if the one tree is worth that much, I think you would get a helicopter in there.

Mr. HESSEL. It is still pretty hard to get them in for one tree, but normally there is probably other trees in the area which then have to go through the normal process of NEPA and all the other things that happen. And it probably was in an HCA habitat conservation area.

Mr. DEFAZIO. But are we allowing firewood cutting in there? I mean, that was what puzzled me. I can understand with all the things we have going on the west side why you wouldn't be able to get in there, but when he said that it went for firewood, that was when it just sort of——

Mr. HESSEL. Let me go on to say that looking at the process and knowing full well to go and sell all these trees and still with Judge Dwyer's probable injunction couldn't sell them anyway, but by selling one tree under a permit didn't have to go through all that process and could get a tree sold for firewood for personal use and/or commercial use.

Mr. DEFAZIO. You know, it is not my district, but I would just be curious in some little follow-up on this in a written explanation because I remain a bit puzzled because, again, if it had that much value, I believe you could have sold it, you know, for the full value. And if it is that valuable, I think they would have flown a helicopter in.

Mr. HESSEL. The answer is I don't know, but we will find out.

Mr. DEFAZIO. Okay. Thank you.

Mr. ALLARD. The committee is in recess until we get back from this vote.

[Recess.]

Mr. ALLARD. I would like to go ahead and call the committee back to order. I will call on Congressman Doolittle for questions.

Mr. DOOLITTLE. Dr. Thomas, we heard testimony about the $60,000 tree that went for $150. Can you comment upon the policy that allowed that type of thing to happen and your familiarity with how widespread that may or may not be?

Mr. THOMAS. Congressman, I do not know, but I will find out.

Mr. DOOLITTLE. Thank you. Mr. Carlson referred, and unfortunately the time was up, I couldn't pursue it, but he referred to the destruction of the infrastructure that it takes to engage in a timber sale program. I am very concerned about that. We have been given to understand that in this round of early layoffs at the Forest Service that foresters and engineers have been targeted within the Forest Service, that biologists have been exempted from layoffs I think was what I heard. What I would like to know is what are the facts about that as far as you understand them?

Mr. THOMAS. We will leave you a piece of paper, congressman, that describes this perfectly, but the timber program between 1992 and present went down 64 percent. Road construction went down 51 percent. We took our foresters down by 19 percent and the engineers by 21 percent. That was the part of the program that was declining. The part where the people were exempted was the part of the program that was increasing. A simple business decision.

Mr. DOOLITTLE. Well, has anything happened within the last few months to change the pattern of layoffs that you just described to accelerate the percentages, for example?

Mr. THOMAS. No, sir.

Mr. DOOLITTLE. I will look forward to seeing the material.

Mr. THOMAS. I do think we should make a point here. We had reduced our work force from 1992 to the present by 4,000 positions. That is our share of downsizing. We make no complaint about that. We downsized in those areas that were declining as Congress instructed us in the appropriations. However, that is not without consequence. Also, when they went down by regulation, we had to offer early retirement, et cetera, by class. We were unable to go to particular places and pick people. Now that we are down to 4,000 people, we have a problem that the people are not distributed as we would like, but we are working on that.

Mr. DOOLITTLE. When you say by class, you are referring to——

Mr. THOMAS. By foresters, by road engineers, by ecologists and so on. So now we are trying to arrange that work force. In the meantime, we are scheduled to go down by 1999 by another 3,000 positions. There was some earlier comments made about taking out workers while sparing the brass. Actually, at the moment, we are disproportionately reducing people in grade 14's and above, and that is also by edict.

In this next round of cuts, we will take the heaviest hits in the Washington office and at the regions. But that is largely an illusion in the sense that only 2 percent of our work force is inside the beltway. So if we reduce that by 25 percent, we reduce the regions by an equivalent amount, even after you take off your shoes so you can count real high, 2,200 to 2,400 positions will still come out of field operations.

Mr. DOOLITTLE. You may have given me the figure, and I just didn't focus on it, but let me ask you this. Was the percentage reduction in biologists and ecologists equal to the percentage reduction in foresters and engineers?

Mr. THOMAS. No, sir. For example, foresters went down from about 5,300 to 4,300; civil engineers from about 1,050 to 816; fisheries biologists, because of our huge demands now with listed salmon, went up 87 percent, but that was an increase from 294 to 381. You start from a much smaller base. Wildlife biologists went down 17 percent. Botanists, given the endangered and threatened plants and operations, went up 38 percent, but that only is a difference between 99 and 137. And I can leave these numbers with you.

Mr. DOOLITTLE. Okay. My concern is that we have a crisis in our forests as you well know. We have talked about the Tahoe area before. Somebody has given me some pictures of forests. This is the Tahoe area, and this is a forest in Oregon. Now, I understand that the climates are different, but, I mean, this picture here on your left points out how brown the Tahoe situation is. And in many of these areas, we have got forests that are up to 50 percent dead and dying. As I have listened to the testimony, to me the system is clearly broken. We have seen a four-fifths reduction in the amount of timber being harvested since the 1980's. I have not heard anything here that suggests that that is going to change. These poor gentlemen that showed up from working in the forests and the mills and so forth and doing the logging are just going to look apparently for more and more jobs. What do you see? What can we do to fix this broken system and to expedite beginning with the salvaged timber?

Mr. THOMAS. Well, first, you have to be the people to define whether the system is indeed broken.

Mr. DOOLITTLE. Well, as one member, it is clear to me it is broken, and I think that is the opinion of a majority of this committee.

Mr. THOMAS. Well, I wouldn't argue about that, congressman. That is for you to decide. One should note that the Federal Judge said that opting is a legal plan, just barely. We complied with the law, just barely, which is as close to balance as you can get under the law. If that is not satisfactory and if there is a new law, we will, obviously, obey it.

The thing in the shorter term is that we are working with everything, and, again, we start again on Monday to figure out how we can do these things under the present law the most effectively, efficiently that we can. But even with the utmost in efficiency, the timber yields in the part of the country that you are talking about are not going back under current situations to anywhere close to previous levels.

Mr. DOOLITTLE. My time is up. I just want to pose this question, and maybe you can answer it later on. We want to change the law. The laws are clearly flawed, in my opinion, and needs to be changed. We would like to get some help from the Forest Service. Otherwise, as Chairman Young indicated, we will write them ourselves, but we could do it better with your help. Thank you.

Mr. ALLARD. The other gentleman from California, Congressman Pombo.

Mr. POMBO. Thank you. Mr. Thomas, I would like to get back to the line of questioning that Mr. Williams had before about the salvage timber and so on just to clear this up in my own mind. He talked about 3.7 billion board feet that were available. Was that just burned because of burned timber, or was that total because of dead, dying, diseased and burned?

Mr. THOMAS. That is just the fire-damaged volume.

Mr. POMBO. How much do you estimate actually burned up and went up in smoke versus what was left with the 3.7 billion?

Mr. THOMAS. The 3.7 billion is the salvageable or potentially salvageable volume.

Mr. POMBO. How much went up in smoke?

Mr. THOMAS. I don't know. There is no way for us to know. If it is not there, we can't inventory it.

Mr. POMBO. It was not inventoried prior to it burning?

Mr. THOMAS. Well, I don't know the answer to the question because it is not a question that we would have any reason to compute.

Mr. POMBO. Well, let me give you a reason to compute it, and you can follow along with my thinking on this. If we had done proper management and you had been allowed to do your job as far as the laws allowed you to do that, and you were able to go in and clean out the dead, dying, and diseased timber so that the fire would not have reached the point that it did. How much could we have saved of the forests so that we would have had enough trees not only for wildlife but enough timber for the mills to continue to operate?

See, one of the things I don't understand, just last summer we were in California and it had a fire, and the CDF and the Department of Forestry were fighting to try to stop the fire before it hit the wildlife preserve because once it hit the wildlife preserve, they were not allowed to go in with their tractors and equipment to stop the fire once it hit that.

And it seemed kind of, I guess, strange in a way that we had laws that would allow the forests to burn up. That can't be good for wildlife. That can't be good for our economy. That can't be good for the social well being of the West to allow that to happen, and what I am wondering is if we actually did manage the forests properly, could we stop the fires from occurring?

Mr. THOMAS. No.

Mr. POMBO. And if we did that, how much would we save?

Mr. THOMAS. The answer is no. We could diminish the risk, but I don't think we could ever tell you under even the best of management that we could prevent fire. But we could certainly reduce the risk and reduce the nature of the fire.

Mr. POMBO. I think that there are other foresters that although there is no way to stop all fires and I realize that, but there are other foresters who have told me that if the forests were properly managed, they could cut back substantially on the loss. And even though a fire may start, it may only burn a few hundred acres instead of several hundred thousand acres.

Mr. THOMAS. I would agree that one can reduce fire risk through management. There is not any doubt about that.

Mr. POMBO. I guess maybe you can understand why I am a little puzzled at allowing timber to burn versus properly managing it.

Mr. THOMAS. Congressman, if you request it, we will be happy to come back and tell you what that cost. It has cost and it has benefits, and I think one of the reasons that it has not been done is that Congress has not seen fit to fund it, and it will not be cheap.

Mr. POMBO. I would like to know what we are losing in fire and what the cost is. The environmental cost has to be astronomical for allowing that to happen.

Mr. THOMAS. Well, congressman, this is considerably more complex than is emerging from this hearing. For example, "that can't be good for wildlife." Oh, yes, it can. It can be absolutely marvelous for some species of wildlife that are well adapted to successional change. We even do intentional burning for wildlife, but the part of it is I understand your point that good management can provide a wide array of benefits, but these things are not as clearly simple as are being described.

But if the point it is can we, with appropriate management, move a considerable way toward providing that entire spectrum of benefits and habitats, the answer is yes. Can we do it totally? Probably not. There are probably some species that would be better related to so far as know the conditions that we have no capability yet proven to produce through silviculture.

Mr. POMBO. Unfortunately, the time is shorted in this process that we go through on hearings. There are 100 questions I would like to ask you about decisions that are made in management of our forests and whether other ways of approaching those problems would be more effective. And I guess I would like to reiterate some of the comments that have been made before by other members that we do want to work with you in establishing. We are going to reauthorize the Endangered Species Act. We are going to look at all of the environmental legislation that you are operating under right now.

It would be a lot easier and a lot more effective to work with you and to have suggestions from you. I am opening myself up to you to work with you on those issues so that what we do come up with will work better than what we are doing today. And I would strongly encourage you and your staff and the other members of your staff to work with us on trying to find a better answer for what we are trying to do.

Mr. THOMAS. Thank you, sir. We would, of course, respond to any requests that the committee makes. I will also pass on the points being made here. However, in the shorter term, we do obey the law. One thing I would suggest, Mr. Chairman, is if we do look at the laws, please don't look at them individually. They were put together individually without understanding or appreciation of how they might interact. And if you do choose to look at the law and if you choose to make any changes, I strongly encourage that they be done in an overview of all the operative legislation and how it might fit together.

Mr. DOOLITTLE. Will the gentleman yield?

Mr. ALLARD. Time is up. Let me go ahead and call on Mr. Cooley and then we can come back. Mr. Cooley, if you would like, you can yield to Mr. Doolittle.

Mr. COOLEY. Yes, I will yield.

Mr. DOOLITTLE. I appreciate that. Dr. Thomas, that is exactly what we are looking for. I understand that the laws were made individually and it has created a hopeless morass that has mired us down into a situation we are never going to get out of without changing the laws. We need that expertise. You understand we have these laws. We have the Courts that are attempting to enforce them. I don't think things are going to get much better. I don't care how good a job the Forest Service does. It is the laws ultimately that are the problem. We need that input, and if there is a way that we can collaborate with you in drafting this legislation, we really would welcome it. Thank you.

Mr. COOLEY. Mr. Chairman, thank you very much. Dr. Thomas, you know, we have listened to testimony from Congressman Wally Herger earlier, and he talked about a fire back in 1987. And I can tell you about some fire damage in eastern Oregon dating back into the 1980s where the Forest Service has never done anything about replanting or anything like that, and it is still dead from burn. What is the rationale, what is the position by the Service of not going in there and replanting in some of these areas that had fire devastation?

Mr. THOMAS. Well, let me turn you over to Mr. Hessel. But for the committee, Mr. Cooley is my new congressman from the 2nd District of Oregon so, welcome, Mr. Cooley.

Mr. HESSEL. What was said this morning, I would have to go back and look at the numbers, but our objective under salvage and restoration of forested lands is to not only salvage but it is to restore those lands, and part of that restoration comes about from planting of trees. The 1987 fires in California, and I was out and visited most of those fires, and I know for a fact that we have done a tremendous job in follow-up reforestation on those burns.

Some of the problems that we ran into on those burns and delays were caused by the fact that we did not have the authority to use herbicides on some of the brushlands in competition that would create an uneconomic situation in planting trees. We now have that authority, and we are moving back into replanting even some of the older burns. So I am not familiar with the Region 6 burns you are talking about, but I will certainly want to follow up to answer your question.

Mr. COOLEY. Above La Grande and into the other areas, we had some burns back in the 1980s, and they are still just as dead as they were then, and no reforestation is going on at all. And it is not steep terrain either. It is high, but it is not steep; pretty smooth.

Dr. Thomas, the 3.7 billion we keep talking about here, and I was gone so I might have missed it, is that total fire and bug and dying, or is that strictly just fire?

Mr. HESSEL. The number 3.7 billion came from an estimate last December of fire by forest fires; strictly fire, not other damage.

Mr. COOLEY. Could you give us an estimate on what we have out there that is not just dead and dying from bug infestation, drought, et cetera? Do we have any figures on that at all?

Mr. HESSEL. We haven't made an estimate on what total dead and dying material we have out there. Most of our estimates come about from forests as it relates to what they feel they can salvage, not total-wise, but we could probably give you some estimates on that. But I would guess it would be in the range of—just as one example, our estimate on national forest lands is that on an annual basis we lose about five billion board feet a year across all national forest lands.

Mr. COOLEY. What percentage would that be of a particular forest on an average?

Mr. HESSEL. It depends on the forest. Certainly forests in the West are much higher to loss than it might be in——

Mr. COOLEY. Well, give me a forest from the West.

Mr. HESSEL. And it depends on the forest in the West. East side of Oregon——

Mr. COOLEY. Well, give me the Ochoco.

Mr. HESSEL. What is that?

Mr. COOLEY. Ochoco.

Mr. HESSEL. Percentage-wise, it is probably in the range of five to ten percent of their growing stock—could be that high. It depends on the drought, and a whole host of things are factored in to how much is lost on an annual basis, but it is probably in that vicinity of 10 percent or less—growing stock; not counting the loss strictly to fires.

Mr. COOLEY. Right, not even talking the loss of fire. I think that you should ask your forester there what the percentage is, and I think you are going to find that it is up in the 25 percent.

Mr. HESSEL. On an annual basis?

Mr. COOLEY. No, right now, visually you can see, I mean, because we are not taking care of it. That is what I am trying to. If we were doing a good job of stewardship, we should be in there for that dead and dying that is not fire-ridden which does have more value right now and take that out, and it is not being done. I think that is something we need to address as well. And when we are talking about the figures——

Mr. ALLARD. The gentleman's time has expired. I will come back to the gentleman.

Mr. COOLEY. Okay. Fine. Thank you.

Mr. ALLARD. I want to give Mrs. Chenoweth a chance, and then we will come back to the gentleman.

Mr. COOLEY. Thank you, Mr. Chairman.

Mr. ALLARD. Mrs. Chenoweth.

Mrs. CHENOWETH. Mr. Chairman, because of the manner in which we have had to have votes, we have lost a number of members. And I too may have more than five minutes' worth of questions. I will try very hard to adhere to the time.

Mr. ALLARD. Well, what I will do is I want to give everybody a chance to ask questions. We will come back in for a second round and give even a third shot if you feel that you need it.

Mrs. CHENOWETH. All right. Thank you, Mr. Chairman. Mr. Thomas, you did say that only 50 percent of the timber damaged by fire lack commercial value for one reason or another. I know that in Idaho a lot of the timber that was burned and certainly timber that has been destroyed by disease and insect infestation is not in areas that are environmentally sensitive directly with regards to the Endangered Species Act, and yet we are not able to get in and restore those timberlands to the health that is required in the Forest Resource and Renewable Resources Act of 1978.

And I know that you have also testified that many of the subsequent laws passed to the Multiple Use Sustained Yield Act and the RPA and the Forest Management Planning Act have tied your hands. Can you tell me, sir, what Act ties your hands to the degree that you cannot move ahead on the allowable cut, the annual yield for allowable cut that maintains a healthy, sustainable forest as required in the RPA?

Mr. THOMAS. Ma'am, I would just as soon not have my hands tied. I would just say that it might impede our rapid progress toward where we would want to go—your term "tied your hands," but that is all right. I would say, of course, anything that is in a total exclusion that we don't go there anyway.

I think the thing particularly in terms of salvage that might cause us the most delay and the most expense is the preparation of the National Environmental Policy Act documents; the EA, Environmental Assessments are—environmental impact statements.

Coupled on top of that in Idaho where you are within the salmon range of listed species is the consultation not only on the forest plans but on all individual actions with the National Marine Fisheries Services. We also are looking forward perhaps if we are not very careful to the listing of bull trout which would move that concern outside of the anadromous fish range into streams that do not have anadromous fish.

So I would say it is the combination of our compliance with preparation of the environmental documents and the consultations that slows us down most.

Mrs. CHENOWETH. Thank you, Dr. Thomas. Doesn't the National Environmental Policy Act allow for emergency procedures?

Mr. THOMAS. It does allow for emergency procedures, but those emergencies are usually built around the protection of health and safety. We have only utilized those six times, something like that, under regulation. It is not as an available avenue as would appear superficially.

Mrs. CHENOWETH. And according to Senator Larry Craig in his speech on the floor of the Senate last October we lost the lives of he said 26 firefighters. I have heard as high as 33 firefighters.

Mr. THOMAS. It is 35.

Mrs. CHENOWETH. Thirty-five. Thank you, sir. When our forests are in the critical condition that they are, don't you think that under the environment, health, and safety of not only humans, the habitat, and so forth that we could move ahead on an expedited basis under NEPA?

Mr. THOMAS. I will answer the question by saying this, ma'am, we will move as rapidly as we can under the law and comply with NEPA, and we will move expeditiously and in compliance and in combination of those two things. I would point out one thing in terms of the fatalities last summer. Forest health had something to do with that, but our biggest loss of the 14 firefighters in Colorado wasn't even on timber ground. It was ground that we would not have even considered fighting fire in order to protect forests or production of timber. It was a totally different question, but, nonetheless, the point is fighting fire is a dangerous business, and we had fire all over the country. It just happened to be there rather than somewhere else.

Mrs. CHENOWETH. Mr. Chairman, if I might, I have some pictures I want to use in my questioning. May I ask the indulgence of the committee, or would you like for me to come back to them?

Mr. ALLARD. In the spirit of fairness to the rest of the committee, let me get back to Mr. Cooley and see if anybody else wants to ask, and then we will come back to you on a second round. Mr. Cooley.

Mr. COOLEY. Thank you, Mr. Chairman. Dr. Thomas, I am sure you are familiar with the east side screen projects, and according to Forest Service scientists' recent publication, and you are probably aware of, it said that your own scientists said that the screen system—the east side screen project had a loss of 135,000 acres of old growth forest, and it places a risk of another 500,000 acres of old growth forest in the Northwest. And this was put out. There was quite a bit of publicity, and it ran in the papers. Wouldn't you say that this sort of proves an issue that this so-called science is essentially "killing" what we are trying to protect?

Mr. THOMAS. Sir, I wouldn't call it so-called science. I would say that the science information is constraining, but that word has been used several times by the committee. As a scientist, I would not refer to that as science. It is technical evaluations. Science is the proposal and testing of hypotheses, but those screens, we believe, were necessary to keep us moving in a direction where we could react—it was not designed to do the opposite. It was designed to get us past the blocks.

Mr. COOLEY. But isn't it doing the opposite, sir?

Mr. THOMAS. Well, I don't know if the opposite is—I don't think so. And we are in the process right now of modifying those screens based on experience, and when we come out of the consultations with NMFS on the 15th of this month, I think we should be cleared where we can go on.

Mr. COOLEY. Are you privilege to the article put out by your own Forest Service scientists concerning the screens and how they have affected the Northwest?

Mr. THOMAS. Yes, sir. I have seen the information on the screens. I am not sure we are talking about the same document.

Mr. COOLEY. But did you see that publication that was put out?

Mr. THOMAS. I am not sure we are talking about the same—I don't know, but I have seen a publication.

Mr. COOLEY. I will make sure that you get a copy of that from your department that shows that this is occurring. Another thing I wanted to ask you, and I am kind of a little bit confused, and maybe you can help me out. When we talk about 3.7 billion board feet available of fire, and there is a possibility of another billion board feet with this bug and dying, are we talking about what we call gross or are we talking about net? Are we talking about gross availability, or are we talking about net availability?

Mr. THOMAS. Gross.

Mr. COOLEY. Talking about gross availability. Okay.

Mr. THOMAS. Net is at least 50 percent less than that, and then whatever else we run into is a matter of constraints.

Mr. COOLEY. We are cutting everything at least in half that is available according to your estimations. Okay. One other thing I would like to ask, and I wasn't here so I didn't hear the answer, and you might have already asked this, but if we pass some legislation, and I think that we will some way or another with the help of Congressman Doolittle and other people at this table, to address the problem we have in dead and dying timber in this country and try to bring it back and some economic value to put people back to work, do you think that you have the resources, both monetarily and people-wise, experienced personnel, to facilitate salvage sales?

Mr. THOMAS. Yes. We are getting close to the wire, but we still retain a quite formidable work force. I did answer that question earlier, and I will be happy to give you the details of what our status is. But right now with black salvage, burn salvage, people and money are not the problem. It is the process of getting it up fast enough. If we were to move to extensive or intensive forest health operations, then we would be short.

Mr. COOLEY. We have been talking mostly about Forest Service. Would you say that the ratios of BLM are pretty much the same as the Forest Service as far as dead and dying timber?

Ms. MERIDITH. No. I think we have a very different situation in BLM, and I don't want to exaggerate the negative impacts of environmental laws on what we are dealing with in BLM. We don't have the density of forests that they are talking about. Even as far as impacts of fire, we only lost about 770,000 acres last year of which only 32,000 were commercial forests. So it is quite a different level of scope.

And our environmental document preparations are going pretty well. We are able to usually in most cases complete an EA in 60 days so we feel we are doing pretty well. Of the 96 million board feet outside of Alaska, this year we are able to offer 64 or 65 million. So we don't really face the same, you know, intensity of situation I think that the Forest Service does.

Mr. COOLEY. Now, you are talking about forest——

Mr. ALLARD. The gentleman's time has expired.

Mr. COOLEY. I am sorry. Pardon me. Thank you very much. Thank you, Mr. Chairman.

Mr. ALLARD. Mrs. Chenoweth.

Mrs. CHENOWETH. Mr. Chairman, I am still confused about the issue of the burn and damaged timber in Idaho because I know that country. I have lived in it, worked in it. Sir, would you commit to me that you would have your foresters reevaluate the potential of removing the damaged timber that have been damaged by these forest fires in Idaho and other states? Because the information that we are receiving is that we can use a lot of that timber. Even if it doesn't have commercial value for structural purposes, we can use it for pulp and chips and so forth. Would you commit on a speedy time frame to have your people work with industry to reevaluate that?

Mr. THOMAS. Well, certainly I would commit to that, but I don't think the chips are the part that is not merchantable, it is that nobody will buy the material. We would be happy to sell it if somebody wants to buy it. That is not our determination—what is merchantable. It is usually industry's determination or a joint one. But certainly I would commit to this. Looking at whether the timber is merchantable is always open for reevaluation. It is a matter of market, whether somebody wants to buy it.

Mrs. CHENOWETH. And so you will commit on a speedy time frame to get out there and let industry make the determination as to whether they want to buy it or not? I mean, you can put the sales up. If you don't get anybody to bid, it is not viable.

Mr. THOMAS. Well, the part of it is—we will put the sales up as fast as we can put them up. The ones that we would put up, of course, would go through our own screens on merchantability estimating that people would indeed buy it. I don't think you could assume that we have—now, if you ask the question the other way around, could I go and examine every acre and put every acre up that is potential, not counting merchantability, we don't have the personnel or time to do that. So we would put those up first that had the biggest opportunity for sale and for environmental protection and for fire reduction purposes and to put high sites back into production.

Mrs. CHENOWETH. Dr. Thomas, you testified to Mr. Pombo and to Mr. Cooley too and as well as to me that you simply don't have the money to do what is necessary to do for forest health. What was your budget 10 years ago and 20 years ago?

Mr. THOMAS. For forest health?

Mrs. CHENOWETH. Your overall United States Forest Service budget.

Mr. THOMAS. I don't know.

Mrs. CHENOWETH. Will you get that information for the committee within 48 hours?

Mr. THOMAS. I don't know about 48 hours, but I will get the information for you.

Mrs. CHENOWETH. I think I can get it in 48 hours, sir.

Mr. THOMAS. I will do my best, but that is Monday.

Mrs. CHENOWETH. Well, let us make it Tuesday.

Mr. THOMAS. How about Wednesday? I will get it for you as quickly as I possibly can.

Mrs. CHENOWETH. Yes.

Mr. THOMAS. I don't think that is going to be a hard number to find, but I have broken myself for promising things that I don't deliver on so I think we can get that for you very quickly.

Mrs. CHENOWITH. I want to show you a demonstration of 20 years ago when your budget was considerably less. This is a picture from the Forest Service of a well-managed forest. I mean, we have roads. You can see we have clear cuts, patchwork clear cuts; a healthy forest. And as you can see from the way the clear cuts have been recovered, your overall budget was much less then, but you targeted the health of the forest 20 years ago.

Mr. THOMAS. Ma'am, we targeted putting timber out, and that is what we got, and that is fine. But, I mean, that was my real aim.

Mrs. CHENOWITH. And this is a picture from the Forest Service of a healthy forest and healthy multiple use.

Mr. THOMAS. That is correct.

Mrs. CHENOWITH. One of our problems, as you testified, was to the fact that you must comply with the environmental regulations and the laws such as the Clean Water Act. You know, I look at this picture, and I think of these firefighters as perhaps those who were lucky enough to live. And I look at the forest and how it was damaged, and I look at the soil and how it has been damaged from the fire. And yet you are prohibited from doing anything in terms of reforestation or timber salvage or whatever.

And yet what we are really facing in Idaho is this, Dr. Thomas. Watershed management is going to be at an all time high because in Idaho we are experiencing 160 percent of snowpack, and yet you have not moved ahead except to assess and consult with National Marine Fisheries Service to make sure that our watersheds are protected. And yet, sir, you testified that because of the habitat of the salmon and potentially the Dolly Varden or you called it the bull trout, you couldn't move ahead because it might damage the spawning habitat, rearing habitat in the streams.

Don't you think, Dr. Thomas, that this situation that has come about in comparison to the other picture really will do more damage to the salmon than anything else if we don't get in there and harvest and reforest?

Mr. THOMAS. I don't know where that is.

Mr. ALLARD. We need to move on. Your time has expired.

Mrs. CHENOWITH. It is in the Boise National Forest. It came from the Forest Service.

Mr. THOMAS. Oh, I understand that. If your point of it is do I condone burning up watersheds and not treating them? No, I don't. But I would assume that we were on that with rehab and revegetation almost immediately, and that it will be replanted whether or not it is in a protected zone or not. So the point of it is am I fond of burning up watersheds? No, ma'am, I am not.

Mr. ALLARD. The gentlewoman's time has expired. Mr. Baldacci.

Mr. BALDACCI. Thank you very much, Mr. Chairman. I am relatively new at this, and there is one question I am interested in an answer to if you can give it to me, and I would appreciate it in 20 words or less. But I am being told on the one side that it doesn't make sense to go in and get this unsalvageable timber out. And then on the other side I am being told that that is an exaggeration, that it can be, and there is a lot of it there, and we want to get it out. You are the person that has been doing this for a period of time. What is your analysis?

Mr. THOMAS. I would answer you, but I don't understand the question.

Mr. BALDACCI. Well, I am reading a report from the Congressional Research Service which is telling me that salvage sales often cost more than the revenues they can generate. We are under a five-minute requirement so I just assumed that you were with me on the uptake of it.

Mr. THOMAS. Oh, I understand the question now. I didn't at the beginning.

Mr. BALDACCI. Okay. But what was the answer?

Mr. THOMAS. The question is you are into the below-cost aspect of timber management, of forest management, and I think in my personal opinion cost and benefit should be extended in their analysis beyond dollars in and dollars out. We should not make the decision totally on, "I put in this much money; I got this much money out." There should be other purposes, though salvage should be good enough in and of itself if it is feasible to provide jobs, to provide timber, to protect from reburn.

However, there are also other aspects to it that can be put in there particularly when you are dealing with forest health. Does it reduce fire risk? Does it have other benefits? It should be, in my estimation, an estimate of net benefit as opposed to dollars in, dollars out. For this year, we estimate that we would receive 175 million on fire salvage, and that it would cost us about $103 million. We would get about a $72 million profit.

Mr. BALDACCI. Now, as far as the Treasury is concerned, most of us are fiscally oriented. I am being told by the Congressional Research Service that it is possible that if you have a more aggressive policy in harvesting or being told to harvest by either helicopter or expensive roads that you can actually lose money by the proposition under the way this formula is established.

Mr. THOMAS. That is indeed possible, that we could take in less money than we spend. However, if you looked at the assessment of net effect including jobs, secondary jobs, fire protection, environmental protection——

Mr. BALDACCI. Well, a lot of us were interested in balancing the budget. A lot of us were interested in that. If there was some way to be able to score that with the Congressional Budget Office, we could score that. But given the way we have it to do now, we would end up losing money to the Treasury and further going into debt if we became more aggressive with forest harvesting that was more expensive unless there is something I am not reading in the formula here.

Mr. THOMAS. Well, I am not looking at it. I don't know what the formula is, but I do know that earlier testimony I would agree with completely, one can either spend that money up front, or we can spend it fighting fire later. I don't know how you score that.

Mr. BALDACCI. Well, I am just saying that this budget that we are dealing with and we are trying to reduce and cut the deficit, and some of us want a balanced budget, I am asking you if you were given a more aggressive policy to cut that wood and to get it out, would it increase the cost of that, and we can actually lose money in the Treasury?

Mr. THOMAS. I think the more intensively we went at it, the more marginal it would become because we would capture our best opportunities up front. But I do think that that would diminish with an aggressive policy. However, I think there is something to do with the balanced budget of whether you pay us now or pay us later. Do we spend 100 units to reduce fire risk, or do we spend 200 units later to fight the fire and rehabilitate it?

Mr. BALDACCI. Well, I appreciate that, but that is not what we are dealing with for ground rules now. Thank you, Mr. Chairman.

Mr. THOMAS. Well, we have forestry ground rules and congressional ground rules, and we both have to look at our own, I guess.

Mr. BALDACCI. Thank you very much.

Mr. ALLARD. Mr. Doolittle, did you have a second question?

Mr. DOOLITTLE. Yes.

Mr. ALLARD. Mr. Doolittle and then, Mr. Pombo. Then to the rest of the committee, we have six panels today. We have gone through two, and so if we could maybe visit with Dr. Thomas in our offices or something, but let us get your pertinent questions out.

Mr. DOOLITTLE. Dr. Thomas, the timber sale program produces a net revenue to the Treasury, does it not?

Mr. THOMAS. Yes.

Mr. DOOLITTLE. Has there ever been a time that you are aware of when that has not, in fact, been the case?

Mr. THOMAS. In total?

Mr. DOOLITTLE. Yes.

Mr. THOMAS. No.

Mr. DOOLITTLE. So every single year, the timber program has produced net revenue to the Treasury so when specious reports like this one, the so-called Green Scissors report, come out which call for the total elimination of funds for timber roads, in your opinion, does that advance either revenue to the Treasury or the cause of forest health?

Mr. THOMAS. I would have to answer the question with the word no. The question—they probably try to make, I haven't read the report, is that we make more money some places than we do others, and some of our sales are deficit.

Mr. DOOLITTLE. Let me ask you this. There are also other purposes, are there not, for timber sales than simply the removal of timber?

Mr. THOMAS. Yes. That was the point I was making about net benefit.

Mr. DOOLITTLE. So that in point of fact, timber sales are done to advance forest health or to help wildlife or recreation? I mean, I haven't even enumerated all of them, but there are a variety of reasons this is done. Right?

Mr. THOMAS. Yes, sir.

Mr. DOOLITTLE. Does the Forest Service regard the construction of a road—does the recovery of costs have to occur in the same year the road is constructed, or do you view that as a capital asset with a long term life span that can be amortized over a period of years?

Mr. THOMAS. It is amortized over a period of years. I don't recall exactly what it is.

Mr. DOOLITTLE. So you would disagree with the Wilderness Society and the authors of this "Green Scissors" which asserts that in their calculation of below-cost timber sales that the recovery of the cost to build a road is a cost that is to be recovered in the same year the road is built?

Mr. THOMAS. That is not the way we keep the books.

Mr. DOOLITTLE. Are you satisfied that the way you keep the books is reasonable and consistent with reality?

Mr. THOMAS. No, but this gets to be a very complex question. I do believe roads should be amortized. They can either be put in and considered as a value and sometimes are. Other times, we have roads that if we have to go back and look at them, we wish we had never put them there, and we have to go back and essentially spend money to take them out. But I think we are getting better and better at that, and if we do build a road, we figure that it has got some other uses besides removal of timber, and we amortize it over time, and that makes sense.

Mr. DOOLITTLE. Our time is short so I would like to ask more, but I am going to switch subjects. I want to go back to something else we talked about. You have agreed that the interaction of all this complex network of laws has produced a difficult situation that will never allow us, say, to get back to harvest levels we have known in previous times. Knowing what you know, what would be the most significant reform that could occur in those laws in order to break this log jam?

Mr. THOMAS. I think the most significant interaction that we are getting now is between the ESA consultation, recovery planning, ESA consultation, and the preparation of environmental analysis documents. And they are hard to pull apart. They are very close and woven together. But I think those two in combination, either singularly or in combination, are the ones that are the most costly in time and in resources. I would want to say though I agree in principle with those laws, but to answer your question, those are the ones that cost us the most in both time and money.

Mr. DOOLITTLE. Well, I hope maybe later on privately or in a letter or something we can get your further thoughts on how to deal with that problem with the interaction. Thank you.

Mr. ALLARD. Congressman Pombo.

Mr. POMBO. Thank you. And I guess taking off from there, I would like to ask a couple of questions about the endangered species consultation process that you go through. How long does it take for the consultation process on petitions for listed species associated with the salvage of timber sales? How long does that process take right now?

Mr. THOMAS. It really varies. We have to go in with the initial analysis, and then the consultation question is the one that can take some time. It depends on the area of land we are managing and what the potential impacts are on the habitat of that species that has been listed and our ability to accommodate those needs in order to reach agreement on consultation and still have a project that is worthwhile. I think it only to be fair that as we go into these things, the agencies with which we have to consult usually get much better and faster at it as time goes on. We are down now to sometimes consultations can be done in several weeks. We do have some that have been pending for over a year.

Mr. POMBO. And in regards to other agencies, why do you feel it is necessary for two or three different sets of biologists to review the same process; you know, the Forest Service, you know, the National Marine Fisheries Service, and the Fish and Wildlife Service to have three separate sets of biologists to look at the same?

Mr. THOMAS. Our biologists, for example, will prepare the information. Then it goes to the National Marine Fisheries Service for consultation, and their biologists give us their opinion, and then we come to a conclusion. I think maybe there are some ways we can be more efficient with that particularly when we are short on biologists and short on time and short on money.

Mr. POMBO. Do you feel comfortable with the capabilities of the Forest Service biologists to properly assess the situation?

Mr. THOMAS. In my opinion, of course, there is a bit of bias and prejudice here and a little pride, but I think we probably have the best cadre of fish and wildlife specialists in the country. And we have a number of them, and they are very good and highly experienced. I have a lot of confidence in them.

Mr. POMBO. And by your previous statements you would do nothing that would be outside of the law in terms of the current loss so you would not in any way encourage your biologists to come up with answers that might not be exactly within the law?

Mr. THOMAS. Absolutely not. I am a biologist myself, and we have fought a long time, and the Forest Service has been a leader that we are to the point now where we have technical specialists that are listened to and are very good, and I have got confidence in them. Now, I ought to make one thing perfectly clear. Sometimes when we follow our best instincts, our best knowledge and we think we are right, we go to Court and we find out we are wrong. But when I say obey the law, I mean when we act, I think we are obeying the law. Sometimes we don't win in Court. We change our operation.

Mr. POMBO. Well, I would tend to give you the same benefit of the doubt that I gave the timberworkers who testified before you in that I don't feel that you are going to do anything that is going to damage the forests either, and that we do need to trust your judgment and let the experts make determinations based on what they believe. I do feel that the laws that we have placed before you are contradictory and sometimes not correct, and we will work to hopefully streamline that process and change that process so that we can reach different conclusions, and we are not back here having this same hearing a year from now.

Mr. THOMAS. I appreciate your comments. That is the nicest thing anybody said to me in a week.

Mr. ALLARD. I believe we will move on to the next panel. I want to thank you gentlemen. You have been very patient with this committee. I hope we haven't disrupted your schedule too much today.

Mr. THOMAS. Thank you, sir.

Mr. ALLARD. Thank you.

Mr. MERIDITH. Thank you.

Mr. ALLARD. The next panel that we will have coming up is a panel of scientists; Dr. Chad Oliver from the University of Washington; Dr. Vic Kaczynski, Fisheries Consultant; Dr. Sampson, American Forests; and Dr. Partridge, University of Idaho. If you gentlemen would join us here at the table please?

Gentlemen, I just remind you that we have some lights there in front of you that indicate your time limits. We would like to give you each five minutes to summarize your testimony for this committee. Your comments in full that you have submitted in writing will be put in the record. The yellow light indicates you have got to be winding down your comments and summarizing when it comes on, and then the red light, we will ask you to stop. Let me go ahead and start with Dr. Oliver first.

STATEMENT OF CHAD OLIVER, UNIVERSITY OF WASHINGTON; ACCOMPANIED BY VIC KACZYNSKI, FISHERIES CONSULTANT; R. NEIL SAMPSON, AMERICAN FORESTS; ARTHUR PARTRIDGE, UNIVERSITY OF IDAHO

Mr. OLIVER. Thank you very much. My name is Chad Oliver. I am a Professor of Silviculture and Forest Ecology at the University of Washington. I would like to say that if we use our latest understanding of science, then it is not necessary to have this polarization between protecting the environment and biodiversity and producing commodity products such as timber as well as employment and protecting such things as private property rights and doing this in a very economical manner.

What I would like to do is first describe to you the changing scientific paradigm or understanding, then tell you the present condition of the inland West, and then tell you some of our alternatives that would allow us to maintain all of these values.

First of all, we have changed from the idea that the forests exist in a steady state referred to by such terms as old growth, ancient forest, climax forest. Without humans around, the forest would exist as in the right-hand side, the old growth stage. By that idea, what we thought was that humans basically had disturbed this condition, and since this was the natural condition, that all species would live in it, and we could maintain all species simply by excluding humans from forest areas. This was the idea behind the preservation-reservation perspective.

What we now realize is that natural disturbances occur over large areas, and these disturbances can be quite large in places; hundreds of thousands of acres and not in others. Now, what happens is that after those disturbances, your forest goes through an open condition, the stand initiation structure, and then grows to the stem exclusion, the understory, and the old growth condition.

Now, what we now appreciate is that each of these structures has certain species that require it in order to live, and we have lost species when we have lost any of these structures, and I can describe that in detail. What we see is that nature behaved over a large area and a long time scale. Now, so what we see is nature maintained all these species in very much of a boom and bust and a long changing from one of these structures to the other.

Now, in the inland West, what we have done is by excluding fire, which was a natural disturbance, and by a lot of selective harvesting, we have moved a lot of stands to that stem exclusion or dense stage where they become crowded, have insects in them.

We also have a lot of forests in the old growth stage by selective cutting there. And what this has done is this has created habitat for a lot of the old growth species, but it is also very susceptible to fire. And we are lacking quite a bit of that stand initiation stage, but because we have this imbalance, many stands and certain structures and overly dense were susceptible to insects and fires which will move us very rapidly and in a very catastrophic way back to the stand initiation stage.

Now, what we appreciate then is this imbalance is what we call the problem with forest health. Now, we also notice that these imbalances occur elsewhere. The Kenai Peninsula of Alaska is in sad shape for similar reasons. Coastal Washington, that wind-through, if not picked up, will have what used to occur naturally in many parts of this country; insects get to the downed trees, then to the trees that are still living. Then you get very catastrophic fires.

Now, we have three ways we can approach this. We can either set aside large preserves, and we will get catastrophic fires as well as the unemployment and other things that you have heard of earlier. The second approach that we have generally done is what we call commodity-base management where we expect timber to pay for all of our values. And by that, it means where you have many of these dense stands, if timber can't pay for it being thinned, then we don't thin it, and, therefore, we don't get the values of reduced fire danger, reduced fire costs, and better habitat.

However, if we turn to an approach where we call landscape management, which is maintaining all of the different structures through a variety of silvicultural operations, looking at the joint production of forest health, fire prevention, habitat, and timber, we can do it all at a quite low cost relative to the others.

Now, the forest health issue. Because much of our inland West has been in a condition where we haven't been harvesting very much, the green shows the amount of growth in the inland West; the yellow shows the amount of harvest; the red shows the amount of mortality. We are harvesting about 2 billion board feet, and we are growing about 10 billion board feet. This isn't going to last. It is going to burn up.

Just very quickly, we can provide all of these values, and salvage is a very integral part of that proactive approach. Then I could suggest very specifics during the question and answer period. Thank you very much.

[The statement of Mr. Oliver appears at the conclusion of the hearing.]

Mr. ALLARD. Thank you. I will now call on Dr. Kaczynski.

STATEMENT OF VIC KACZYNSKI

Mr. KACZYNSKI. Thank you. My comments are a summary of a paper I presented last year at the Forest Health Symposium in Spokane, Washington.

Wildfires are natural disturbance events, but the results of these catastrophic wildfires we have been having in the western United States are anything but natural. Dr. Thomas and Dr. Oliver and others have briefly described the broad situation of very poor forest health that we have in our western states.

Forest health is the key to the probability and the severity of wildfire. Forest health will affect the frequency, the area, and especially the intensity of the burn. And catastrophic wildfires have catastrophic impacts on salmon and bull trout and steelhead habitat in our Pacific Northwest. And these stream impacts just simply have not received the appropriate attention that they deserve.

Today, the potential for catastrophic stream impact is very high. Wildfires impact streams in three ways: First, they decrease vegetative cover; that is, the vegetation gets burned up and the roots get destroyed. Secondly, they increase the storm runoff. The rainfall cannot absorb into the soils, and it runs off on the surface. And, third, you increase the runoff of the sediment, and you increase the landslide rate bringing all of that debris into the streams. My written testimony summarizes these impacts in more detail, and I refer those to you.

Now, I would like to move to an illustration of a catastrophic wildfire that occurred in northeast Oregon. This was the wildfire that affected the spring Chinook spawning population in the upper Grande Ronde River. This population is about 10 percent of the

Snake River endangered spring Chinook salmon. This is a tributary to the Snake River.

All of the adults and eggs from the 1989 spawning were killed outright in a 36-mile reach of this river. All of the fry from the 1988 spawning were killed in this stretch of the river. All of the smolts from the 1987 spawning that had not migrated yet were killed in this stretch of the river. And we have had impacts on the spawning gravels ever since then including last year when I was there, and in some nearby streams, we had this situation. So the spawning success has been impacted since that time.

Spring Chinook are particularly vulnerable to this type of habitat. They occur in the low gradient floodplains, and forest fires in any one of these tributaries can sluff off these materials and go down, and that material gets transported down into these reaches that these fish prefer. So they are particularly vulnerable to wildfires.

I would like to give one more quantitative example of wildfires. I will use northeast Oregon again, and that is in the north half of the Wallowa–Whitman National Forest. Not counting 1994, but the previous eight years, we had 20 percent of that area affected by wildfires. Using some simple mathematics, we have a 100-percent probability of a wildfire impacting our stream habitat where we are trying to rebuild these fish in the next 40 years if we don't do something about this deleterious condition of poor forest health.

In summary, if you don't remember anything else from this talk, please remember forest health is complementary with our fish protection and our fish restoration goals that we want. Salvage logging, prescription thinning are tools that the professional foresters can use to get us into a better situation. Thank you.

[The statement of Mr. Kaczynski appears at the conclusion of the hearing.]

Mr. ALLARD. Thank you. Dr. Sampson.

STATEMENT OF R. NEIL SAMPSON

Mr. SAMPSON. Thank you. I am Neil Sampson. I am here on behalf of American Forests which is the oldest nonpartisan, nonprofit citizens conservation organization at the national level. I have been personally involved in this a lot of ways including chairing and being principal author of that National Commission on Wildfire Disasters report, and I thank the Chairman for his courtesy in mentioning that yesterday when the hearing started, and I really appreciate that. We worked very hard on that.

We have also done a lot to deal with scientific studies of the inland West; did a cooperative project with the Boise and published a book recently that we did at a symposium in Sun Valley. In addition, we worked a great deal with the legislation in the 102nd and 103rd Congress that has been mentioned. So there is a lot of history involved in the subject from our point of action.

Today, I must apologize for having only brought this morning because I was only really told last night, but I brought a copy of a public opinion survey that we did in October of this year. I think you will find some of the findings fairly interesting. There is a lot of data underneath that. It is all publicly available if you would like to read it and make any interpretation different or the same from what we did.

I also brought a copy of a reprint from the Sacramento Bee of a series that was run in November and December in Sacramento last year, and it was our judgment that this was just about the best job that the public media did around the country last year trying to explain a situation to people that is darn hard to explain in 20 second sound bites and on which there is a lot of broad complexity and information.

I am going to skip through my testimony. I put it in two parts. I am always uncomfortable when we talk about salvage and forest health because they are different, in my judgment. Salvage is an attempt to make something out of a very bad deal, and, in my judgment, forest health is an attempt to get ahead of the problem and to try to do something to manage those lands correctly.

We are not going to eliminate fire, but we can change its intensity, change its spread, change its scale, and we have anecdote after anecdote of treated stands where roaring crownfires hit them, dropped to the ground, burned through, didn't kill the standing dominant timber, went right on through. You didn't have the environmental damage, but you have got a different kind of fire. So I think that we are talking about things here that you are on the right track to consider that we have got a problem.

We have tried to outline the problem. You have identified a couple problems that as a commission we were never able to identify. We could not quantify the degree of risk reduction. What is an investment in forest health treatment worth in terms of reducing this billion dollar outlay that we laid last year? How can we ascribe it? We thought if the insurance companies can surely do it on a smoke alarm in your house, we ought to be able to do it on this one. But the numbers eluded us, and I gathered from the testimony today that you weren't getting any better numbers and that that was frustrating to some of the members of the committee.

There is a lot of frustration on the pace at which the Forest Service does this stuff, but I hope this hearing, if nothing else, showed you that that is a part of the process that they go through. And what was hinted at but not said here is it is one thing to do an environmental assessment; it is another thing to lawyer-proof it. And to get an assessment bulletproofed against trial lawyers is much more expensive, and I think that is part of what we need to look at today. I don't believe any of us are proposing skimping environmental assessment, but we are proposing that two and three years sometimes sounds like a very long time.

Well, I commend you to the work that has been done in the Congress on forest health. There have been hearings all over the country. Mrs. Chenoweth's district has hosted two in Idaho, one in Coeur d'Alene in 1992 and one in Boise in 1993.

I think the bulk of information that has been developed and the work that has been done in this Congress sets the stage for the kind of legislative process Mr. Craig started yesterday in the Senate and I hope these committees will take up in this coming Congress. I have attached a whole lot of reading here that I don't expect you to go through, but we would be very happy to respond in other ways when and if it is appropriate. Thank you, Mr. Chairman.

[The statement of Mr. Sampson appears at the conclusion of the hearing.]

Mr. DOOLITTLE [presiding]. Thank you. Dr. Partridge.

STATEMENT OF ARTHUR PARTRIDGE

Mr. PARTRIDGE. I am Dr. Partridge, Professor of Forest Disease and Insect Problems at the University of Idaho. I present to you today primarily the findings of 34 years of research on disease and insect problems. And I am afraid my findings don't justify emergency measures.

At the present time, we are losing to disease and insects less than one percent of our standing trees per year. Actually, that figure is .176 percent if you need. It is strange that in 1974 we were losing 12 percent of our trees per year. That peak at that time rose to about six percent in the early '80s and has since declined.

Now, I am not opposed to salvage, but I am opposed to salvage using figures that are untrue. And what you have been presented thus far is primarily material from inventories or surveys developed by the Forest Service to count the number and amount of trees on a piece of land, not to give you an idea of the dynamics of forest insect and disease activities. We indeed need more work on these things, but there is no imminent emergency. This has not been demonstrated, not by scientific work, only by inventory of materials.

And I am not alone in that assessment. I call your attention to the Forest Service publication entitled, "America's Forests: 1994 Health Update," page five. "Update shows that overall the condition of our forests has improved significantly over the past 70 years." This is in contrast to that emergency outlook. We don't at the present time need to implement what to me looks like a breach of some of the contracts we have heard recently.

If indeed we implement emergency salvage, it will mean that the Forest Service will have to stop working on its immediate plans, implement salvage plans or immediately do so which takes people away from doing their jobs. This will also necessarily then increase the budget for that agency. It looks to me like some of the proposals here do two things: Increased bureaucracy taking away our democratic rights to appeal and increasing the amount of money that that bureaucracy will have to spend to implement what is proposed. Now, there are other ways to handle this, and I suggest the main problem here is that the managing agencies in the past have not properly consulted with many of the outside units who could properly provide them the information I have given you today. I also have given you a 14-page statement of all these things showing you the trends and some of the data as it has been analyzed.

I think we should be focusing on public involvement, not taking away the rights of the people but making them more involved in the processes of land management. I think we should be sure that every dollar spent is spent to do what we have substantial evidence for doing. At the present time, the data you have before you are very spurious. Thank you.

[The statement of Mr. Partridge appears at the conclusion of the hearing.]

Mr. DOOLITTLE. I think in light of the present situation, maybe it would be best if we all go vote.

[Recess.]

Mr. ALLARD. I will call the meeting back to order. Dr. Partridge, did you get an opportunity to complete your testimony?

Mr. PARTRIDGE. Yes, sir.

Mr. ALLARD. So we are to questions. We understand that the practice of leaving 300-foot buffers of dead timber along the stream for fish habitat and monitoring the streams from past salvage projects has shown very little, if any, increase in sediment or stream temperature. Is there any justification for this policy? Does anybody want to respond? Do you want me to try it again? Did you get the question?

Mr. KACZYNSKI. Is there any justification for the PAC fish policy of 300-foot buffers?

Mr. ALLARD. Yes, buffers.

Mr. KACZYNSKI. As a fisheries biologist, I can follow the logic developed in FEMAT which is where PAC fish came from. For the necessity of a buffer strip, something in the neighborhood of one leafed tree. FEMAT and PAC fish both arbitrarily double that distance to something approaching 300 feet. I don't think there are any magical buffer distances.

I think you should do a lot of site-specific analysis, and you should set your buffers appropriate for the conditions you encounter. And we submitted to the Forest Service just recently, a week ago, an alternative to PAC fish which does just that. And if it would be of value to you, I would obtain a copy for you, and I will submit it to you as well.

Mr. ALLARD. I would appreciate it if you would provide that for the committee.

Mr. KACZYNSKI. Sir, I will do that.

Mr. OLIVER. From a forest ecology and silviculture perspective, I would be a bit concerned about presuming that you can preserve this 300-foot area and assume a steady state condition will exist there, that being one of the most productive areas that is most likely to build up in fuel. And there have been cases where a fire moves through this continuity of fuel and burns all the trees which was just the opposite of what Dr. Kaczynski would say would be desirable.

Mr. KACZYNSKI. And the other thing I did not mention, within the philosophy of PAC fish, and I have to speak to the draft of PAC fish—I have not seen the final—I am not sure it is out—but the main strategy of PAC fish is one of preservation. And preservation of riparian areas is simply a prescription for disaster. These riparian areas burn in our western United States, and they burn hot.

Mr. ALLARD. Okay. Anybody else want to comment on that question? I have got another question. Would you expect higher risk to wildfire suppression actions in the future without treatment today?

Mr. SAMPSON. That was the inescapable conclusion that the commission came to in the hearings that we held with people all over the country. And keep in mind that the wildfire situation in the inland West is not just a forest situation. The BLM talked this morning about not having very much forest, but, boy, do they have a lot of brushland that had normally under natural cycles probably 10—15-year fire frequencies which some of it has gone 100 or 120 years without burning, and it is really dangerous now.

So, yes, our conclusion is is that for every acre that burned in 1994, there is probably five or six out there that are in that overfueled condition so that a combination of dry weather, which is about an 80 percent certainty in the west, and lightning, which is a very high certainty as well, is just simply going to trigger fires that are going to burn as intensively or more intensively than what we have been seeing in recent years. It is just there.

Mr. OLIVER. The combination of natural cycles and past management has definitely created the situation. I agree with Dr. Sampson.

Mr. SAMPSON. The other thing, if I might follow up, people have built homes in through that former wildland in an intermixed way now which both heightens the chance of ignition because of human activities and raises the costs of both fighting and disasters that happen. And so of all the problems that face them out there today, we have been talking about forest health, but where people and forests intersect in those forests, which is becoming a very complex mix, is a huge risk and cost problem that remains a real challenge.

Mr. ALLARD. Dr. Oliver, on page three in your testimony, you indicate that past management, that is, commodity-base management, has led to timber production paying the full price of all forest values, forest health, biodiversity, and others. Would you elaborate on that statement?

Mr. OLIVER. Yes. What happens is it gets to that below-cost timber sale problem where if you have an area that you may want to have thinned because it will reduce the fire risk, if it is a below-cost sale, either it can't be done or if it is done, it has to be done in such a way that the timber that could be removed from there isn't sold. So you end up with either doing those operations that can be paid for by the timber alone although it may provide other values, or you end up not doing an operation or throwing the wood away after the operation is done.

Mr. ALLARD. So going ahead and providing for these values, in effect, could lead or would lead to below-cost timber sales?

Mr. OLIVER. It would. Yes.

Mr. ALLARD. Well, can you suggest mechanisms to prevent subsidizing the timber industry while doing below-cost timber sales?

Mr. OLIVER. One way to do it would be to not sell timber on the stump, that basically you would hire loggers to do the thinning or the other operations and move the wood to a landing. And at that landing or a log yard or a saw yard or something, then the wood would be sold to the highest bidder so then what you are doing is you are separating the logging operation from the actual sales. This is what is done in parts of Europe, and it has several benefits to it. But among others, you basically do the best operation for the stand for these multiple purposes and remove the wood where it is in excess. And then once removed, you treat that as whatever you can recover from it.

Mr. ALLARD. Would you comment further on using incentives versus using regulations to provide the public values on private lands?

Mr. OLIVER. On private lands, if you want to provide these public values, doing such operations as thinning and longer rotations provide the public values of this higher quality wood which means more employment, greater biodiversity. But it is a cost to the landowner because if you look at the economics, it is not quite economically feasible now.

Now, if you put in a regulation requiring these people to do these operations, then it just becomes a tax on the land. It makes it more costly to produce timber which means it reduces the profit and is a disincentive to manage land at all.

However, if you give the landowner an incentive, and I have worked with Professor Lipky at the University of Washington to look at efficient ways to do these incentives and we may be doing some trials of these through the State of Washington, if you give them incentives for them to provide these public values on the private lands, you will find that you will have many more — it would be much more efficient and much more opportunities for them to provide them.

I would like to give one example of a present regulation that is a disincentive, and that is that thinning or extending rotations in western Washington would provide some of the habitat for the spotted owl. However, there is a law on the books right now that if a spotted owl lands in your forest, you can't harvest your timber. So that is an incredible disincentive for people not to produce the habitat. They are basically harvesting their forests when they are young at a faster rate than before to avoid creating the habitat because they will be penalized for creating it.

Mr. ALLARD. Dr. Kaczynski, if you could do one thing to prevent these catastrophic wildfires, what would you do?

Mr. KACZYNSKI. I would do everything I could to restore forest health and the upland forest health on the riparian forest, and I would do it just as fast as I could.

Mr. ALLARD. And would you go in a little more detail on how you would do that?

Mr. KACZYNSKI. Yes. It would be the combinations of thinning to reduce both. The species have changed in many of the western forests from fire-resistant species. The stand density is greater, the age structure has changed, and we have these tremendous fuel loads on the forest floor. So we have got to get back to the species mix that reflected the natural disturbance regime before European settlement.

We have got to get back to those stand densities that reflected the disturbance regime before European settlement. And we have got to do something with that excess of fuel load on the forest floor which, in pact, you can approach that mechanically and, in part, you can approach that with prescribed burning during seasons of the year and during where you can control both the intensity and the extent of your control burn so you do not get a catastrophic wildfire. And I would defer very much to the professional foresters as to how they would accomplish these specific things.

Mr. ALLARD. Are you familiar with the east side forest screens?

Mr. KACZYNSKI. Yes, I am.

Mr. ALLARD. If so, then have they been a help or a hindrance to forest health potential stream impacts?

Mr. KACZYNSKI. I think they have been a hindrance to forest health and the corresponding high risk of stream impact. The forest screens have done a good job of maintaining the status quo, keeping us in this situation of high risk, tying the hands of the professional foresters within the Forest Service to get in there and attack this problem of poor health in our forests. I have been hearing this poor health in our forests for the last four years, and it is not getting any better.

Mr. ALLARD. Now, Dr. Kaczynski, are you familiar with the consultation process of the Forest Service on the Endangered Species Act?

Mr. KACZYNSKI. Yes, I am.

Mr. ALLARD. What do you think of the process?

Mr. KACZYNSKI. I think we have got the wrong horse in front of the cart. I think the professional fisheries biologists in the Forest Service, the professional hydrologists in the Forest Service, and the professional foresters in the Forest Service know a heck of a lot more about the field situation, the reality of the situation than the biologists and the lawyers and the National Marine Fisheries Service. And if we had anyone who should be taking a stronger lead, I would give that stronger lead to the professionals in the Forest Service.

And somehow we have got to educate the people, the lawyers and the biologists and the National Marine Fisheries Service to be more realistic, to listen more carefully, and somehow to get these young people more realism in terms of experience in the field somehow. That is a pipe dream.

Mr. ALLARD. I have got one more question. This gets back to the wildfire suppression actions. Would you expect a higher risk to wildfire suppression actions in the future without treatment today?

Mr. KACZYNSKI. Would I expect——

Mr. ALLARD. Yes. Would you expect a higher risk to wildfire with suppression actions in the future without treatment today?

Mr. KACZYNSKI. If we don't get treatments, we absolutely are going to get higher incidents of wildfire, and, again, I would defer to the gentlemen that work more closely with the forestry aspects of that.

Mr. ALLARD. I think whoever formatted this question is trying to ask what you would think of the risk to additional fires without the suppressive actions and treatment today?

Mr. KACZYNSKI. We would get substantially increased risk of wildfire and substantial increased risk of stream habitat and the detriment to the very fish species we are trying to recover if we do not get in there and actively treat the situation.

Mr. ALLARD. Does anybody else on the panel want to comment on that question?

Mr. OLIVER. I would like to make one comment that it may get to in that sometime the idea if we let them all burn up today, we won't have to burn about them burning up next year. But we do have this problem of reburns in that the first fire that burns in an area will kill the trees, and then over the years, the trees will fall on the ground and create high fuel loads on the ground.

Then if you get a second fire going through there, one, two, three, or four decades later, without any salvage, there is a lot of dry logs on the ground that then burn extremely hot and cook the soil and very often end up eliminating any of the new trees that had begun to grow, and you end up very frequently with brush fields. So this idea of reburns is very much of a problem.

Mr. ALLARD. Good comment. Can anybody on the panel see in any way how dead or dying timber would be beneficial to fish and wildlife habitat?

Mr. SAMPSON. Well, I think we have all run into the fact that some dead and dying timber out there is a very important part of the component. And I don't think anybody is proposing the notion that you go out there and sweep up every dead and dying stick. That is a very important part of the cycle.

The problem that we face are areas that grew as near as we can tell for centuries with 25 and 30 trees per acre now have 5 and 600. They are highly specie shifted toward firs. They are stressed and moisture stressed during dry periods, and instead of burning at low temperatures and fairly low to the ground with the consequence of recycling of nutrients, you have these long periods of no burn and then you have this catastrophic burn.

We are seeing trees with 600 years of age and perhaps a fire scar every 13 years up until about 1870 that weren't touched by fire since 1870 and then were killed dead after living for 600 years. That is not very good evidence that what they were seeing was a standard intensity burn. So it is pretty clear that those forests have shifted.

It is more than we want to go into today, but the nutrient cycles are clearly shifted, the hydrologic cycles are clearly shifted, and while we have an eruption of trees as part of that system, the trees are not the only thing that are affected. The whole system is affected at this stage, and so as we talk forest health, let us talk about the nutrients because those nutrients run downhill and get in those creeks and feed the benthic organisms that support those salmon that we are so worried about being endangered.

That is what a system looks like, and those systems are out of whack. And just staying away from the creek 300 feet and protecting it from sediment. As important as protecting it from sediment is, if there is no spawning fish to come, saving all the spawning beds are going to be a really, you know, low-benefit effort.

Mr. KACZYNSKI. And, Mr. Chairman, there is a lot of benefit to the fish to having large logs and trees drop into the stream. That makes the stream habitat more complex, and a more complex stream habitat is more productive, and is refuge for the fish. Also, these trees near the stream do provide us with the shade to keep the streams cool. The input of litter and leaves is part of the food chain.

When we move into the riparian area, we want to move in carefully, but we cannot just have riparian preserves. We must balance the objectives of the interaction with the riparian ecology with the stream ecology, and we must balance that with fire and the disastrous fire risk. But we do get benefit from logs in the streams.

Mr. ALLARD. Any other comments on that question? Okay. Yes, Dr. Partridge.

Mr. PARTRIDGE. In regard to the business of leaving snags, you may or may not realize that it is the very organisms living in those snags that protect us from the very bark beetles and bugworms and so forth that cause the damage you are talking about.

Mr. ALLARD. Good comment. Let me call on some members of the committee. Congressman Doolittle from California please.

Mr. DOOLITTLE. Dr. Oliver, you described I think it was a four-phase process with forest growth and indicated that a stand-removing fire takes you back to the stand initiation phase. I have read that we have in many parts of our forests a density that is 10 or 20 times what it used to be. And I am aware of a fire in Mrs. Chenoweth's area back in 1910 I think it was which was so hot that it burned below the ground, like seven feet below the ground, and I don't know any more about the fire than that.

But when you get a severely hot forest fire, and I guess I will have two questions; one is, with all the dead and dying trees we have got today and the increased density, is the likelihood of that type of a fire substantially increased? And, secondly, if a fire of that nature occurs, then what happens to the stand initiation phase?

Mr. OLIVER. A couple of things. One is you are right. What has happened is that the high amount of fuel that we have as a close number of standing, drying trees create very hot fires relative to some of them that were normally there. We have seen in the Tyhee Creek fire near Wenatchee that the fire was much hotter, and I can go into details of how we know that. And what that will do, of course, is that will do a lot more cooking of the soil.

Now, the other thing that we brought up when you weren't here is if we don't salvage that, preferably remove some of it before it burns, if you didn't salvage after it after burned, then the trees, as I mentioned, the first fire simply kills them. The trees then over the decades fall down and create high densities of downed material. We get these very hot reburns which then cook the soil extremely.

So some of the high densities we will be creating soils that end up being hydrophobic on the top which cause runoff rather than infiltration of water. It will be creating some hot spots that probably will come back into brush fields for a long while, and other areas will come back to trees.

Mr. DOOLITTLE. You also mentioned when you were talking about species—let me just ask this panel of experts—part of nature is that species go extinct and new ones come along, isn't it? And is that something that is not natural?

Mr. OLIVER. It happens. The concern is that some of our alteration of habitat may be causing the species to go extinct at a faster rate than has happened historically or prehistorically except in some of those extreme conditions. And some of the concern I want to point out is that we have had species become endangered and others go extinct where we have eliminated each of those structures including that stem exclusion stage. We almost had the Kirkland's warbler go extinct when we eliminated that, and we have had species go extinct when we eliminated the stand initiation and species go extinct when we eliminated the old growth. So the concern is to maintain some kind of a balance.

Mr. DOOLITTLE. Thank you.

Mr. ALLARD. I will call on the other gentleman from California, Mr. Pombo.

Mr. POMBO. I will pass.

Mr. ALLARD. Mrs. Chenoweth.

Mrs. CHENOWETH. Mr. Chairman, I wanted to ask Mr. Sampson who is highly regarded in the industry—and I appreciate all of your testimony very, very much; it is very informative and educational to me—you made the statement though that we can't really crash through what Judges are going to do to us as far as moving the process along. And that seems to be where we are stymied. What would you suggest? The law seems to be so clear, and yet we have rules and regulations written that are in exact opposite of what the Congress has stated. What do you suggest, Dr. Sampson?

Mr. SAMPSON. Wow. That is a big question. That is more of a question for a longer discourse, but let me just simply say that on the back of the napkin when we talk about these things, what I tend to draw is inverted pyramids, pyramids standing on their point. And the points are the law, and we have scattered them over this issue landscape one at a time; endangered species here and NEPA there. They make eminent good sense, and I don't think anybody has a sense that that was the wrong thing to do.

But each year gets a bigger and bigger layer of case law, judicial decisions and administrative regulations, and, of course, congressional budgets all of which play into that. And pretty quick what you have got over 20 years now that we have been doing that is you get these larger and larger triangles—pyramids that build on those one single points until you have got tremendous overlapping and complexity.

If you are in the field today as a Federal manager, you are not caring about what the law said 20 years ago. You are looking at today's complex interaction of judicial decisions. And the other thing that we talk about is decentralizing, getting decisions out on the land because the decision you make when you look at a watershed is pretty easy sometimes compared to the decision you make in here.

But I might hasten to point out that every time somebody sues somebody in the Forest Service, they sue the Secretary of Agriculture. They do not sue the district ranger, and every time the Secretary of Agriculture loses, his lawyers figure out another three-page memorandum to tell people not to get the Secretary in that position again. And so the fact of the matter is over 20 years we have totally centralized this because of those lawsuits coming back here at this point.

Now, how do you get out of that? The answer, I think, has eluded us so far. It is very complex. Our best bet in the forest health legislation was to pick some small spots and experiment with expedited process and try to demonstrate that with expedited process we can get both good environmental and economic results.

To clean up the whole mess has, in fact, been one that has eluded these committees in the past. It crosses jurisdictions. Those laws cross jurisdictions of several committees at once, and it is an enormous challenge for this Congress to take a look at. I would be happy to go through some other stuff later with you on some specific ideas. But if you are looking for magic bullets, I don't have any.

Mrs. CHENOWETH. Thank you, Dr. Sampson. I am not looking for magic bullets truly but some solutions. Dr. Partridge, I have not ever met you before or been able to hear you testify. What do you teach at the University of Idaho?

Mr. PARTRIDGE. Just about everything. Wildland resource conservation, urban forestry, insect and disease material. I have advanced graduate courses in all of these and a number of others as well.

Mrs. CHENOWETH. Are you a department head?

Mr. PARTRIDGE. No.

Mrs. CHENOWETH. Do you teach full time there or——

Mr. PARTRIDGE. I have just been there 450 years. That is all.

Mrs. CHENOWETH. No, truly, could you——

Mr. PARTRIDGE. I am a full professor well beyond retirement age. I can do and say about what I please.

Mrs. CHENOWETH. You know, I think that is wonderful. Thank you, Mr. Chairman.

Mr. ALLARD. Mr. Cooley.

Mr. COOLEY. Thank you, Mr. Chairman. Vic, I have some things I would like to ask you to make some comments on. As you probably know, I served on the Columbia Gorge Task Force for two years as a state senator in the State of Oregon, part of that group. And, of course, we have spent a great deal like $2 billion on mitigation of the salmon, and many times I went through this process of talking to the expertise on this area trying to evaluate their judgment as to how we can mitigate this particular species, and nothing has ever happened.

Could you give me your idea of what you think about the Endangered Species Act and what is happening to the Coho salmon and things like that in that area? Because this is directly affecting our forests' livelihood in the Columbia Gorge and its viability and its interpretation. And we seem to have alluded to a lot of things, and nothing is happening.

Mr. KACZYNSKI. Well, as a practicing fisheries biologist and ecologist and my training and that, I professionally see a lot of abuse of the Endangered Species Act at the administrative level. The biggest single abuse I think is the taking of the species concept to smaller and smaller subunits until with fish, we are starting to talk about every single fish population in every single stream as an endangered species.

And I went back and read the Endangered Species Act in the record, and that record said one of the things we want to avoid is naming every single squirrel in every single park in the United States as an endangered species under the Act, and we are approaching that administratively the way the Act is being administered.

The Columbia River situation is an extremely complex situation. I believe the fish—our salmon that go up the Columbia River are worth having. I don't want to see those fish get lost, and it is really a challenge to us how we can do that without disrupting our civilization and our economy in the Pacific Northwest. We have gotten a tremendous amount of benefit from that flood control irrigation and hydroelectric system. It is really a part of our civilization, and there is going to be a lot of disruption there before we get past that.

And those are the main challenges for those Snake River salmon. Our forest situation with our Snake River salmon—this is not really the critical problem. We could make the forests into the best salmon habitat in the world. It would be like preparing a bridal chamber with silk sheets and the bride never showing up.

Mr. COOLEY. Thank you. I appreciate that. You heard Dr. Thomas. I think you were here when he was testifying——

Mr. KACZYNSKI. Yes.

Mr. COOLEY [continuing]. About the east side screens in the forest things, you know, and I think you are probably pretty familiar with that process. Do you think that those screens have really helped or hindered the forest health or the potential stream impact?

Mr. KACZYNSKI. We talked about this a little bit while you were gone, and I personally believe that they are a hindrance to forest health. They basically maintain the status quo. We still have the same unhealthy forest situation that we had before we started that process. We haven't moved off the dime.

Mr. COOLEY. And yet the Forest Service seems to defend that every time we talk about it. Even some of their own scientists are starting to put out articles saying that the screens are detrimental to the forest's health, and yet when you talk to the people in a hearing such as this, they defend those screens right to the hilt. I mean, those are the best things that ever happened. And we just can't seem to get them to come off of this center point to realize what is really happening.

Do we have a conflict between management and science here, or what, in your opinion, is going on that creates this on one side the scientists that are working there are saying, "This is not working. It is ruining our forest industry," and on the other side we have the management saying, "No, no, they are wrong," and yet they claim that they are really abiding by science and doing everything possible to make everything as best as they possibly can?

Mr. KACZYNSKI. I suspect we have some bureaucrats defending their bureaucracy.

Mr. ALLARD. Time has expired. If we don't have any other questions from the members of the committee, I would like to move on to the other panel. Thank you, gentlemen, for your time and your responses in your testimony.

I would like to call on the fourth panel that is the timber firms; Mr. Roy Grossen, Mr. Connell, Mr. Johnson, Mr. Lindsay, and Mr. Olson. Again, gentlemen, I just remind you that you have got three lights there in front of you. And as long as that green light is on, it is a go; and when they hit the yellow, it is time to wind up remarks; and when it is red, I will ask you to stop your testimony.

And we will ask each one of you to go ahead and give your testimony, and then I will ask for members of the committee if they would like to ask you any questions. I thought I would start with, first of all, Mr. Grossen. Is there one member of this panel that wants to start off, or should we just start down the line? Mr. Grossen, you are on first then.

STATEMENT OF ROY GROSSEN, BOISE CASCADE CORPORATION, COUNCIL, IDAHO; ACCOMPANIED BY PATRICK CONNELL, V.P. ROCKY MOUNTAIN LOG HOMES, HAMILTON, MONTANA; D.R. JOHNSON, D.R. JOHNSON LUMBER COMPANY, RIDDLE, OREGON; ROBERT LINDSAY, ROBERT LINDSAY AND ASSOCIATES, EUGENE, OREGON; DON OLSON, KAIBAB FOREST PRODUCTS, PHOENIX, ARIZONA

Mr. GROSSEN. Thank you, Mr. Chairman, and committee members, Helen Chenoweth from my home state of Idaho. My name is Roy Grossen. I reside in Council, Idaho. I am also mayor for the City of Council and President of Northwest Timber, but those are just volunteer jobs. My main job is I work in a sawmill there in Council, the only sawmill in the Council area.

Three weeks ago I found out as of March 31 that the sawmill will be closed down permanently. Fifty-six employees including myself will be out of work. It is very devastating to a small community of only 800 individuals in a county where a work force in Adams County is only 1,800 people. That is about 30 percent of the income for that area.

As you know, small, rural community hospitals are in trouble. This will absolutely devastate that hospital. I predict it will shut down probably within a year. Our railroad system into that area, which is the only main transportation we have for central Idaho, will cease to exist. My neighbors up to the north, Grangeville, within the last 24 months, that mill there shut down with 200 employees being gone. My neighbors to the west, Joseph, Oregon, which you heard about earlier, over 100 employees right there. They are gone forever.

These are small, rural communities that have no other diversification. I have been in diversification programs for over 10 years. There is nothing there but the natural resources. That is all we have to rely on. What we are seeing in the sad tragedy of this whole thing is that every one of these communities, including my own, sit right in the heart of the Payette National Forest—dead center of that forest; timber all the way around us, and I seen much of it burn up last summer. And we can't touch a stick of it, and our mills are going down. It is hard to explain to our people why we cannot log those areas.

Many of those reasons all fall back to one, the Endangered Species Act. Salmon in our area we have seen shut down much of that. The Chinook salmon, the sockeye salmon, it really don't make any difference though. Those are nothing more than surrogate species.

We have in the head of the Lochsa River, and some of the other reaches of northern Idaho—Selway is one primary stream—that is pristine and never had logging or cattle grazing in it. There is no fish, folks. It is not logging. It is not cattle grazing. It is just the fact that there are other things going on in the system, and it is all blamed upon the habitat, and that is not true. The habitat is there, but the fish are not.

Another fact that we may look at is at endangered species. I have mentioned before no matter whether it is salmon, whether it be the

89-215 O - 95 - 4

wolf, it could be a three-legged grasshopper for all that matters, the preservation community will continue to appeal any activity on those forests. These appeals have completely shut down our forests all the way through. We are not moving any timber out there that should be moved.

And it is because of the appeal system, the Endangered Species Act, the intervention of other governmental agencies such as the National Marine Fisheries Service—the good old U.S. Fish and Wildlife Service dictates almost everything we do, it seems like, in our country anymore—and it is very hard for my people to understand why we can't make a living out there because of the Federal regulations.

I am very concerned. I think there is a lot that we can do out there. The fires of last summer burnt 3.7 million acres. You have heard some conservative figures here of saying only about 3.7 billion board feet. Folks, it was over 5 billion board feet. The Payette National Forest—I have an EIS right here for the proposed fires up there. To give you an idea, on the Lower Salmon River, 56,000 acres. Of the 56,000 acres, only 1,000 acres proposed to harvest timber on. No volumes are included within that. I can show you all four documents on the Payette National Forest. No volumes are included. Our neighbors to the south in the Boise National Forest has already prepared theirs and ready to sell at 275 million Board feet. The Payette is doing nothing. They are scared to partially because of the salmon.

What we need, we need some corrections out there. We need revisions to the Endangered Species Act. We must have those. It must be immediate, not like the other Congressman said earlier, "Why don't we wait?" We can't wait. Hey, we are losing jobs now, folks. We have to move now. And it is very important that we move now.

The other one is have people in the equation. People make a big difference. We all live there. That is my home. I need to live there too as well as those animals. I love all animals out there. I love to hunt and fish, and I love the wilderness—all areas. But we need to live there too. Make people part of that equation. Make it communities and restoration of those communities as well as the forest when we look at forest health. And we should do the very same also when we look at the Endangered Species Act. People are part of that equation.

I ask you that you look at these two Acts. One is to pass an emergency forest health bill, and for salvage, it used to be prior to 1993 when the Clinton Administration controlled everything, the local forest supervisors had the authority at that time to declare an emergency and sell those sales nonappealable. I would ask that you reinstate that again. The other one is make changes to the Endangered Species Act to include the human factors in my local communities. So please take that into consideration. I am sorry I went over, Mr. Chairman. I am also looking for a job.

[The statement of Mr. Grossen appears at the conclusion of the hearing.]

Mr. ALLARD. The gentleman's time has expired. Mr. Connell.

STATEMENT OF PATRICK CONNELL

Mr. CONNELL. Mr. Chairman, my name is Pat Connell. I work for Rocky Mountain Log Homes which is located in Hamilton, Montana. These aren't Daniel Boone-type structures that we produce nowadays. We have grown from a backyard business to the premier manufacturer of solid wood homes along with our affiliate, Pioneer Log Homes. We employ over 100 workers. I am here also representing the Independent Forest Products Association with another 100-member companies throughout the West.

I came to testify because I am concerned about the slow process we have all been hearing about today about trying to put out salvage of dead timber. I would like to see Congress pass legislation that removes all procedural roadblocks to getting these forests salvaged. Without such legislation, I really do agree with Roy, we are going to have less than five percent of the timber which burned this summer reach market.

Now, my company has salvaged timber sales the last few years in regions one, two, and four including Utah, Wyoming, Idaho, and Montana. Two of our Spruce Bark Beetle salvage sales were within the 280,000 acre Corral Fire. Now, this picture—these type of fires produce a habitat crisis for all species which live in or near our forests whether they are legally mandated as endangered or not.

This is Cloochman Creek. It is a class one fisheries stream. As you can see, it has a lot of shade. It is the headwaters of the north fork of the Payette River. This is a primary headwater spring for the Payette River. Mrs. Chenoweth, this is a constituent, Ken Walters, my contractor, Shorts Bar Logging out of Riggins. As you can see, it is gummed up and contaminated by ash. It would be like drinking out of a used cigarette ashtray.

Previous to the fire, there was a 75-foot buffer strip protecting the spring from the impact band. It was fire, Mr. Chairman, not logging or any other activity, that destroyed this spring. We are going to experience a succession of fire seasons like 1994 and destroy more class one fisheries if Congress does not address the underlying forest health problem. Here is Ken with a recently killed burn that was a green subalpine fir. We do not have a long time in which to salvage this material.

Different species along with different size of trees really react to fire differently. Smaller diameter white wood species began checking or cracking immediately after the fire, and except for limited uses like house logs, they really need to be harvested immediately. Millions of dollars will be foregone if salvage of this material does not occur this summer; not next summer, this summer.

Unfortunately, most of the recently announced salvage proposals like Roy was speaking about on the Payette are talking about a targeted execution date of their plans in September. That means maybe bidding the sale or advertising the sale then, not starting to harvest. You know, the cow is already out of the back door of the barn.

Now, this is road construction for the Brundage Ski Area on the Payette Forest for their parking lot expansion, and it is within an anadromous fishery. Construction occurred concurrent to this summer's fire suppression efforts in the next drainage to the north. NMFS allowed the use of heavy equipment during this project, but they would not allow the Forest Service to fight fire with heavy equipment in any anadromous fishery. I don't understand how NMFS can defend this decision, but the results are clear. Due to minimal impact suppression tactics, which were developed by the Forest Service and NMFS, equipment and expertise of local Idaho loggers were virtually ignored.

Mr. DOOLITTLE. Mr. Chairman, I know we are not asking questions, but I want to understand that picture. What is that? A ditch or something they dug there?

Mr. CONNELL. No, sir. That is a road.

Mr. DOOLITTLE. Okay. Thank you.

Mr. CONNELL. Mr. Chairman, it is a brand new road that is going over a creek to access the parking lot. We can pass these to you, sir.

Mr. DOOLITTLE. Thank you.

Mr. CONNELL. This is a picture taken three days after the Corral Fire started to blow up in the end of September after it had been burning. On the very morning that the fire ravaged my company's Hendricks Creek salvage sale, which, by the way, was not in an anadromous fishery, this equipment was 15 minutes away from the fire. Rather than use this equipment to build a fireline and potentially stop the fire before it reached our sales, the Forest Service directed my crews and me that this equipment had to be evacuated.

I believe that the order from NMFS to fight Idaho fires without bulldozers is absurd. I understand the need to protect salmon, the habitat of endangered species, but letting fires burn millions of acres of habitat will not protect endangered species.

My final point. I urge this committee to consider an oversight hearing to review the Forest Service 1994 fire suppression costs, management, and the results of that suppression. Thank you, Mr. Chairman.

[The statement of Mr. Connell appears at the conclusion of the hearing.]

Mr. ALLARD. I thank the gentleman. Mr. Johnson.

STATEMENT OF D.R. JOHNSON

Mr. JOHNSON. I want to extend my thanks to both Chairmen for holding this very important meeting. The issue of timber salvage is timely and needs to be addressed immediately by Congress. I cannot speak on the issue from a national aspect, but I think what we in Oregon call the east side forests are representative of the problem we are all facing in the timber industry when it comes to the harvest of salvage timber.

First, let me give you some background. My name is Don Johnson. I own a mill and operate it in Grant County, Oregon. It is part of the Blue Mountain area where we have one of the greatest bug killed, potential fire hazards as there is I am sure anywhere. Our mill employs 200 people, and in a small area like ours, it is the heart and soul of the economy.

Oregon has led the world in timber productions for years, and we pride ourselves for harvesting timber and maintaining the healthiest forests in the world. In the past few years, timber production has come to a virtual halt which has crippled our industry and put thousands of hardworking Oregonians out of work. We want to continue to provide jobs with good pay. If something is not done soon, we will lose our jobs, a solid tax base, and a community.

I want to briefly make five major points: First, the harvest of salvage timber and the immediate reforestation of an area is a plus for the environment. This is a win-win situation. This will show the speed of disease, lower the fire danger, and start the process for improving forest health.

Second, the system for offering timber sales is broken. The Forest Service will not move quickly enough to offer salvage timber sales. When you place all the requirements of planning screens, many self-imposed such as PAC fish consideration and current NEPA compliance standards, along with the Endangered Species Act, sales do not get offered; and if they do, they end up in Court.

I know the issues surrounding timber sales is complex, but we should not stand by and let this resource go to waste. It is a crime to let dead and dying trees go to waste when there is such a shortage of logs for our mills to supply our nation with lumber. The salvage timber puts dollars in the local economy and provides a huge amount of money for the United States Treasury.

Third, the window of opportunity is now open to make meaningful use of the salvage timber resource. Between six and twelve months is the time frame. Any program not producing timber within that time frame will really do very little good. We need relief now from the current system of offering timber sales or nothing can or will be accomplished.

Fourth, we need to set the goals for salvage timber sales forest by forest. Those goals can be tracked by those of us closest to the resource. Currently, there is no accountability, and each forest seems to set its own standards and limits for what can or cannot be done. Any bill coming out of Congress must give specific goals and place accountability. If that does not happen, we will end up with another messy program with no one really in charge and no meaningful results.

Fifth, I encourage the subcommittee to dig deep and find out just how much salvage volume is really out there. The volume numbers provided by the agency that I have reviewed totally underestimate what I know exists in the forests in my area.

For example, the Forest Service says there is only 30 million board feet on the Malheur National Forest that should be salvaged. I think the number is much closer and could be much beyond 200 million board feet. A great deal of salvage timber resources are being placed off limits by letting the agency continue business as usual. The committees need to clear away all the chaff and find out what is really there. I think everyone will be surprised. This is why my fourth point of assigning targets is so important.

In closing, I want to, again, extend my thanks to all who helped make this hearing possible and encourage you to move with the utmost haste to get a reasonable piece of legislation passed. By doing nothing, a great deal of timber resources will be lost. Your efforts are on the right track, and all of us who make our daily living in the forest products industry stand willing to help in any possible way. Thank you.

[The statement of Mr. Johnson appears at the conclusion of the hearing.]

Mr. ALLARD. Thank you for your testimony. Mr. Lindsay.

STATEMENT OF ROBERT LINDSAY

Mr. LINDSAY. Mr. Chairman and members of the committee, I am Robert Lindsay, a forest resource consultant from Eugene, Oregon. I am here today to detail for you the increasing complexity of salvaging dead and dying material from our national forests.

An excellent example of the complexity is the comparison of two forest fires on the Willamette National Forest. In September 1988, the Shady Beach Fire burned roughly 9,000 acres. In October 1991, the Warner Creek Fire burned roughly 9,000 acres. The two fires are six miles apart. The suppression cost for the Shady Beach Fire was $14.5 million and on the Warner Creek Fire $11 million.

The Shady Beach Fire contained a total of 166 million board feet of dead and dying timber. The EIS or environmental impact statement was completed, timber sales prepared and sold, and harvesting began by July 1989. Ten months is what it took. We harvested 131 million board feet or 80 percent of the salvage timber. That timber sold for $36 million. The local governments received $9.4 million in lieu of tax payments, and roughly 1,100 jobs were created out of that salvage material. Currently, 95 plus percent of the fire area meets or exceeds reforestation standards, and other environmental damage has been ameliorated.

The Warner Creek Fire contains 180 million board feet of dead and dying timber. Today, some 40 months after the fire, the environmental impact statement is being challenged in Court. No salvage sales or operations are occurring. A large percentage of the timber on this fire is of species which deteriorate very rapidly following a fire. Why the dramatic differences in these recovery operations? Mostly, it is the difference in land allocations, the spotted owl, Court injunctions, Option 9, and constantly changing rules and regulations concerning forest management.

Shady Beach was primarily forest land and timber production land. But for the fire recovery, we retained wildlife trees, maintained stream buffers, required logging systems that did not disturb the soil. We addressed the growing spotted owl controversy. We monitored stream temperatures and sediment and implemented many of the ecosystem management features we are calling for today. And it met the soon to be adopted 1990 Willamette National Forest Management Plan.

Warner Creek occurred in October of 1991, three years later, but after a whole bunch of laws that I won't read for you and judicial opinions concerning the spotted owl, this area of the Warner Creek was a habitat conservation area under the Spotted Owl Management Plan. This was the first fire that occurred in an HCA. There were no guidelines, rules, regulations, or policies from anybody on what to do with it.

The purpose of the project was supposedly to provide or recreate owl habitat, but the process was hampered by constant review and change by the Northern Spotted Owl Oversight Committee, the Oversight Steering Committee, the Interagency Northern Spotted Owl Conservation Group, the Regional Ecosystem Office, the Regional Interagency Executive Committee, as well as consultation with the United States Fish and Wildlife Service.

Thus, the EIS and recovery process for Warner Creek stands at 40 months, still counting. The environmental impact statements proposes to harvest 9 million board feet, five percent of what is dead and dying. Under the utmost optimistic scenario, the Forest Service could recover $3 million from this salvage sale. That would mean only $800,000 to the county and 81 jobs. Well, you have got to remember the bottom line is that taxpayers spent over $10 million on fire suppression and the other items involved, and $30 million worth of timber is sitting there going to rot.

What is the important prognosis out of the Warner Creek Fire? Are we going to gain anything by letting it sit there? No. We are going to have reburns. It is going to burn hot. We are going to have worse environment than if we had done a good salvage job.

The one thing I want to get across to you, the current requirements for completion of an environmental assessment or an environmental impact statement on the Forest Service is a minimum of two years. That is from the time somebody thinks something should be done till somebody signs a document saying they can do it. Then you add another year or another year plus for a total of four years before any operations begin. We have got to change that. Congress has to do something to streamline this process so that we can return our land to productivity and salvage these forest products.

[The statement of Mr. Lindsay appears at the conclusion ot the hearing.]

Mr. ALLARD. I thank the gentleman. The time for the gentleman has expired. Mr. Olson.

STATEMENT OF DONALD OLSON

Mr. OLSON. Chairman Allard and other members of the subcommittee, I very much appreciate the opportunity to be here to testify. My name is Don Olson. I am president of Kaibab Forest Products, a small Arizona-based company. I am also here representing the Region 3 Management Committee for our area, and, finally, as the Chairman of the Public Timber Board of our national organization AF&PA.

We have all heard repeatedly about the forest health issues in the Northwest and in the inland areas, the acres burned and the costs, et cetera. But one area of the country we don't hear much about is the Southwest. In addition to our deserts, there are extensive national forests in our part of the country. And the issues we have been talking about are every bit as severe on our national forests as they are in other parts of the country; the overgrown forest conditions, the extremely high fuel loads, the insects and disease problems. And there certainly is not a lack of scientific evidence and information about the conditions of these forests.

Fortunately, I guess, in the last couple of years in the Southwest we have been fairly lucky in that we have not had any major wildfires. Our last major one was in 1990. It was the Dude Fire. It burned about 24,000 acres at a cost to us of about $12 million. Six lives were lost in that fire. It burned with such intensity that it sterilized many parts of the soil, destroyed four Mexican spotted owl habitat areas which is a listed species, and one of the common things we hear from the scientists in our area certainly is it is not a matter of if the forest will burn, it is only when.

In 1990 when I accepted the position that I have, we had three very good mills operating in the Southwest. They were all in small, rural communities. We employed about 500 people. With the position I have had, I have certainly been intimately involved in the last couple of years of having to shut down two of those facilities permanently. And by midyear of this year, we will be down to one very small facility that is going to really struggle with less than 70 employees.

I certainly understand that we are not unique in mill closures and layoffs, but I think it is really important to understand in the Southwest that as an industry, we are basically 100 percent dependent on public timber. We don't have alternatives of private lands. We don't have nonindustrial forested lands. It is all from our national forests.

In our region, the growth out of that region from Forest Service numbers is around 800 million board feet. It used to be the sale volume was somewhere around 400 million a year. Today, we are down to less than 50, and I am afraid it is going to go to zero very shortly when they come up with the designation for critical habitat for the Mexican spotted owl.

We have permanently, and I mean permanently by mills shutting down, auctioning off the equipment, leveling the ground, using it for other purposes. We have permanently dismantled more than 50 percent of our industry in the Southwest, and I think there is another good portion that I am certain is not far behind that. And I guess if we do see a turn around and we can get something moving in terms of proactive management on our forests, I have a real concern that in the Southwest that we will have an industry that will be able to help out in that endeavor.

I think from all the testimony we have certainly seen that in every region of the country we have proven the common need for aggressive hands-on management, and letting nature take its course has proven foolhardy economically, environmentally, and in the human sense tragically. For a problem this widespread, the solution must be national in scope.

Your committees have the opportunity to restore the needed leadership and bring sense back to our legal system. We need a thorough oversight and reform of the conflicting laws which govern the management of our Federal lands. We need better accountability and leadership in our Federal agencies. And while oversight and development of appropriate legislative solutions may take some time, we need immediate action to enable the Forest Service to attend quickly to our most urgent forest health and salvage needs. Thank you very much for the interest in this issue, and I would appreciate any questions you might have.

[The statement of Donald Olson appears at the conclusion of the hearing.]

Mr. ALLARD. Thank you all for your testimony. I guess I have one basic question I want to address to all of you. Do you think the Forest Service has been as responsive to the needs of your industry today as they were 40 years ago?

Mr. GROSSEN. No.

Mr. ALLARD. Forty years ago would you describe their relationship to you as more of a partnership as opposed to today which is perhaps more adversarial? Let the record show that they were agreeing with that statement. Do you believe the Forest Service can do more to facilitate your needs, or do you think that their hands are really tied by lawsuits, that it continually gets threatened if they don't work more with your interests?

Mr. JOHNSON. I think they can do more if they just would.

Mr. ALLARD. You think that the lawsuits that they mention is, you know, as big a concern as they make it out to be?

Mr. JOHNSON. Well, they are hindered to a great degree by that all right, but there are still many areas and many things they can do to help us.

Mr. ALLARD. Let the record show that was Mr. Johnson responding. Mr. Connell.

Mr. CONNELL. Yes. Mr. Chairman, consider a Forest Service mid-management individual that has the opportunity to choose between doing nothing or something, and if he does something, he is at risk for lawsuit, for failure for career advancement, and opened up to all sorts of diatribe of members in his community or out of the nation for mismanaging his responsibility. By doing nothing or extending that, he does not have to face that risk of lawsuit.

Mr. ALLARD. At one time, the Forest Service had more of a multiple use sort of a concept. Do you think that exists today?

Mr. CONNELL. The law is still on the books, but it doesn't seem like the output indicates that they are aware of that.

Mr. ALLARD. Mr. Lindsay.

Mr. LINDSAY. Yes. I would like to comment on that. Chief Thomas said earlier at this committee that they had taken a certain number of losses within the Forest Service, and he quoted foresters and he quoted civil engineers. Being a field-type person and working with the Forest Service in the field, what has happened, yes, they have lost foresters. Most of the job loss has been in timber, but the real tragedy is they have lost the trained technicians who do the job on the ground.

The Willamette National Forest, which used to produce the most timber of any forest in the United States, now has one logging specialist. They have three people, in my estimation, on the whole forest who really know how to lay out a timber sale. Congress can pass laws and regulations to change the way the Forest Service is supposed to manage. But unless you do something to get the Forest Service to train people or retrain the few people that you have left, those laws are not going to accomplish anything.

Mr. ALLARD. I thank the gentleman for his response. Mr. Doolittle from California.

Mr. DOOLITTLE. I am very concerned that the Forest Service has become a hopelessly paralyzed organization. And even if they were functioning well, of which they are not, the laws are such that hamstring to a large degree what can be done. I have two questions. What single thing specifically would be the most important reform we could make? I don't believe that this is hopeless or that it is so complex that we just are going to have to limp along. That is not my world view. We make the laws. We can solve this problem completely. So what single reform would you, ladies and gentlemen, care to suggest would be necessary to get things going again?

Mr. JOHNSON. Well, I would like to talk a little bit about how a regular company is made up, and I don't think the Forest Service organization could be run that much different than that. We, in our company, also have specialists such as the Forest Service has biologists. They have the reports and all of these kinds of things.

They are there for the purpose of being the specialists in those fields. But we still have to have common sense and someone to make the decision of what ultimately is going rule, whether it is going to be fish or it is going to be sales in our company or timber in our company or the accounting department or whatever it is. Somebody has to coordinate those things and decide which is the best route to go. A common sense approach is what we are really void of.

Mr. DOOLITTLE. Well, the problem is—I mean, how do we legislate a common sense approach? You may not have the plan. Let me invite you to communicate with us on this committee because if you don't, we will just have to make it up ourselves. Give us your plan for what you would like to see this mess straightened out so we can get back to how it ought to be.

Mr. OLSON. If you are wanting one thing, I think certainly from my perspective it is got to be some change in the Endangered Species Act.

Mr. DOOLITTLE. Okay.

Mr. OLSON. That is basically—truly, the law or abiding by the law or the lawsuits or the designation of critical habitat or the things involved, that is what is going to shut down the Southwest.

Mr. DOOLITTLE. Well, we are going under the direction of Mr. Pombo here to make dramatic reforms to the Endangered Species Act. However, as Dr. Thomas testified, that alone will not solve the problem of timber in the forests. And so we are going to have to have a more comprehensive solution than that. We will do that. Better than that, I invite the affected interests to study this carefully and to let us hear from you. We want to do it. This is the year to do it.

I also want to say, Mr. Chairman, I would love to engage—it is too bad we haven't had the time today to really go into the things that we need to delve into more. I am going to have to leave at 4:30 for a meeting I cannot miss so in the interests of moving along, I am going to stop asking questions.

Mr. ALLARD. Mr. Pombo.

Mr. POMBO. Thank you, Mr. Chairman.

Mr. ALLARD. Excuse me. Mr. Johnson, were you trying to get my attention to respond?

Mr. JOHNSON. No. The Endangered Species Act is the key to it all right, but, again, with the Endangered Species Act eliminated, you still lack the leadership in the Forest Service to do these jobs out there.

Mr. ALLARD. Okay. Now, Mr. Pombo.

Mr. POMBO. Thank you. As Mr. Doolittle said and as you have heard testified previously, we are going to make changes. And it is extremely important that it happen this year, and I think that there are a lot of issues that have been brought up today, a lot of testimony that we have had today that shows that Congress as a whole has basically ignored a lot of these problems for a long time. And I don't think that our actions in the past and the actions of the Executive Branch have led to where we are right now.

I am open to the suggestions that you have as to changes that can be made not only in the ESA but in other areas of environmental law and environmental regulation on streamlining the process and making the system so that it works. I do not believe that any of you want to see harm come to the fish and wildlife in your area, nor harm to the forests which are the habitat of that fish and wildlife.

And I place a lot of faith in you and will count on your advice and counsel in the changes that we are going to make in the coming year. And it is going to be extremely important that you work with us, that you let us know what changes can be made, and what can help to streamline the process so that you can proceed as quickly as you can.

You just heard testimony just a couple of minutes ago from someone who said that this is not a crisis, that we do not have a crisis, that it is a political crisis, that it is the rhetoric of the time. That is the kind of testimony that we normally heard here, and, you know, the chance to hear testimony from you about the problems that have come up is extremely important for Congress to hear, for the committees to hear so that we can move on in a positive manner and try to make the changes that need to be made.

I would just like to conclude by thanking all of you for being here and hope that we can make the changes that are needed in the next year. Thank you very much.

Mr. ALLARD. I will just make an additional comment. We still have a presidential veto on any legislation that may come out of this committee so, you know, we always have to keep that in mind too. Mrs. Chenoweth, you are next.

Mrs. CHENOWETH. Mr. Chairman, gentlemen, I have just heard such compelling testimony, and, of course, Mr. Grossen's testimony hits home, but they all do. I would like to ask Mr. Connell, in your estimation as a man who makes a living off of the forest products, knowing the state of the forests today, would you feel that this is an emergency?

Mr. CONNELL. Absolutely. The health conditions of the forests that exist today are as a result of fire suppression that was done out of hopefully the right idea since the inception of Forest Service activity in the West especially built up after the 1910 fire in your state. And part of the idea of the suppression of fire was that the timber that would not be burned up would then find its way to be used in society as wood fiber, whether it is chips or sawlogs, house logs, or what have you.

So the health condition has never existed as it does now, and this forest health condition is going to create catastrophic conditions that we have heard the scientists talk about that haven't been seen ever in the field of forestry.

Mrs. CHENOWETH. Mr. Connell, do you believe that that should influence the legislation that we put forth—the emergency situation?

Mr. CONNELL. Yes. I hope so. The opportunity to minimize the financial and resource losses due to the fires that we have seen in 1994 can only occur if the salvage effort goes forward, as I spoke in my testimony, this year. This is the type of wood that burned in Idaho and Montana where I am familiar with, and it just does not have a long time frame to salvage it. It is an emergency. When you have someone come into an ER room from an accident, you do not analyze. You triage instantly, and then you instantly react to save the patient. And we need to save the patient and salvage.

Mrs. CHENOWETH. Do you believe that this is an emergency of such proportions that even though it didn't happen as suddenly as an earthquake, it should get our attention as a natural emergency which has economic ramifications would have?

Mr. CONNELL. Congresswoman Chenoweth, first off, I am sure the families of the firefighters that died this last summer considered it an emergency. The industry that has not received the wood that could have come off of these areas over the next many, many years consider it an emergency. I consider it an emergency. And the response of the bureau that managed it should be reflecting the emergency condition.

Mrs. CHENOWETH. Thank you. Mr. Chairman, I have one more question, and I will try very hard not to run over my five minutes. Mr. Lindsay, you testified that the process was hampered by constant review and change by the Northern Spotted Owl Oversight Team, the Oversight Steering Committee, the Interagency Northern Spotted Owl Conservation Group, the Regional Ecosystem Office, and the Regional Interagency Executive Committee as well as consultation with U.S. Fish and Wildlife Service. Was this all done in open hearings? Was this an open process; this consultation?

Mr. LINDSAY. No, it was not. The consultation and the overviews of the progress of the environmental analysis team was basically a closed process.

Mrs. CHENOWETH. Mr. Lindsay, can you tell me where the authority came for these people to make these decisions behind closed doors?

Mr. LINDSAY. No, I cannot. I was involved with Shady Beach. I was an official member of the analysis team. On Warner Creek, we were told by legal—or the Forest Service was told by legal counsel that no one other than a Forest Service employee could be on an environmental analysis team. And during any consultation periods or otherwise, we were, as an observer, excluded from those conversations.

Mrs. CHENOWETH. And you are saying that as a matter of record to this committee?

Mr. LINDSAY. Yes.

Mrs. CHENOWETH. That is very significant. Do you feel your civil rights have been abused?

Mr. LINDSAY. Well, that is a difficult question, but I think the process has broken down. The Shady Beach process were myself, other people from the environmental groups, et cetera, were involved. Many of the problems which now are being sued or appealed were taken care of on the ground before they became major confrontations. And when we exclude these people and do not allow them to do anything until the official comment on the EIS, then we have these head-knockings because we are beyond the point that we can make minor adjustments on the ground to hopefully satisfy the two sides.

Mrs. CHENOWETH. And my last question, Mr. Chairman. Mr. Lindsay, do you understand the seven elements of a RICO lawsuit?

Mr. LINDSAY. No, I do not.

Mrs. CHENOWETH. You might ask your attorneys about it. Thank you, Mr. Chairman.

Mr. ALLARD. Thank you. Mr. Cooley.

Mr. COOLEY. Thank you, Mr. Chairman. I would like to address my questions to D.R. since he is a mill owner in my district. I want to make a comment before I ask him a question. He is very modest because I want to tell you that his ingenuity and entrepreneurship has kept Prairie City basically alive and part of an area of John Day.

What is happening, and I want to ask you, Don, this, is that under the current sales program, if there is any in your area as far as the public lands are concerned, is there anything going on at all now?

Mr. JOHNSON. Well, they keep promising from the Forest Service that there will be something going on, but it never develops. For example, last year was supposed to be 155 million feet sold. It ended up at 17 million feet net volume.

Mr. COOLEY. When they have these hearings and discuss the different programs that they do in order to evaluate the salvage or the cutting of timber, be it green or otherwise, do they include any of your people—allowed to attend those meetings such as your foresters——

Mr. JOHNSON. No.

Mr. COOLEY [continuing]. Or your scientists or anything to attend those?

Mr. JOHNSON. No.

Mr. COOLEY. So you only receive the results of those after it is completely finished without any input at all?

Mr. JOHNSON. We do not. That is right.

Mr. COOLEY. Have you ever, sir, asked them if you could at least be a witness—I mean, not testify but just an observer in that process?

Mr. JOHNSON. Well, we didn't even know they were going on for a long time, and when we found out by talk off the street, frankly, that it was going on, that the other side—the preservation group was being consulted about the whole thing, we asked to be in there. And they said, "Well, you just didn't show up." Well, we didn't show up because we weren't invited. We didn't even know that the meetings were going on.

Mr. COOLEY. So what you are saying is that under testimony here that the forest people in your district at sometime or another have consulted with the preservationist, obstructionists, whatever group you want to talk about, before decisions were made, but you were never invited to attend those meetings?

Mr. JOHNSON. That is right. That is what the screening process is really about.

Mr. COOLEY. So you think that your problems with the current forest management programs in your area are directly directed to lack of some kind of authority or communications or participation by you involved in the process so you know what is going on?

Mr. JOHNSON. Yes. I personally feel very much so that the people in command of those areas there aren't going to sell any timber if there is any way that they can avoid it, salvage, green, or otherwise. And they just keep us out of the process.

Mr. COOLEY. Now, some of those people live right in your district. You know these people. They know your workers. They know the families. The kids all go to school together and everything else. Do you think that this is their desire, or is it the desire from something that is sort of unknown outside that is putting this kind of pressure on the locals as we have already talked and several gentlemen have alluded to the fact is that if you don't do anything, you don't get in trouble; if you do anything, you are going to be in trouble so let us not do anything?

Mr. JOHNSON. I think there is quite a bit of the element that if you don't do anything, you are not going to get in trouble. All the Forest Service people don't feel that way, but I think the leadership does in that area.

Mr. COOLEY. Are you familiar with the scientific report coming out of the Forest Service concerning the screening and how it is destroying old growth?

Mr. JOHNSON. I have read it. Yes. I know of it.

Mr. COOLEY. I thought it was strange that the head of that group had not seen that. Very strange.

Mr. JOHNSON. Yes.

Mr. COOLEY. Let me ask you one final question. Do you believe that the people in Congress have the ability to do something to make your situation better?

Mr. JOHNSON. Well, I am very impressed after coming to Washington this time to watch you people operate. I think there is a light at the end of the tunnel, and I think that you do have the ability and the power and I see the desire now to make that change to put people in the equation and put this thing back on track to some degree certainly from what it is now and has been in the immediate past.

Mr. COOLEY. Well, I want to thank you for coming and all you gentlemen, and I will say something even though Mr. Pombo is still here and Mr. Doolittle is gone, but we are going to rewrite the Endangered Species Act.

Mr. JOHNSON. Well, thank you very much. We certainly need it.

Mr. COOLEY. Diligently we are working on it, and I tell you we will spend the time to make sure that that happens.

Mr. JOHNSON. Let me say something. In order to get an emergency situation out, we have to bypass the laws. We have to get some sufficiency language in there somewhere where they can't tie us up in court from now till doomsday, and that is what has really been hindering us dramatically up to this point even if they did sell a sale.

Mr. COOLEY. Thank you, Mr. Chairman.

Mr. ALLARD. Thank you. I just might add to this conversation, as far as my committee is concerned and I think other committee chairmen are taking a similar attitude is that we want to hear from you. And if you have noticed the panels this morning instead of having the bureaucrats on first, we had the people that would be the most severely affected, whose jobs were affected as the first panel. And then later on we did bring on the bureaucrats, and I apologize to you that you are later on in the day. But I think that reflects a change in the Congress in general that we are going to be much more sensitive to what is happening outside the beltway.

Mr. JOHNSON. And I think we can speak for the industry, we appreciate that very, very much. And if there is anything in the world any of us can do, I am sure we would be very happy to do that.

Mr. ALLARD. Thank you. Thank you for being with us. I will call ahead and call the next panel. This is the fire and grassroots panel. We have Mr. Gerald Adams, Mrs. Rita Carlson, and Mr. Jim Irvine. Okay. We have got Mrs. Carlson and Mr. Adams. Mrs. Carlson, would you like to start off the testimony for this panel?

Ms. CARLSON. I would love to. Thank you.

STATEMENT OF RITA CARLSON, ALLIANCE FOR AMERICA, CAROGA LAKE, NEW YORK; ACCOMPANIED BY GERALD ADAMS, FIRE MARSHALL, NORTH LAKE TAHOE FIRE PROTECTION DISTRICT, CRYSTAL BAY, NEVADA

Ms. CARLSON. Well, thank you, Mr. Chairman, and members of the subcommittee for the opportunity for me to be here today and testify. My name is Rita Carlson. I work in Lewiston, Idaho, for a company called Potlatch Corporation. I am also a member of UPIU Local 712. In addition to that, I am vice president of a nationwide grassroots organization called the Alliance for America. Today, I represent my fellow workers and the Alliance for America.

I am not a scientist. If I am an expert at anything, it is on the impact that the failing forest policies, failing forest health, and failing forest products companies have on individual families, communities in the intermountain West. My expertise has been earned because of my personal involvement in a number of local and national grassroots organizations that are trying to cope with the Federal environmental policy gone seriously wrong.

In my testimony today, I want to put a human face on the issue of forest health, and I encourage you to keep that face in mind as you discuss ways to untangle the mess our forests are in.

Thousands of people live and work throughout the area where serious forest problems exist. We have built lives, families, homes, and towns in and around our national forests. We live and work in areas of the intermountain West, and we have planned our communities' futures around the Federal Government's promise of a sustainable supply of raw wood products from the National Forest System.

During the forest planning process, we were assured that our Federal forest managers could protect the many values that we enjoy in the forests. The Federal Government promised that the forests we are dependent upon would continue to be managed for the most good for the most people. The forest planning process seems to have been thrown out the window in favor of current systems of forest management gridlock, analysis paralysis, and out-of-control litigation. It is now clear that in our towns, those forest policy failures and broken promises threaten our economic and environmental futures.

The first to pay the price of all the broken promises are the people closest to the forest; people like Errol Roberts of Joseph, Oregon. Errol worked for the Boise Cascade Mill in Joseph. That mill closed last summer. With more than a little frustration, Errol and his coworkers now stand in the unemployment line. The job prospects in Joseph are nonexistent except for the seasonal work like battling the 100,000 acre fire that burned around their community last summer. Isn't it stupid that we have to pay our people unemployment while we have got our timber sitting in the forest rotting? I had hoped that we had sent you guys here to do better than that for us.

Dr. Bob Lee, University of Washington, has long warned the state and Federal Governments that many rural care-giving services are woefully unprepared for the human wave that was generated by a collapse of the national forest sale program. He and others have warned of increases in the abuse of drugs, alcohol, spouses and children, and increases in heart attacks and suicides, and we are now learning that Dr. Lee and others were right.

In Libby, Montana, the crisis hotline has seen a 300 percent increase in usage since the beginning of their mill closure 18 months ago. A recent headline in their paper indicated that the food pantries were running dry, and according to the county officials, they don't know what to do. They have families living in their cars in campgrounds.

We have a history of fires in the West, but with the mounting fuel load on the forest floors, those fires are now burning with such intensity that they destroy everything in their path. We not only have animals as victims of the negligence, but the soil itself is damaged to the bedrock. Under these conditions, soil regeneration is extremely damaged.

We believe that without action from this Congress, it is only a matter of time before we will be forced to live through another summer of dismay as our future, our children's future, and their heritage goes up in smoke. We are a proud people, and we are paying the price of failed Federal policy. We don't want government handouts. We want to return to work, and we are frustrated by the situation that seems so unnecessary.

We believe that if you help us, we can conserve our forests and protect their health while still providing for ourselves and our families. We are asking Congress to give us the tools to take back our way of life, but we don't have much time and neither do our forests. Thank you.

[The statement of Ms. Carlson appears at the conclusion of the hearing.]

Mr. ALLARD. Thank you for your testimony. Mr. Adams.

STATEMENT OF GERALD ADAMS

Mr. ADAMS. My name is Gerald Adams. I am a fire marshal from a small, little town in North Lake Tahoe, Nevada. I guess I am here representing the wildland urban interface communities. Back in 1988, we recognized that we had a fuel problem, and we started to do something about it. We developed a grassroots program that allowed us to go in on sensitive lands within the Tahoe Basin and develop a pilot project, kind of an experiment, to see if we could meet the environmental concerns and the fires protection needs.

We went into a 20-acre parcel in 1988 and 1989. We were able to take about 480 trees off of 20 acres, and that was the first couple years of our drought period. Since that time, even through our drought period in the Lake Tahoe Basin, I haven't had more than maybe a dozen trees on that 20 acres die. So just from the management standpoint, we were able to hang onto some of the trees that in other areas we have lost complete acreages of.

That little pilot project we basically got an A+ on from the Tahoe Regional Planning Agency which is our environmental regulatory agency in the Tahoe Basin. That allowed us to do another 20 acres the next year, and then that steppingstone allowed us to do a 750-acre project in 1991. We did a helicopter selective timber harvest operation.

And these are in our drainages where—this is not my community, but these are some pictures of some of the issues that are going on in the Tahoe Basin. But it allowed us to take and reduce the risk. We understand that we are not going to totally eliminate the fire risk itself, but we can at least reduce the risk within our community.

One of the things that I have worked a lot in in the basin is we have done this through a lot of public education and different grassroots projects. In trying to educate the decision-makers within the Tahoe Basin, in 1992, we had a wildland fire in the El Dorado National Forest that was called the Cleveland Fire. And it was only a small fire compared to some of the ones we have last year. It was 24,500 acres. But it made the list of being the nation's largest loss wildland fire in 1992.

The property losses amounted to 245,525,000. It cost $16.4 million to suppress it for four days of operations, and we lost two air tanker pilots in that process. If you take those figures and divide them into the 24,500, you come up with a $10,700 an acre. And then in tracking costs, the dollars stop there, but they really don't because then there are other revegetation programs that will go on for five or ten years.

In our operation in the last five to six years, my largest or my average cost for the work that we have done has been $800 an acre, and I still have my forests. We have got to start looking at how we are dealing with the way that we are dealing with our forests and our fire situations today. I think one of the other issues too that needs to be brought to the table is that we were able to accomplish what we did through joining partnerships and coordinations and cooperations. I was concerned about this program that eventually took off in 1988. I started it in 1986. But until I started working with other people of different professions, I wasn't getting anywhere. I joined forces with the cooperative extensions, the U & R Cooperative Extension, and since then, you know, we have been able to build on that. And now we have a regional program that is looked at as a model. And I thank you for listening to me.

[The statement of Mr. Adams appears at the conclusion of the hearing.]

Mr. ALLARD. Mr. Adams, your fire district, your revenues are local taxpayer funded?

Mr. ADAMS. Everything we have done has been out of the individual property owner's pocket, and their 1991 operation was taxpayer dollars. Yes.

Mr. ALLARD. Now, you have been involved in some of the forest fires in your area, fighting them?

Mr. ADAMS. Absolutely.

Mr. ALLARD. And did you get reimbursed by the Federal Government for that, or was that all local dollars?

Mr. ADAMS. We have mutual aid agreements. We have an agency or a group that is called the Sierra Nevada or the—it has been a long day for me too—we get reimbursed after the first 24 hours through our mutual aid pacts.

Mr. ALLARD. From the Forest Service?

Mr. ADAMS. Yes.

Mr. ALLARD. Do you feel that you get fully reimbursed for your costs, or do the local taxpayers pick up part of that cost?

Mr. ADAMS. There is a minor amount that is not reimbursed, but it is pretty much reimbursed.

Mr. ALLARD. Okay. And how much does it cost you when you get involved with a forest fire in your district?

Mr. ADAMS. It depends on how many personnel we send, how much equipment we send, and how long they stay.

Mr. ALLARD. Okay. And you had a fire nearly every year or every other year or every three years on the average?

Mr. ADAMS. We have had fires within our region every year since 1991. When I say our region, we responded into California, and California responds into Nevada. That is our agreement.

Mr. ALLARD. I see.

Mr. ADAMS. We had people on the Cottonwood Fire which was 48,000 acres which was kind of interesting. It 1961, they had the Donner Lake Fire that was a $1 million expenditure. It had 48,000 acres approximately. And the Cottonwood Fire was additionally about 48,000 acres, and that was a $13 million fire.

Mr. ALLARD. Is there a lot of forest health plans in your area as far as you know? Is the Forest Service doing much to promote things that would improve the health of forests to make it less susceptible to fire?

Mr. ADAMS. I think the Forest Service is doing what they can with their cutbacks in funding and personnel. I personally and the Forest Service also has sat on what is called the Forest Health Consensus Group, and we are in our 29th month of sitting on that.

And our objective is to take some new recommendations back to the Tahoe Regional Planning Agency on how the ordinances should be written on the fuels reduction ordinances that they have or the fuels management ordinances that they have. And I think we are going to be quite successful in that. It is just taking a long time to do. Twenty-nine months ago it was a room of adversaries. Today, that is not so.

Mr. ALLARD. Okay. Mr. Pombo.

Mr. POMBO. Thank you. Mr. Adams, you were talking about the pilot program that you had in Tahoe. From your experience, it did reduce the fire danger on the initial 20 acres I believe you said, and then it was expanded to 750 acres?

Mr. ADAMS. Correct. The original pilot project was 20 acres, and we had a situation where our community is designed for disaster like most of the other ones that have been allowed to be built in the wildlands without any other provisions tied into the approval process. But what we did was we had areas, and the First Creek drainage was our worst drainage. Like I said, we went in on 20 acres and took out 480 trees, approximately, and it is anywhere from a 45 to 70 percent slope in there.

So the spread on that fire, if we had had a fire in the bottom of that drainage, was—we have done some hypothetical runs on that, and within the first hour and a half, we would have been on a defensive mode more than anything else and just trying to get as many people out as possible in a rescue effort.

Mr. POMBO. On the area in the pilot program, what was the result of the wildlife in the area where you did go in and manage it in that way?

Mr. ADAMS. Interestingly enough, since we have worked on all of our drainages, we now have more raptors. Since we have opened the forest up, we have more raptors. We see more game; raccoons which—I have lived in this community for 25 years, and I have seen more wildlife than I have before we started.

Mr. POMBO. Thank you. Mrs. Carlson, I guess I will just put it to you this way. In the past several years, a lot of what has happened has been to remove any incentives for production, to remove the incentives for the individual to take care of themselves, but at the same time we have increased the other side of the agenda considerably.

I can remember last year, I know the Chairman and I went through some real good battles in the Ag Committee over this where anything that had anything at all to do with production and jobs we were cutting, and on the other side, the welfare side, we were increasing dramatically. And I think that in a community like yours, you can see that they went in and removed the production side at the same time that they increased the need for welfare and for emergency services.

Ms. CARLSON. That is correct. And in our communities, as I stated in my testimony here, we are in real big trouble. It also was stated earlier today that we have like our insurance systems—those are all things that are all paying the price all the while we are leaving our dead and dying, our burnt up timber that is salvageable that we are not being able to access it.

Mr. POMBO. And I know the people in your community would rather be working than in the situation they are in.

Ms. CARLSON. Yes, prefer especially when you look at the little kids.

Mr. POMBO. Thank you very much.

Mr. ALLARD. Mrs. Chenoweth.

Mrs. CHENOWETH. Thank you, Mr. Chairman. Mrs. Carlson, you have testified that you work in a mill that produces paper and tissue products. These are made out of chips. Right?

Ms. CARLSON. That is right.

Mrs. CHENOWETH. And pulp. Are you asking that the burnt timber in your area be sent to your mill to be chipped for pulp?

Ms. CARLSON. No, not necessarily. Our mill has a sawmill attached to it, and the salvage logs are taken to the sawmill. They are converted into sawlogs. The waste product, the sawdust and the chips that are left after that process, is taken or sent to the tissue mill or to the pulp mill where it is made into pulp and then sent to either the paper mill or the tissue mill. Therefore, we are employing a multitude of facets in our economy.

Mrs. CHENOWETH. Mrs. Carlson, you heard upon my questioning of the Forest Service that they would be willing to take another look at the areas that have been devastated by fires in our northwestern states. Would you and your people that you are in touch with in the industry be willing to work with the Forest Service on doing another assessment and urging that process along?

Ms. CARLSON. I heard him make that commitment that he would do that, and it excited me because we have been trying for many years to get not only the Chief of the Forest Service but many of the staff people and the members here on the Hill to come to our area to take a woods tour, to walk these areas.

In part of Mr. Thomas's testimony, he talked about the inaccessibility of a lot of the burnt timber. But in my area, that is just not true. And if they could come, I would be more than happy to walk those areas with them and show them. All we are waiting for is something to stop the appeal system, something to open up these areas that are locked up with grizzlies and wolves and PAC fish so that we can get in there to get that timber out.

Mrs. CHENOWETH. Mrs. Carlson, I notice there is a pile of papers there at your arm and some videos. Could you explain that? Have you entered everything you need to into the record?

Ms. CARLSON. No, and I would like to do that now. I have two videos here, and I encourage you to watch them if you want to see exactly what it is like to close a mill down. These are the heartfelt stories. These are the people you can look into their eyes. You can hear the stories from their point of view. Also, I have here 676 letters which I was able to gather starting last Sunday from people in my area and the West Coast asking this Congress to please do something about the salvage sales.

And also, in addition, I have a copy of the Vision for Resource Management which a group of us from the West Coast got together and put this together. We feel it is very well done, and it provides a litmus test for what we can do in bringing our forests back to health, not only on a level of United States but on a global level as well.

[The videotapes, letters, and resource management report are on file with the Committee.]

Mrs. CHENOWETH. That is very impressive. I do have a question for our fire marshal, Mr. Adams. I think it is commendable what you have done there at Lake Tahoe. It seems to me what your testimony brought to my mind was that there seems to be an incentive—the way the Forest Service is being financed right now, there seems to be an incentive to let fires get larger than they should rather than being there when the fire is small enough to contain it. And because of the community interest that you were able to generate in your pilot program, you have been able to suppress the fires and save the resources. My hat is off to you. It is a model.

I want to understand it better and study it better, and I thank you very much.

Mr. ADAMS. I did bring a couple of handbooks. We wrote a defensible space handbook, and it was so technical that when we first wrote it, we had to rewrite it the fourth time. And I think Mr. Darren Gibson has one of those maybe you could look at. And the other thing that is of concern to us now is that from the Forest Service's standpoint is we have this brown halo around us, and we are trying to get rid of that, and we need some help with that one.

Mrs. CHENOWETH. Thank you, sir.

Mr. ALLARD. Time has expired. Mr. Cooley.

Mr. COOLEY. Thank you, Mr. Chairman. Rita, I have been long watching the Alliance for America, and I commend you on your ability to inform people about the problems we have in the Northwest in the timber industry.

Ms. CARLSON. Thank you.

Mr. COOLEY. And I think you have done a very good job of that. I am glad you brought this along, and I look forward to watching the videos. I, basically, don't have many things to ask you because I think that the people who testified before you have pretty well said pretty much the same thing so I will use my time for the fire marshal here. I have some fascinating things reading your testimony. I didn't know anything like this had happened in this country anywhere. How did you get around all of the Federal regulations? I mean, you know, why didn't you have the Endangered Species Act? When you pull a tree out, you are going to endanger something. How did you get away with that?

Mr. ADAMS. We followed all the same rules that the U.S. Forest Service had to.

TRPA is a unique organization. It has six members from California and six members from Nevada and one member that represents the United States. The primary objective is to protect the quality of Lake Tahoe, you know, the water quality. And everything that we did, we met every single environmental requirement——

Mr. COOLEY. Did you fill out a statement?

Mr. ADAMS. It was done by the Improvement District. We hired consultants, you know, to do that. We did environmental assessments. We did archaeological assessments. We had 17 Chinese camps that were in the Comstock area, and we worked around those. Basically, they were flagged off, and we just didn't go in there, and no trees were dropped in there. But we met every environmental regulation the Tahoe Regional Planning Agency has, and I am assured that they are probably as restrictive as the Federal Government's.

Mr. COOLEY. Let me go back for a minute. I didn't address my question, I guess, to you properly. You met all the environmental, you say, requirements. Did you submit these to the U.S. Forest Service, or where did they go? Did you just do the record and say, "Here they are. If somebody comes and asks us, we have got them"?

Mr. ADAMS. No. The approving authority is the Tahoe Regional Planning Agency.

They are the organization that we would report to or provide our documents for.

Mr. COOLEY. How do they circumvent—in other words, what I am saying is that maybe you have told us something we didn't know about before. Why aren't any other districts doing this? Why don't we just set up the same thing for any district we want, get the fire marshal, and go through the same thing? The people that have testified today, I guarantee you, have spent more time and money and energy than you did, and they can't get anything. So maybe we are approaching this from a different way. Who brought you on to the idea that you could do these things without intervention from all of the "Federal laws"?

Mr. ADAMS. I don't know if I have the answer to that question. I know that when I needed to get something done or I needed to get this fuels reduction program started, I went to the TRPA and said, "Here is what we want to do. How do we do this? What within the law can we do to do this?" And, again, I have to think that the Tahoe Regional Planning Agency, which basically shuts down U.S. Forest Service projects sometimes based upon some of the submittals, that their requirements must be the same as anybody else's.

Mr. COOLEY. You had no challenges in Court for removal of trees or worried about the habitat or endangered species in that 750 acres? You are right in the middle of the spotted owl habitat.

Mr. ADAMS. We have spotted owls. Yes.

Mr. COOLEY. Yes. I know you do.

Mr. ADAMS. Yes.

Mr. COOLEY. I am very familiar with your area. That is why I want to know how you did this because you are telling me something that I don't think anybody else has ever been able to accomplish.

Mr. ADAMS. You make me feel lucky now. I didn't know how lucky we were. I really didn't.

Mr. COOLEY. Well, you are not lucky. You have shown us that you have done a good job of managing even under the present system we have. So maybe there is some way we can skirt around it.

Mr. ADAMS. We did a lot of public education. One of the other things that we have done is the Tahoe Regional Planning Agency has an image problem. And so they went into a cooperative effort with U & R Cooperative Extension, and they put out a seasonal, little newspaper every month in the summertime called, "The Tahoe Landscape." And every June, we would put out a fire issue, and we would talk about the components of fire, the problem, the solutions, and those went to 48,000 homeowners. So we had——

Mr. COOLEY. Excuse me, Mr. Adams.

Mr. ALLARD. Time has expired.

Mr. COOLEY. One question. Could you make that information available to us? I would like to look at it, and I know some other members on this committee would like to look at it as well. Is that available?

Mr. ADAMS. Sure. You mean the Landscape?

Mr. COOLEY. I am sorry, Mr. Chairman. Excuse me. I would appreciate that. Thank you.

Mr. ALLARD. Let us go ahead and proceed on to the next panel. Thank you both for being here; appreciate it. Next panel is environmental groups. We have Dr. DellaSala and Dr. Franklin. Do either one of you have a preference as to who goes first? Dr. DellaSala, if you would please.

STATEMENT OF DOMINICK DELLASALA, WORLD WILDLIFE FUND, WASHINGTON, DC; ACCOMPANIED BY THOMAS FRANKLIN, THE WILDLIFE SOCIETY, BETHESDA, MARYLAND

Mr. DELLASALA. I will try to be brief. I am sure everybody wants to go out and have pizza at this point. My name is Dr. Dominick Della Sala. I am a senior forest ecologist with the World Wildlife Fund. The World Wildlife Fund is the largest international conservation organization in the United States with over 1.2 million members and 5 million members located across the globe.

I would like to thank the Chairman and members of the committee for inviting me in to testify on this very important subject. As a doctor of forest ecology, I lived and worked for eight years in the Pacific Northwest investigating the impacts of logging operations, including thinning and salvage, on fish and wildlife populations.

I understand that although this hearing was originally intended to address forest health, the members of this committee would prefer testimony focusing on salvage and thinning. While I am quite qualified to do that, I think it is imperative that members of this committee understand that thinning and salvage are merely components of forest health in general and can only be dealt with within that context. Because of the interconnectedness of forest functions, thinning and salvage cannot be dealt with independently.

While I realize that this hearing was conceived of in the aftermath of the tragic effects of last year's fires in the Northwest, thinning and salvage practices alone will not prevent forest fires or control the spread of forest diseases. While we agree that there is opportunity to use thinning and salvage to boost local economies, such activities must be conducted within the framework of NEPA and scientific assessments currently underway in the region. Similarly, it is imperative that these appropriate safeguards be taken to ensure that economic gains are also sustainable and not just short term.

Having worked on salvage effects, I realize that there are opportunities to remove some trees damaged by last year's fires through salvage. However, salvage operations should be conducted outside remaining roadless areas and late-successional forests, that is, forests that are older than 200 years old and undisturbed by logging, and we should also leave large, old trees behind.

This is because the large trees are typically resistant to fires—typically the low-intensity fires—and, therefore, act as natural fire breaks and are often resistent to disease and provide essential habitat for species that feed on destructive insects.

Salvage operations must also utilize appropriate logging techniques that minimize soil damage. If we continue to cause soils to run off into streams, we will not only destroy salmon spawning beds, but we will reduce the ability of forests to recover from logging.

Lastly, while some level of salvage may be acceptable, maintaining adequate amounts of coarse, woody debris is essential for cycling nutrients back into soils and providing structural habitat for many insect-eating species that will help reduce costly insect outbreaks. The Forest Service has some scientifically credible guidelines in place for leaving trees within salvage areas to reduce these impacts.

While thinning and salvage may appear to reduce the intensity and frequency of fires or insect outbreaks, there is no agreement from the scientific community that this is, in fact, true particularly during periods of drought like last year. On the contrary, there is evidence that extensive thinning, salvage, and spraying with insecticides diminishes the ability of a forest to respond to insect outbreaks.

Many species such as ants, wasps, bats, and birds feed on destructive insects and are more effective and economical at keeping these insects in check than are pesticide applications. Most of these species live in late-successional forests, further supporting the position that those areas should not be logged or salvaged.

I have also worked on numerous thinning projects, and it is my professional opinion that thinning will result in even greater forest health problems and fire risks over the long term. Thinning can dry out the forest understory and increase fuels by leaving behind slash. Road building to access areas for thinning also increases fire risks. In fact, many of last year's fires were caused by careless people having access to fire-prone areas through the already extensive road network crisscrossing our national forests.

In closing, I am not advocating that thinning and salvage be prohibited on Federal lands. However, it is vital that roadless areas and late-successional forests be exempt from these activities. These few remaining natural areas are absolutely critical in maintaining salmon populations on which local communities are economically dependent.

We urge the committee to resist the temptation to use salvage and thinning as a primary means for increasing the dollars generated from our national forests and for achieving forest health objectives. The committee should instead concentrate on logging practices that will protect remaining late-successional forests and restoring salmon populations, both of which are essential for keeping the inland Northwest forests healthy, functional, and prosperous for future generations.

I would like to note that there is strong public support for restoring salmon populations in the region for economic reasons. A recent study by the group, "Save Our Salmon," a northwest conglomeration of environmental and fisheries organizations, indicated that restoring Chinook salmon in the Columbia River Basin would generate $349 million in additional revenues and return fishing jobs to the region. I have provided more extensive information in support of my testimony, and I welcome any questions you might have. Thank you for your patience.

[The statement of Mr. DellaSala appears at the conclusion of the hearing.]

Mr. ALLARD. Dr. Franklin.

STATEMENT OF THOMAS FRANKLIN

Mr. FRANKLIN. Thank you, Mr. Chairman, members of the subcommittee. My name is Tom Franklin. I am a certified wildlife biologist, and I am not really representing an environmental group here today. I am representing the profession of wildlife management. Our members or biologists work for Federal agencies and also in the private sector. But I was pleased to be invited to speak about the issue of salvage timber sales in the American West and their implications for wildlife and wildlife habitat.

My testimony includes a summary of a report from an independent panel of scientists that carefully studied the east side old growth forests in Oregon and Washington. I will conclude my comments with some observations and recommendations on behalf of the Wildlife Society.

A panel of ecologists I mentioned from five scientific societies conducted this study and found that east of the Cascade Crest in Oregon and Washington old growth forests are more fragmented than at anytime during European settlement leaving native fish populations severely depleted and watersheds extensively degraded. The scientists concluded that the findings point to poor health of entire landscapes, not just forests.

The panel's report, which I will make available to the committee, analyzes current conditions in 10 national forests east of the Cascades. It covers forestry sources, resident and migratory fishes, aquatic systems and wildlife. The findings demonstrate the diversity of habitat species and histories in these national forests and make clear that comprehensive interdisciplinary approaches to landscape management are essential to halt degradation of east side resources.

Concerns about management of forests throughout the West rose, of course, with the wildfires of 1994. Some scientists, resource managers, and citizens are calling for immediate intervention through logging to improve forest health. To alleviate these threats, many are advocating widespread salvage and thinning but with inadequate analysis we believe.

The panel's report that I referred to earlier concludes that such narrowly conceived approaches to forest management are inadequate for protecting forest resources, whether water, fish, timber, or wildlife. Salvage and thinning may benefit some dense tree stands, but these techniques may at the same time increase risk to forest resources other than timber.

The panel developed a series of recommendations that fall into five categories: One is protecting remaining late-successional old growth forests, large old trees, and dominant ponderosa pines. Second is protect aquatic diversity areas, roadless regions, and stream corridors.

The third is to limit timber harvest on steep slopes, fragile soils, and unique or vulnerable sites. Fourth is to create multiorganizational teams with broad expertise to develop long range management plans for all east side forests, and to set up monitoring program for the region in order to ensure that we can do proper management.

Now, independent of the panel report, the Wildlife Society has some ideas to offer concerning timber salvage sales. Much of the concern of wildlife professionals is due to the focus on dead trees instead of the forest. They wish to capture the dead standing timber while it is still valuable, and the consequences of opening more road access and effects on other resources are not getting the attention they deserve.

There seems to be little concern for wildlife or fish resources among those who support aggressive salvage operations. Their focus is only on how the burned area stands are vulnerable to fire, how much timber volume has been lost, and how something needs to be done about it immediately. The problem with forest health is not new. It has been recognized for about 30 years.

So I would just conclude by saying that the wildlife profession believes that the Forest Service is moving ahead with post-fire rehabilitation and timber salvage sales without a long-term plan for restoring forest health, protecting riparian habitat, providing connectivity for wildlife habitat, or protecting old growth or managing roadless areas.

Actions are being driven by each year's fires. We recognize the dilemma they face with the threat of wildfires, but are concerned that the Forest Service may be foregoing long-term options for fish and wildlife conservation and ecosystem health. Salvage timber sales should be limited to previously roaded areas where they can do the most good at regenerating the forest while protecting old growth and restoring the ecological integrity of watersheds. Thank you.

[The statement of Mr. Franklin appears at the conclusion of the hearing.]

Mr. ALLARD. Thank you both for your testimony.

I can see from one end of the alphabet to the other. That is a long step. If all things being equal, say we didn't open any more—I mean, you raised some concerns about more roads into the area, for example. If you saw that as static, could be assured that no roads would open up, would you support timber sales as we are talking about here—the salvage timber where you have wood that is basically hitting the ground; the tree is dead? Or are you both opposed to that no matter what the situation?

Mr. DELLASALA. If I could take the lead on that, maybe you can jump in, Tom. I am not opposed to timber sales. What I am opposed to is further fragmenting our remaining late-successional forests. And if that means going into those areas and removing timber in late-successional forests even without roads, such as with helicopter logging, I would not like to see that mainly because we have very little of that left.

And Tom can correct me if I am wrong, but the East Side Scientific Society Panel study report had demonstrated quite clearly that most of the basins that they had studied, the amount of late-successional forests left has dropped to about one-quarter to one-third of their original extent. We don't have a lot left out there, and I encourage anybody on this committee to get up in an airplane and fly over that region and take a look at the level of cutting that has been done from airplane. There is not much left out there in the way of large areas of undisturbed or unlogged habitat for wildlife and fish populations.

Mr. ALLARD. Dr. Franklin.

Mr. FRANKLIN. I would just say that the Wildlife Society also is not opposed to timber sales or even salvage sales or even thinning in some cases. And one issue that hasn't been brought to light very much today is the possibility of doing prescribed burns under certain controlled situations to simulate the effects of natural fires and to reduce some of the hazard from wildfires. So we would support that.

But, again, we have a situation, as Dr. DellaSala mentioned, that the old growth forest, the ponderosa pine forests in the so-called east side region are much reduced, as he mentioned, and we have documented that with maps for each national forest in eastern Oregon and Washington. And we think that they are so far reduced and fragmented as to make them extremely susceptible to inappropriate management.

So we are suggesting that we be very careful in how we manage those areas in and around the old growth forests and protect them in the interim until we can get a very thorough analysis of really what the best science says and the most effective way to manage these resources. Some of that is occurring in the east side—the Columbia River Basin effort that is going on right now, but there needs to be a great deal more analysis.

Mr. ALLARD. Science is a continuing phenomena. I am a scientist myself by training, and there is always new information and everything. Where do you say that that body of knowledge is substantial enough that we move ahead?

Mr. FRANKLIN. I would say that it is not the question of whether the body of knowledge is substantial enough to move ahead. I think what we need at this point is to take the existing knowledge that we have and have an open, careful analysis with participation by the Forest Service, the public, both industry and the scientific community, the conservation community to come to some kind of consensus on how we should move forward in these very sensitive areas. Get the best information we have together, use the best minds we have to analyze it, and put it before the public for a decision.

Mr. ALLARD. Mrs. Chenoweth.

Mrs. CHENOWETH. Thank you, Mr. Chairman. I find this testimony very fascinating. Dr. DellaSala, you are the senior forest ecologist for the World Wildlife Fund?

Mr. DELLASALA. Yes.

Mrs. CHENOWETH. What is your degree in and where did you receive your degree?

Mr. DELLASALA. I got my Ph.D. from the University of Michigan in Forest Ecology. I have two post-docs, one from the University of Wyoming and one from Oregon State University, both forest ecology programs and wildlife ecology programs.

Mrs. CHENOWETH. Now, I want to clearly understand your testimony. Did I hear it from you that if we took a flight over the east side area we would find fewer trees standing today?

Mr. DELLASALA. That is not correct, Mrs. Chenoweth.

Mrs. CHENOWETH. Okay. For the record, please make sure I understand this.

Mr. DELLASALA. Sure. What I was referring to, in fact, if you take out that picture that you had, the framed picture, I could even show it to you without taking an airplane flight.

Mrs. CHENOWETH. The one on the forest health——

Mr. DELLASALA. The one that you had framed—that beautiful picture of the managed forest lands—that one there. And what you see in the background there are extensive clear cuts and a roading system. That is all a heavily fragmented forest. It is precisely those conditions that are unhealthy from a biodiversity standpoint. We will lose species over the landscape with that type of disturbance, and that is what I was referring to.

It is not the question of trees out there. This is a question of habitat for certain species, and clearly there are some species—there are many species that can persist in intensively managed systems, but those aren't the ones that are in trouble. The ones that we are losing are those that occur in late-successional forests.

For instance, we know from the studies that have been done out there, there are about 174 listed species in the inland Northwest. It is about one-quarter of all endangered species in the inland Northwest—I mean, in the U.S.—occur in that region. 1,100 Federal candidate species also occupy that same area. Most of those species are associated with the older forest types. Those are the ones that we are concerned about that is a warning signal that we have pushed those systems too far. We stretched the limits of the resiliency of those systems.

Mrs. CHENOWETH. Doctor, could you tell me what species we will lose with this kind of——

Mr. DELLASALA. I can't really fully——

Mrs. CHENOWETH. You can't tell me specifically?

Mr. DELLASALA. I can give you some probabilities.

Mrs. CHENOWETH. No. I want specifics. Can you tell me what species we are going to lose with this kind of management? And let me ask you do you understand what the prey base for the spotted owl is?

Mr. DELLASALA. I studied the spotted owl for two years over on the Willamette National Forest looking at the prey base.

Mrs. CHENOWETH. What is the prey base for the spotted owl? And don't tell me the flying squirrel.

Mr. DELLASALA. The flying squirrel is a chief component of the owl's prey base in certain portions of its range. The owl has got quite a bit of geographic variation in its prey selection. In the northern part of its range, it feeds on flying squirrels to be very general. In the southern part of its range, it feeds on wood rats to a large extent. It also feeds on voles and a variety of other small mammals.

Mrs. CHENOWETH. Could you help explain to me—do you understand what this picture is?

Mr. DELLASALA. I am not sure what I am looking at, but it looks like a burned area.

Mrs. CHENOWETH. This is an elk cow. This is her calf. It has been burned, sir. Do you think that is healthy for the wildlife?

Mr. DELLASALA. The one thing that I think——

Mrs. CHENOWETH. Well, that is natural. Right?

Mr. DELLASALA. Right. To fully answer that question, what we are dealing with here is a system that—it is fire habitat. Fire was a part of the natural ecology of those forests. We are in fire habitat, and those areas are going to burn regardless of what we do there. We will lose wildlife through fire, and there are a number of species that are adapted to that system. Although individuals may burn up, populations persist even in fire habitat.

Mrs. CHENOWETH. Can you please tell me what the Save Our Salmon, a northwest conglomeration of environmental fisheries, organization is?

Mr. DELLASALA. That is exactly what it is. It is a group of environmental groups and fishing organizations that have been looking at how much we would gain economically by restoring salmon in the Pacific Northwest.

Mrs. CHENOWETH. Can you tell me where their funding comes from?

Mr. DELLASALA. I cannot tell you where their funding comes from.

Mrs. CHENOWETH. I know that I have gone over my time, but I would like to ask the committee's indulgence to ask Mr. Franklin just one question, Mr. Chairman?

Mr. ALLARD. You may go ahead.

Mrs. CHENOWETH. You speak about a panel of ecologists from five scientific societies, and yet in your oral testimony you didn't tell us exactly who that was?

Mr. FRANKLIN. I would be glad to. The societies are the American Fisheries Society, which represents fisheries biologists; the American Ornithologists Union, which represents bird scientists and biologists; the Ecological Society of America, which represents ecologists throughout the country; the Society for Conservation Biology, which represents the fairly new discipline of conservation biology; and the Wildlife Society, which I did mention, represents the wildlife biologists and scientists.

Mrs. CHENOWETH. And the Sierra Biodiversity Institute?

Mr. FRANKLIN. The Sierra Biodiversity Institute is an organization that primarily for us produced the GIS system analysis that we used in the study.

Mrs. CHENOWETH. Thank you.

Mr. ALLARD. Dr. DellaSala, I would like to follow up a little bit. You talked about the total ecological phenomena that burning was part of it and wildlife being burnt up was part of that ecological. If there are human beings in the area, is that part of the ecological phenomena?

Mr. DELLASALA. Absolutely. Humans are part of the system. There is no question.

Mr. ALLARD. So if a human burns up, that is just part of the natural phenomena?

Mr. DELLASALA. I did not imply that.

Mr. ALLARD. I mean, that is my question.

Mr. DELLASALA. I don't think that humans should burn up in fires. I am not somebody that would ever advocate that, and as I mentioned in my testimony——

Mr. ALLARD. I am just wanting to know how far your philosophy went——

Mr. DELLASALA. It doesn't cover that.

Mr. ALLARD [continuing]. On nonintervention in the ecology because, obviously, there is human life that is going to be lost from time to time in a forest fire.

Mr. DELLASALA. Mr. Chairman, I would be the first one to run into a burning building and take somebody out, to answer your question. And I realize that there are human concerns here, and I think that what we need to do is look at this as a buffering solution, that in areas near towns we need to do some thinning and reduce those fuels.

Mr. ALLARD. So it is appropriate for humans to intervene from time to time?

Mr. DELLASALA. Yes. But I think as we move further away from human settlement, we need to set more fires in a controlled manner, and we need to let some burn particularly in wilderness areas.

Mr. ALLARD. Thank you. Mr. Cooley.

Mr. COOLEY. Dr. DellaSala, well, number 1 is I will tell you that I live in the area that you fly over and determine that all the trees are dead and dying and it should not be properly managed and nature will do it. Are you familiar with some of these reports by the U.S. Department of Forest Service? See, this is the State of Oregon. See the dark spots. Can you see those?

Mr. DELLASALA. Yes.

Mr. COOLEY. Okay. Do you know what those dark spots represent? That is eastern Oregon that you flew over. Okay. That represents the spruce bug worm defoliation of that amount of timber in that part of the state. That is not proper management.

Mr. DELLASALA. Agreed.

Mr. COOLEY. Oh, wonderful. This is also a picture of the same part of the state. Do you see that overlay?

Mr. DELLASALA. Yes.

Mr. COOLEY. That is the pine beetle kill. Now, you take both of those and put them together, and we are losing most of the timbers that you are such an expert on the east side because we don't manage that area. Now, how can you sit there and tell me that this is good management of a natural resource that belongs to everybody in this country including the environmentalists and those who want to cut this timber and allow that to be devastated by disease and think this is good? How do you get to that equation? How can you say allowing this renewable asset to be destroyed by bugs and disease, which this is by your own people, and say that is good? I don't understand that logic. Would you explain that to me?

Mr. DELLASALA. I think you misinterpreted my testimony, congressman. I was not implying that we should not manage those forests. And your overlays there don't tell the whole story because a lot of those lands are managed lands. They are not all set-asides.

Mr. COOLEY. This is U.S. Forest Service, sir. I didn't draw these maps. They drew them, and this is their information.

Mr. DELLASALA. Respectfully so, I think you need to look at the land use designations within those areas to see if those are managed or they are set-asides. I would be willing to stake my reputation on most of that land that you have pointed out is managed land.

Mr. COOLEY. But it is not managed. If it was managed, it wouldn't be dying. It is not managed. That is what we are talking about here. We are trying to salvage an asset that belongs to all the people of this country to get some economic recovery of it instead of allowing it to deteriorate and turn into bug wood. That is what we are trying to do here. If this was managed, we wouldn't have this percentage.

This is almost the entire east side of the State of Oregon. I represent 72,000 square miles, larger than 33 states in this country, and we are cutting no trees because we are having them dead and dying or they are burnt, and this is an asset. It is a renewable asset, and we are not doing anything because we are destroying or disturbing natural—nature's way.

Mr. DELLASALA. If I could repeat my testimony, I am not opposed to timber sales, salvage, or thinning. And I don't think, to add to that, we are going to manage our way out of this. Once you have got an insect outbreak in that area, there is no evidence that management will reduce insect outbreaks over the long term.

Mr. COOLEY. Okay. Get to one other thing. I was on the Columbia Gorge Task Force for two years as a state senator. You talk about the great rehabilitation of fish and the coming in of $349 million additional revenue to the area. Sir, we have spent $2 billion of our money to try to mitigate the salmon, and they have mitigated not one.

The Fish and Wildlife right now is now proposing a half a billion dollars a year to try to mitigate the salmon with no scientific backup, and we continue to do this. At some point, the people of this country are going to say, "How much are we going to spend to save a species?" And when it starts coming out of their pocketbook into billions of dollars, they are going to make another decision, I believe, because the science is not helping us. We are willing to spend that money, and we have spent it right up to now, $2 billion. Next year a half a billion dollars with no mitigation.

We are just pouring it out there to make people feel good, and we have got to get a handle on this. I mean, there are a lot of things we can do with that money. There are a lot of people that need to be helped, and yet we are doing this, and we are getting nowhere with it. I find that your report is a little hard to take.

And, Dr. Franklin, I certainly wish the panel that you participated in in your evaluation of our forest and its health and everything else included some people other than what I would say obstructionists in the environmental groups—some down-to-earth people who earn a living there, who work in the industry there, are people who related to that industry before you come up with these conclusions.

Because I will tell you, this list here is a list of obstructionists—scientists who have developed an obstructionist attitude, and this is killing the Northwest. We want to manage. We want to live there. We want to raise our families there, and we want a good environment. But what has happened to us—and we were asleep at the switch, and I know it, and I have to compliment you on your ability to shut us down—we are not doing anything, and you are pushing us out of there, and I understand that.

We are here today—some of the people on this panel from the Northwest, and a lot of new people from the Northwest—to try to turn this around. We don't want to turn it around to devastate the species. We want to turn it around so man, animals, and the environment can live together. And under the present program, we are not living together.

We are endangered, and everything else is being considered. And through evolution, you do lose something, and man, because of our necessity for civilization, is going to destroy some other species. But I will tell you as long as I am alive and my 10 grandchildren, I am not going to let a snail ruin this species. And that is what is happening to this country. Some animals are going to have to be sacrificed.

Mr. FRANKLIN. May I respond?

Mr. ALLARD. Dr. Franklin, yes, you may respond.

Mr. FRANKLIN. Okay. First of all, I would just like to say that the groups that participated in this study were not obstructionist environmental groups as they have been called. They are professional and scientific societies. They include the best scientific minds that we had in that region that we could apply to this issue. We did not set out in a way with a predetermined notion that we were in any kind of effort to obstruct or negatively affect communities.

The role of scientists is not to obstruct anything. We believe our role is to lay out the facts as we see them through our collection, review, and analysis of the data, and present the information and some options to you and other decision-makers to make those decisions based on all your other factors including human concerns.

So I would just urge you before attacking this particular report that you recognize that we are not obstructionists, and, in fact, we would like to work with the Congress and anyone else interested to resolve these problems. We are just as much concerned about them as you are.

Mr. ALLARD. I would like to thank the panel for showing up this evening, and I know it has been a long day. I don't know whether you have been sitting in the room for the whole seven and a half hours or not, but it has been a long day. And as you can tell, we have some real concerns that were brought up during the hearing. I am going to go ahead and draw the hearing to a close and adjourn the committee.

[Whereupon, the committee, at 5:25 p.m., was adjourned subject to the call of the Chair.]

STATEMENT BY MARK SIMMONS
PRESIDENT,
WESTERN COUNCIL OF INDUSTRIAL WORKERS LOCAL #2910
UNITED BROTHERHOOD OF CARPENTERS AND JOINERS OF AMERICA
ELGIN, OREGON

BEFORE JOINT HEARING OF THE HOUSE COMMITTEE ON RESOURCES
SUBCOMMITTEE ON NATIONAL PARKS, FORESTS AND LANDS
AND
THE HOUSE AGRICULTURE COMMITTEE
SUBCOMMITTEE ON RESOURCES, CONSERVATION,
RESEARCH AND FORESTRY

Washington, D.C.
February 10, 1995

I want to thank the chairpersons and the members of both committees for allowing me the opportunity to speak in support of an emergency measure to allow salvage operations in federal forests. I also want to recognize Congressman Cooley who represents my district.

I appear before you today on behalf of the 30,000 members of the Western Council of Industrial Workers, including the 325 men and women of WCIW local unions #2780 and #2910 in Elgin, Oregon. And I appear today on behalf of my coworkers at Boise Cascade where I have worked for 18 years. I currently work at Boise as a heavy equipment mechanic.

During the past several years, actions to protect the northern spotted owl and other threatened and endangered species have all but stopped timber harvesting on federal lands in the Pacific Northwest and Northern California. Since 1990, more than 17,930 timber workers have lost their jobs in the region[1].

I'm here today because these job loss figures aren't just numbers to me. These numbers are real people -- people I know -- friends of mine. Over the past year, one hundred and eighteen workers lost their jobs when two sawmills in Joseph, Oregon shut down. The sawmills closed because the companies could not obtain enough timber to keep the facilities up and running. I am here because I have one hundred and eighteen friends who want to work to support themselves and their families but now must rely on unemployment insurance.

I also have seen how the timber supply problems in the West affects workers across the nation. Last year, I traveled around the country to meet with some of my union brothers and sisters who work in the construction trades. They told me how the timber supply problems in the West are raising the cost of lumber. The higher prices slow construction and housing starts in their communities, threatening jobs and upsetting local economies.

89-215 O - 95 - 5

Timber workers like me were raised to believe that economic opportunity lay in the forests surrounding our homes. We believed the mills would remain in operation forever. And we believed we could pursue the American dream so long as we were careful stewards of the forests. So long as we replanted and protected the trees, we could feed the mills, keep our jobs, and help produce lumber to house America. The forests and the trees are still there. But our hope and sense of security have all but disappeared as we wait for a solution to the crisis that will bring timber to our mills and protect our forests.

Some say we should move to the big cities to find new jobs. But these people don't understand our strong ties to our jobs, the land and our heritage. For many of us, working in the forest products industry is a family tradition, passed from generation to generation. We are skilled workers. We take pride in our trade. And we are rural people. We have no desire to move into Portland, Seattle, San Francisco and the like.

I've seen friends of mine forced to make that move. Some are forced to leave their families behind because they can't afford to move their wives and kids with them. And when they get to the city, they feel lost, out of place.

People in my community are frustrated, bitter and angry. Their faith in the federal government has been seriously undermined by the inability of the government to find a balanced solution to the timber supply crisis. We feel the government has betrayed our economic base, our future and our children's future.

Our members, and timber-dependent workers throughout the nation, are extremely concerned about the health of our national forests. As forest products workers, our lives are intertwined with the forests. The forests provide the natural resource that keeps us employed. They provide the natural magnificence that makes our communities such beautiful places to live and raise a family. And they provide a place for recreation.

As the timber supply crisis has worsened, legislative, judicial and administrative actions, combined with a lack of funding, have prevented the removal of damaged, diseased and dead timber from federal forests all across the nation. The damaged timber weakens the health of our national forests, leaving them susceptible to catastrophic wildfire. Last year, catastrophic wildfires destroyed more than 3.7 million acres of federal forest land in the Intermountain West, killing more than five billion board feet of timber. That's five billion board feet of timber that can be salvaged if we act quickly. The costs of catastrophic wildfires are high. Last year's fires in our region cost the government over $1 billion for fire suppression alone. And the fires took the lives of 26 members of our communities[2].

Some of the scientists you'll hear from today will tell you what forest products workers have known for years -- comprehensive, ecosystem-sensitive forest management practices, including salvage logging, are necessary to control and improve forest health.

Salvage logging can help ease the national forest health crisis. Salvage sales enable foresters to remove trees destroyed by disease and insects before they infect other parts of the forest. Dead and dying trees also need to be removed to prevent catastrophic wildfire and to prevent damage to fish and wildlife habitat.

Salvage sales also could provide much needed relief for timber-dependent workers. Harvested in a timely manner, damaged, dead and dying trees can help keep mills open and save jobs. The Forest Service estimates that more than 1.5 billion board feet of timber could be salvaged and sent to mills this year. Our union believes the amount of timber that can be salvaged is actually much higher than the Forest Service estimate. I have to say that people in the West are disgusted about the salvage situation. We walk through our forests and see millions of board feet of salvageable timber just laying on the ground while we see our friends and families lose their jobs. It's an insane situation.

So for the sake of our forests and our families, we urge the Congress to recognize the timber supply and forest health emergency and move quickly to expedite salvage logging operations. We urge you to grant the Forest Service emergency authority to begin the immediate salvage of dead and dying trees in national forests.

We also urge the Congress to develop and pass a long-term, comprehensive forest health bill that will provide for the development of forest health improvement programs to prevent further damage and reduce the risk of wildfire in our federal forests. And we urge you to allocate adequate funding for federal forest management programs under the FY 1996 Interior Appropriations bill.

The Western Council of Industrial Workers and the Carpenters Union have been participating and will continue to participate in efforts to reverse the current trend of deteriorating forest health. Forest products workers want to work and we want to protect the forests. We remain convinced we can do both.

Thank you.

---

[1] "Forest Products Industry Report On Mill Closures, Operations, And Other Related Information," Paul F. Ehinger & Associates and Robert Flynn & Associates, July/August, 1994.

[2] U.S. Forest Service, United States Department of Agriculture.

STATEMENT OF RANDY BESAW
DRYER OPERATOR,
HALSEY, OREGON

BEFORE HOUSE COMMITTEE ON RESOURCES
SUBCOMMITTEE ON NATIONAL PARKS, FORESTS AND LANDS
AND
THE HOUSE AGRICULTURE COMMITTEE
SUBCOMMITTEE ON RESOURCES, CONSERVATION, RESEARCH AND FORESTRY

Washington, D.C.
February 10, 1995

Good morning. I thank the chairman and the committee for allowing me to testify today on such an important topic to pulp and paper workers like myself.

My name is Randy Besaw and I am a dryer operator at the Pope and Talbot pulp mill in Halsey, Oregon. I also am a member of the United Paperworkers International Union, local 1189. I appear here today in support of salvage logging on behalf of my union brothers and sisters and pulp and paper workers throughout the United States.

I first became involved in natural resource issues when I saw the effect the northern spotted owl issue, and the resulting timber supply crisis, is having on working people in Oregon, Washington and Northern California. I've seen mills close and good people lose their jobs. And it's not just timber workers. The truth is, pulp and paper workers in our region also are suffering from the timber supply crisis. The less timber processed by sawmills, the fewer wood chips available for our mills to turn into pulp and paper products.

I've seen the problem first hand. Workers at our mill in Halsey were laid off last summer because of a lack of chip supply. I have friends, close friends, who didn't know how they were going to feed their family. That's a terrible fear. All of us at our facility now live in fear that our mill will soon shut down. We see mills closing all around us. And we see our neighbors on the unemployment line. We know that wood chips are increasingly difficult to come by and those that you can get are extremely expensive. Although pulp and paper prices have skyrocketed -- in some cases, prices are at record levels -- the Douglas Fir chips used by many mills in our area are so expensive, that the high cost of the end products barely covers our production costs. We know that our employers will soon have to make some tough choices. And we know we may lose our jobs as a result.

While we haven't been hit as hard as our friends in the timber industry, we see the writing on the wall. We know that when a sawmill shuts down, our mill is going to have to search even harder for wood chips. And we know that one day, we too may find the mill doors closed.

I don't think people back here in the East fully realize what's going on in our communities. Many seem to think we're about to cut the last tree. That's crazy. We love the forests. We work in the forests. We hunt and fish in the forests. The forests provide for our livelihoods. That's why we care so much about forest health. That's why I've traveled across the country to appear before you today.

For pulp and paper workers in the West, our interest in forest health is two-fold. First, the forests of the Western United States have been desperately dry during the past several summers and falls. Meanwhile, foresters have been prevented by federal restrictions and judicial injunctions from removing damaged, dead and diseased timber from national forests. The buildup of this material threatens forest health and, when combined with the dry conditions, increases the likelihood of wildfire. Wildfires endanger animals, forest ecosystems and surrounding communities where many of our members and their families live.

Second, pulp and paper workers depend on a reliable timber supply for our livelihoods. Public forests and the communities that surround them have a long history of mutual support. We have a keen interest in responsible forest management -- the forests provide jobs and recreation for our workers. Therefore, we want to do everything we can to keep our forests healthy and productive.

Our union strongly believes that with disease and wildfire a natural part of the forest ecosystem, the only way we can control and improve forest health is to conduct comprehensive, ecosystem-sensitive forest management practices, including salvage logging.

Salvage timber sales affect not only the physical health of the forests, but the fiscal health of timber-dependent communities. These sales can provide much needed relief for pulp and paper and timber workers impacted by the spotted owl debate and the timber supply crisis. With green timber supplies so tight and unstable, damaged, dead and dying trees can provide a critical supply of fiber to mills throughout the nation.

But we must move quickly to remove the salvageable timber. Each day we delay, the more we endanger the health of our forests. Each day we delay, the more the timber decays, reducing the chance we can process the fiber.

Moving to salvage dead, dying and diseased timber provides us with a rare opportunity to produce a "win-win." We can protect the health of a vital natural resource and help protect jobs in the pulp and paper industry. I don't see how anyone in their right mind could oppose these goals.

The U.S. Forest Service currently holds the authority to expedite sales of timber killed or damaged by drought, insects, disease or fire. Regional foresters can exempt salvage sales from the normal timber sale procedures because dead and dying trees need to be removed within two years. However, even though the Forest Service recognizes the need to address the current forest health emergency, appeals, legal challenges and inadequate funding often delay and/or prevent salvage sales from proceeding.

On behalf of my brothers and sisters who work in pulp and paper facilities throughout the United States, and on behalf of our national forests, I urge the Congress to pass legislation granting the Forest Service immediate authority and resources to expedite salvage sales immediately.

Workers in my industry and the health of our forests are depending on you.

Thank you.

Our Forest Going Up In Smoke and the Realities of Option 9

Prepared by
Jim Carlson

Executive Summary

The photos in this album reflect our national forest on the Olympic Peninsula as they are being managed under current "science".

Pages 1-4, tell the story of one tree. This particular tree blew down on the Quinault Ranger District several years ago. I, and others, urged the U.S. Forest Service to put this tree up for sale (and thousands of others) but were denied. We also attempted to buy this tree and two others, under a personal use permit, for a interpretive building we wished to construct at our ranch as part of a economic diversification project (tourism). This request was also denied -- in spite of the provision for this contained in the Grays Harbor Federal Sustained Yield Unit Agreement.

Recently, this tree was sold under a fire-wood permit for $5.00 per cord to a local unemployed logger. This particular tree contained approximately 21,000 board feet gross scale, with a net scribner scale of over 18,000 board feet. (800 board feet equals one cord.) Converted by our saw mill this tree would have produced in excess of $60,000 worth of lumber and provided considerable employment for the mill and woods crew. I can only imagine the revenue that could have been generated for the U.S. Forest Service, and our schools and community, from the sale of this tree -- and thousands of others -- for lumber purposes.

The final irony of this story is that on January 13th of the current year, Grays Harbor County sold the home of this unemployed logger for delinquent taxes in the amount of $931.91. Had this tree been processed for lumber, this unemployed worker may have had a job.

The balance of the pictures I have enclosed record how damaged and distressed timber and particularly blow down are being "managed" on the Olympic National Forest. Specifically, this timber is being utilized as fire-wood, fuel for forest fires, dwellings for insect infestations, or is being left to rot. I just don't understand how we can treat these extremely valuable and RENEWABLE resources in this fashion -- particularly when families and communities depend on them to survive.

The Ongoing Destruction of the Infrastructure

As a result of policies like those outlined in page one, over two hundred saw mills, veneer and plywood plants in the Northwest have closed permanently. Most of these facilities have been torn down and junked out. This has impacted over 20,000 timber workers directly to date. The number of victims continue to mount and hardly a week goes by without new plant closures.

More recently, the U.S. Forest Service has embarked on a road obliteration project. The rationale being forwarded by them for this proposition is:

[1.] some of these roads are causing or may cause potential environmental damage. ("more science")

It has been my observation that there are some of these roads that truly qualify for obliteration due to potential environmental reasons. What is unsettling, however, is that these instances can and are used as a "straw-man" to further the objectives of those who want everyone out of the forest.

[2.] under current maintenance methods the USFS is short and is projecting continuing short falls in road maintenance funds provided by logging activities. They are also projecting additional reductions in funds that come through Congressional Appropriations for roads.

Historically, logging operations have provided massive amounts of money to construct and maintain the forest road systems -- which are used by a multitude of user groups. Obviously, if we no longer harvest any timber these funds disappear -- as apparently do the roads.

Interestingly enough, as the USFS sold a $60,000 tree for fire-wood, the Quinault Ranger District had insufficient funds to purchase the necessary diesel fuel for their road grader. Under this scenario it is very difficult to perform road maintenance activities, and ultimately more and more roads will "qualify for obliteration" for which there seems to be funding.

As you can imagine if the current management of the forest continues as it has over the last five years -- the destruction of the industry, the communities, the infrastructure, and in many cases the forest itself will be complete.

I can't emphasize the following enough:

Our communities and families have been living on their equities built up over decades. This equity has now been drained from our communities. We cannot wait any longer for consideration and meaningful action addressing this situation. We desperately need your help now.

Resume
Jim Carlson
716 south Shore Road
Quinault, Washington 98575

PROFESSIONAL EXPERIENCE:

President, CEO, and founder of J & J Forest Products, Inc., a harvester and manufacturer of forest products. Mr. Carlson started this Lake Quinault company in 1968 with hand tools and a vision that evolved into a four division corporation (logging, shakemill, remanufacturing, and sawmill). As CEO Mr. Carlson was a hands on leader that guided the daily activities of the various divisions. J & J Forest Products, Inc. has achieved sales in the excess of 7 million dollars annually.

Today this company which historically employed over 60 direct employees and as many as 40 sub-contractors, is closed.

PROFESSIONAL AFFILIATIONS:

Mr. Carlson serves on the Board of Directors of Woodnet, an organization of over 300 lumber and wood working companies; the Grays Harbor Economic Development Council; and Cintrafor, the center for international trade in forest products at the University of Washington. He actively supports these organizations participating on various committees.

COMMUNITY SERVICE:

Board member of the Lake Quinault Community Task Force, a group that focuses on economic development and diversification as well as other local issues.

Member of the Grays Harbor advisory board for Senator Gorton.

PERSONAL:

Mr. Carlson is married to the former Kay Marie Stephens of Raymond, Washington. The Carlsons' enjoy four daughters - Heather and Mindy who are elementary students, Hollie a high school student, and Kellie who is currently working in Washington D. C. for Senator Slade Gorton.

AVOCATION:

Mr. Carlson's varied recreational interests include his family, fishing, hunting, coaching AAU Girl's Basketball, and raising registered Quarter Horses. His horse, Judge Cash, was a finalist in the All American Futurity in Ruidoso, New Mexico, in 1989.

EDUCATIONS:

Graduated 1966 from Willapa Valley High School in Menlo, Washington.

Participated in numerous seminars, conferences, and colloquies concentrating on production, management, trade, and resource issues.

STATEMENT OF
JACK WARD THOMAS, CHIEF
FOREST SERVICE
UNITED STATES DEPARTMENT OF AGRICULTURE

Before the

Subcommittee on National Parks, Forests and Lands
Committee on Resources
and
Subcommittee on Resource Conservation, Research, and Forestry
Committee on Agriculture
United States House of Representatives

Concerning

Review of the Timber Salvage Program

MR. CHAIRMAN AND MEMBERS OF THE SUBCOMMITTEE:

Thank you for the opportunity to discuss the timber salvage program. I am accompanied by Gray Reynolds, Deputy Chief of National Forest System, and David Hessel, Director of Timber Management.

We share your sense of urgency about the salvage situation in the West especially given the extensive fire damage suffered last year. Last summer 56,000 fires burned over 1.3 million acres of State and private lands, 14,000 fires on National Forest System lands burned over 1.5 million acres, and 8,000 fires burned 1.3 million acres of Department of the Interior lands.

Our current policy emphasizes the quick removal of dead and dying timber where it is consistent with local forest plan standards and guidelines. We are required to follow the same laws for salvage timber sale logging activities as for logging activities associated with the regular timber sale program.

This will help meet public demand for timber, reduce fuels in areas that may be susceptible to wildfire in the future and assist in the reforestation of these areas. We will also salvage where we need to restore areas by planting trees.

<u>The Forest Service Salvage Timber Sale Program</u>

Since the major fires in 1987, the Forest Service has maintained a five-year salvage strategy which is updated annually and funded by the salvage sale fund. The program addresses insect and fire killed, dead, damaged, or down timber and the associated tree removal needed for stand improvement. The best known part of this program is the dead timber harvested after a large wildfire. This fire salvage will be a significant part of the salvage program strategy for the next 2 years.

Historically, approximately 50 percent of timber burned is not salvageable. It is our policy to pursue actively the remaining burned timber for salvage harvest.

For example in 1994, an estimated 3.7 billion board feet were damaged by the fires on National Forest System lands in the West. While this is a large quantity of salvageable material, much of this wood was in small diameter trees or the defect was so severe the trees were of no commercial value. Isolated trees or trees on steep slopes were not reasonably accessible. Fire rehabilitation required anchoring dead trees across slopes to prevent soil erosion. These factors reduced salvageable timber volume from the 1994 fires from an estimated 3.7 billion board feet to about 1.8 billion board feet, a reduction of 50 percent of the total burned timber.

Other factors such as compliance with environmental laws such as the National Environmental Policy Act, Endangered Species Act, National Historic Preservation Act, National Forest Management Act (standards and guidelines of forest plans,) Clean Water Act, Wilderness Act, and Wild and Scenic Rivers Act will reduce the estimated volume further. This reduces the available fire salvage volume from the estimated 1.8 billion board feet to a range of 656 million board feet to 1.5 billion board feet. These figures do not include volume loss that might occur because of lawsuits. In some burned areas, there may be roadless areas we can access only by using alternative logging methods such as helicopter logging.

Over the past five years, the salvage program in the western regions has averaged 1.8 billion board feet per year. In 1995 the Forest Service plans to salvage 1.6 billion board feet and our projection at this time in 1996 is 1.5 billion board feet. These volume figures may change as we complete our analysis of the 1994 fires.

However, pending litigation involving salmon in Oregon and Idaho and bull trout in western Montana, Idaho, Oregon and Washington may affect Forest Service's ability to salvage timber. In response to these suits, I have worked continuously with the National Marine Fisheries Service to complete the required consultation for the listed salmon in the Columbia River Basin.

Forest Health Concerns

The forest health problem and associated high intensity wildfires are indicators of an ecosystem that is outside the expected range of natural variation. Our Western Forest Health Initiative, which would include salvaging timber from fire areas and areas impacted by insects, disease, and drought, highlights the needs to correct short-term high-risk areas as well as actions needed to promote long-term forest health.

Our current ecosystem management assessment in the Columbia River basin is aimed at determining the long-term effects of our actions in terms of future stand conditions and management actions. We will also need to assess the advantages and disadvantages of harvesting versus other management options such as prescribed fire or thinning of trees. Salvage logging is one of several methods available to reduce fuel loading.

Conclusions

In conclusion, we will demonstrate progress toward harvesting salvage timber in addressing the forest health problem. The Under Secretary for Natural Resources and Environment and the Forest Service have committed to convene an interagency team at the highest level to meet next Monday, February 13, to develop a strategy to expedite the preparation of salvage sales and actions that will help solve the forest health problem in the West.

The Forest Service:

- Is moving aggressively to assess timber salvage opportunities from areas burned by wildfire in 1994;

- Is following the law in preparing salvage timber sales; and

- Is continuing its efforts to improve coordination between other State and Federal regulatory agencies and will continue efforts to facilitate the consultation in environmental analysis processes.

The Forest Service will act on the key recommendations of the Western Forest Health Initiative report and ensure that forest health factors are included in forest plan goals and objectives. The Forest Service will also refine, validate, and expand the data base on forest health problems nationally for further policy and budget action.

Not all areas can be managed immediately. However, we have enough knowledge of the forest health problem to restore high risk sites to an acceptable structure and composition in line with long-term goals of sustaining ecological processes. This can be accomplished through a combination of salvage logging, reducing fuels through mechanical means, prescribed fire and thinning of densely stocked stands.

In the long-term, we must consider the economic and ecological results of the management actions we take today on the condition and resource capacity of National Forests in the future.

This completes my testimony. We would be happy to answer any questions you may have.

STATEMENT OF DENISE MERIDITH, DEPUTY DIRECTOR, BUREAU OF LAND MANAGEMENT, DEPARTMENT OF THE INTERIOR, BEFORE THE SUBCOMMITTEE ON NATIONAL PARKS, FORESTS AND LANDS, COMMITTEE ON RESOURCES, AND THE SUBCOMMITTEE ON RESOURCE CONSERVATION, RESEARCH, AND FORESTRY, COMMITTEE ON AGRICULTURE, HOUSE OF REPRESENTATIVES, ON THE OFFERING OF SALVAGE TIMBER SALES.

February 10, 1995

I appreciate the opportunity to appear here today to discuss the Bureau of Land Management's (BLM) timber salvage program.

The timber salvage issue involves BLM forested lands throughout the entire intermountain and Rocky Mountain west, as well as the State of Alaska. It is also integrally linked to the larger issue of forest health that concerns us all.

BLM manages approximately 50 million acres of forested land, of which 28 million acres are in the lower 48 States. Approximately 4 million acres are commercial sawlog species, half of which is in western Oregon. The remainder is woodlands. Of the two million acres outside western Oregon, about half is withdrawn from harvest because of restrictions such as wilderness study areas, designated wilderness areas, special wildlife habitat needs, or is inoperable because of topographic restrictions, fragile sites, and reforestation difficulties. These forests, which are often adjacent to National Forests and in the transition area between rangeland and higher elevations, provide wood fiber, important wildlife and fisheries habitat, recreational opportunities, and important watersheds.

It is BLM policy to place a high priority on timber salvage efforts. This policy recognizes the value of salvaging portions of the merchantable tree volume killed by drought, insects, disease, and wildfire. Both the BLM Forest Product Sales Handbook and the Oregon Timber Sale Procedure Handbook direct our employees to include damaged timber as the highest priority in annual sale plans.

Tree mortality is a symptom of, and not the cause of forest health problems. Historically fire has played an important role in the formation and maintenance of healthy forests. In drier areas of the west where decomposition of organic material by biological processes is slow, frequent low-intensity fire kept fuel loading and stocking levels low. Stand density control, prescribed fire and salvage of mortality are some options for treatment.

In many cases, salvage of dead and dying timber has a short-term benefit to overall ecosystem health by reducing the potential intensity of wildfire and a long-term benefit through conversion of the site to a more stable stand structure. Some mortality is a natural part of succession, and certain amounts of dead material are important for maintaining ecosystem function. The BLM places a priority on salvaging appropriate quantities of dead and dying timber ahead of the sale of green timber.

At the same time, the benefits of dead wood in the environment are recognized. These include standing and down shade necessary for both natural and artificial reforestation, barriers to the movement of sediment, and habitat for numerous life forms necessary for the restoration and sustainability of forest environments.

Over the last 10 years, BLM has given continuing, close attention to the harvesting of valuable salvage timber resources from public lands. Some of BLM's efforts include:

- o sending a crew from Roseburg, Oregon, to Alaska to offer salvage timber for sale;
- o sending a crew of foresters from Montana to California to lay out and cruise over 17 million board feet of salvage already sold this year;
- o immediately dispatching personnel to evaluate fire mortality in Idaho, California, Montana, and Oregon;
- o offering timber for sale without guaranteed access, requiring the purchaser to negotiate a right-of way;
- o offering for sale 13 million board feet of salvage beetle-killed fir in southeastern Idaho in 1991 and 1992, which required personnel sharing;
- o salvaging over 50 million board feet in California since 1988;
- o rapidly responding to needs of local residents to reduce fire risk following a bark beetle outbreak in central Oregon; and
- o successfully reducing fire intensity and severity near Klamath, Oregon, by thinning and underburning pine stands.

In 1992 Congress established the Forest Ecosystem Health and Recovery Fund (Fund) to help BLM address and treat the forest health situation in the interior northwest and overcome funding inadequacies. This Fund was a provision of the Department of the Interior and Related Agencies Appropriations Act of 1993, Public Law 102-381. It is used by BLM for planning and preparing salvage timber for disposal, administration of salvage timber sales, and subsequent site preparation and reforestation. The Fund is perpetuated by the deposit of the Federal share of receipts from the disposition of salvage timber to be used to restore and maintain forest health. In administering the Fund, BLM must assure that expenditures are limited to eligible projects. We have used the Fund in a judicious manner to support salvage efforts.

We have been able to meet our timber salvage goals and objectives through the teamwork of our foresters and other agency specialists. Also, field offices have been encouraged to explore new ways to accomplish this workload.

What would be helpful in facilitating our responses to both forest health and salvage issues would be to expand the Fund's authority to include such practices as prescribed fire, fuels treatment, and density control (thinning). This would not only help improve forest stand structure and maintenance necessary for perpetuation of sustainable forests, but would also contribute to increased employment and provide a source of wood fiber. Since such an expansion of the Fund's authority would require legislation, we are working on a legislative proposal for consideration by the Department, the Administration, and the Congress.

In carrying out timber sale planning and preparation, we must comply with a number of Federal statutes, including the Federal Land Policy and Management Act, Endangered Species Act, National Environmental Policy Act, Clean Air Act, Clean Water Act, National Historic Preservation Act, and Archaeological Resources Protection Act. As the science of forest management has changed, we recognize that many requirements of these laws are considered good for ensuring proper functioning of forest systems.

I should point out that gross figures of existing salvage can be misleading. Dead trees are always present to some extent; they may be scattered or in small bunches. Economics plays a big role. The deterioration of wood quality can be extremely variable even within a single species. Each salvage sale is unique depending on questions such as:

- how steep is the slope and what direction does it face;
- what is the erodability of the soil type;
- what wildlife and plant species are or were present;
- are there threatened and endangered species' considerations;
- how severe was the burn;
- what logging method should be used;
- must land use plans be amended;

- o is there existing access;
- o is a new road necessary;
- o is it economical to harvest;
- o how should volume be measured;
- o how fast will the wood deteriorate;
- o is there a market; and
- o what are the plans of adjacent land owners and agencies?

These are only some of the questions to be answered. Acquiring access alone may take one to three years.

We have attached to our statement BLM's best estimate of timber salvage statistics, as submitted to Committee Chairman Don Young. We are planning to offer approximately 64 million board feet of timber salvage for sale in 1995, based on what the States have requested to do the job and on existing resource capability. The estimated salvageable volume of 156 million board feet is the amount that is physically accessible but, in some cases, would be restricted for economic or environmental reasons.

I want to call your attention to the statistics for Alaska which show an estimate of 60 million board feet of salvageable volume. The majority of the accessible salvageable dead material is located in the Tiekel Block near Glenallen. This land has been selected by the State for possible retention. With uncertain tenure, the BLM is reluctant to take on a major commitment of resources in the area. Also, marketability of the material is questionable, and it is useful primarily for fuelwood and chips. We presently have no personnel capability in Alaska to undertake such an operation.

In closing, we recognize that timber salvage is important to the economic viability of many western communities, and the BLM will continue to commit our available resources to meet the challenge.

This concludes my prepared remarks. I will be pleased to answer questions.

BUREAU OF LAND MANAGEMENT

ESTIMATED SALVAGEABLE TIMBER

State	Salvage Reason	Salvage Species	Gross Vol. (MMBF)	Salvageable Vol. (MMBF)	Salvageable Value (Dollars)
Alaska	Insects	Spruce	400 MMBF	60 MMBF	$ 1,500,000
California	Fire/ Insects	Pine/ Fir	41 MMBF	21 MMBF	$ 1,295,000
Colorado	Fire	Pine/ Fir/ Spruce	1 MMBF	1 MMBF	$ 41,000
Idaho	Fire	Pine/ Fir	16 MMBF	16 MMBF	$ 505,000
Montana	Fire	Pine/ Fir/ Larch	4 MMBF	3 MMBF	$ 538,000
New Mexico	Fire/ Insects	Pine	1 MMBF	1 MMBF	$ 34,000
Oregon-O&C	Fire/ Insects	Pine/ Fir	100 MMBF	35 MMBF	$ 7,000,000
Oregon-Eastside	Fire/ Insects	Pine/ Fir	30 MMBF	15 MMBF	$ 2,760,000
Wyoming	Insects	Pine	9 MMBF	4 MMBF	$ 256,000
Total			602 MMBF	156 MMBF	$13,929,000

STATEMENT OF
CHADWICK D. OLIVER
PROFESSOR OF SILVICULTURE
UNIVERSITY OF WASHINGTON
COLLEGE OF FOREST RESOURCES

Before the
Subcommittee on National Parks, Forests and Lands
of the Committee on Resources
and
the Subcommittee on Resource Conservation, Research, and Forestry
of the Committee on Agriculture

United States House of Representatives

A hearing to investigate the timber salvage situation on Forest Service and BLM land.

February, 10th, 1995

MR. CHAIRMEN AND MEMBERS OF THE SUBCOMMITTEES:

I will address this issue in five parts:

1. CHANGING SCIENTIFIC UNDERSTANDING AND MANAGEMENT APPROACHES
2. PRESENT CONDITION OF THE FOREST
3. SALVAGE AND OTHER PRO-ACTIVE MANAGEMENT
4. EFFECTS OF SALVAGE TO THE FOREST ECOSYSTEM
5. COMPARISON OF MANAGEMENT APPROACHES WITH VALUES

CHANGING SCIENTIFIC UNDERSTANDING AND MANAGEMENT APPROACHES

The scientific understanding of how forests grow has changed dramatically over the past few decades (Figure 1), and this change has dramatically affected our approaches to forest management--including timber salvage. As long as scientists thought (and some still think) forests exist in a "steady state", a hands-off, or preservation approach to forest management seemed appropriate to maintain natural values. Now that scientists realize that the forest always has been dynamic and constantly changing through disturbances, regrowth, climate change, and species migrations, it is possible for active management including salvage to provide timber, biodiversity, forest health, fire protection, and other values simultaneously.

This part of the statement will briefly describe the changing scientific bases of management:

Steady State Theory (now outdated) and "Preserves"

This theory predominated ecology between 30 and 100 years ago but has lost scientific credibility in the past few decades. According to this theory, forest communities were thought to exist naturally in a benign, "stead states", sometimes associated with "climax" or "old-growth" (Stevens 1990). Disturbances were considered external to the system, usually artificial, and generally harmful. The steady-state forest was assumed to be most conducive to stability and diversity, and these forests could only exist where human activities were excluded.

Recent variations of this theory accept natural disturbances as real, but believe nature will create forests so different from human activities that human intervention other than to preserve forests will be irrevocably harmful to the natural system. Large preserves are advocated where natural patterns and processes are assumed to grow to and maintain this old-growth condition with limited human activities. Species dependent on habitat other than old-growth are assumed either not to exist, to be able to survive in old-growth structures, or to exist in geographically distant areas.

This theory led to the concept that human activities are innately disruptive to an otherwise natural system, and that forests need to be preserved from human influence if they are to maintain their intrinsic values. For this reasons, various forms of preserves and reserves have been established as areas to be "free" of human activities.

Preservation management using this theory has led to insect epidemics and past (and future) catastrophic fires, after which old growth habitats will be diminished. Such catastrophic fires as the Foothills Fire (over 140,000 acres) on the Boise National Forest in 1992 (Sampson et al. 1994) are significant examples of the fallacy of assuming natural processes would maintain a steady state and protect all species.

Dynamic theory and Landscape Management

It is now accepted that many large and small natural disturbances occur to forests and there is no stable, natural condition (Botkin 1990, Sprugel 1991). Forests regrow through a succession of structures (Figure 2). Each structure is suitable for some plant and animal species and not for others.

Many forest areas have continuously cycled through large disturbances and regrowth. As the structure changes through growth or disturbances, plant and animal populations change through migration, growth, dormancy, and death. Where large areas of low human populations existed, all plant and animal species were maintained as periodic, random disturbances ensured that all forest structures were represented across a very large area even though of widely varying amounts at different times.

Extreme losses of forest structures for habitats can cause species to become endangered or extinct. Such losses have occurred at various times in nearly all structures--the ivory billed woodpecker when old (old growth) river floodplain forests were diminished in the Southeast; the Kirkland's warbler when the stem exclusion structure was diminished in jack pine stands in the Midwest; the lotus blue butterfly when stand initiation areas regrew to closed forests in California (Fry and Money 1994).

This theory has led to active management in ways compatible with both human needs and ecological processes, referred to by such names as "landscape management" (Oliver 1992a,b,c, Boyce and McNab 1994). With this management, silvicultural operations can be used to coordinate changing forest stand structures to maintain all habitats and to reduce risks of uncontrollable natural disturbances. This coordination is done through a variety of field silvicultural operations such as thinning, uneven-aged harvesting, even-aged harvesting, controlled fires, creating snags, and replanting open areas. Maintaining forests within this variation involves removal of timber and other products and creating employment and other values as byproducts of these efforts.

Commodity-based management

Historically, much forest management has followed a third approach referred to here as "commodity management" where forests have been managed primarily for specific commodities, such as grazing, water, or timber---except for the extreme preservation approach toward fire management. Values such as biodiversity were often not considered, or human impacts were assumed to be so insignificant to forest ecosystems that they would not affect such values. Commodity management has become institutionalized on public forest lands in the United States (and elsewhere in the world) where national forest management practices are funded by timber sales receipts and where various thinning and harvesting operations need to be economically justified. Commodity management has essentially been required on private lands, since landowners must make a profit to pay taxes or their land will be confiscated

This approach has generally promoted just those forest habitats and structures compatible with efficient commodity production. The same economic basis which has led to even-aged management on highly productive sites has led to uneven-aged management on low-productivity sites in the Inland West. Commodity-based management creates less forest health risk than preservation (O'Laughlin et al. 1993), but since the return from timber harvest funds all management, this approach generally provides less biodiversity, timber quality, and employment than "landscape management"--but generally more than "preservation."

Through this approach, commodity (usually timber) removal was expected to pay the full price of providing all values, including forest health, biodiversity, recreation, etc. Consequently, in places where thinning was "below-cost" relative to the value of timber, thinning was not done and the other values which would have been provided by the thinning--reduced fire danger and habitat were lost. Instead, these forests will burn up.

PRESENT CONDITION OF THE FOREST

There are present imbalances of forest structures in many parts of the United States, because of past natural and human factors. I shall describe the Inland West in somewhat detail and several other areas of imbalance: the Pacific Coast, the Kenai Peninsula of Alaska, and the eastern United States.

The Inland West:

The condition of forests of the Inland West is the result of past centuries of natural and human disturbances and regrowth. Most management has been a combination of commodity management and preservation.

Before European-Americans predominated the area, the forests grew as in Figure 2 (Johnson *et al.* 1993). At low elevation, frequent ground fires kept the forests in park-like stands. This type of fire and the park-like forest structure (primarily ponderosa pine forests) were common in the southern Rocky Mountains and at low elevations in the central and northern Cascade Mountains (Covington and Moore 1994, Agee 93). Forests at mid- and upper elevations in the eastern Cascades and central and northern Rocky Mountains burned in hot, stand-replacing fires at intervals of about one or two centuries.

A combination of natural stand-replacing fires, commodity management for sheep, cattle, horses, and timber, and human-caused burning of the late 1800's and early 1900's created conditions of relatively low fire susceptibility in the first few decades of this century. By the 1950's, a preservation approach excluding all fires, natural and otherwise, was effective enough to allow a regrowth of dense forests at both upper and lower elevations. At upper elevations and in the southern Rocky Mountains, the regrowth to dense forests (stem exclusion and later stages of the lower part of Figure 2) created quite abnormal conditions.

Forest management in the Inland West has been through uneven-aged harvesting (often "highgrading") , in contrast to the clearcutting practiced in the faster-growing regions of Western Oregon and Washington (Adams 1980, Daniel 1980). Uneven-aged harvesting removed large trees and allowed growth of smaller trees which were often of different species than the larger trees. This predominance of uneven-aged harvesting has been contrary to the public's perception of clearcutting and to highly publicized cases such as the Bitterroot Controversy, Montana (Burk 1970).

Because of uneven-aged harvesting practices and fire prevention, the Inland

West presently contains many forests of overly-crowded , small-diameter trees and many uneven-aged forests (Figure 3). Standing volume is about 100 times as much as annual growth, indicating the forests have been increasing in volume for many decades. The forest's overcrowded conditions is reflected in the high mortality rate (Figure 4).

These overcrowded forests with many dead trees presently provide habitat for such old-growth-dependent species as the spotted owl (in eastern Washington and the Oregon Cascades); however, they are also extremely susceptible to insects, diseases, and fires (Sampson *et al.* 1994): disturbances which change stand structures very quickly. At the same time, there is a relatively small amount of open forest area. Species which depend on this habitat, such as Canadian lynx, grizzly bear, bighorn sheep, and the grey wolf, are jeopardized.

The Inland West's forest are growing much faster than they are being harvested (Figure 4). Dry summers have prevented dying trees from rotting, leading to a buildup of fuel. Within the next few decades, millions of forested acres of the Inland West can be expected to burn, returning them to the stand initiation stage (Sampson *et al.* 1994). These changes in stand structure will occur either through destructive, stand-replacement wildfires or through active management to reduce the excess fuels in forests in the older stages. After these disturbances occur, there will be larger amounts of open habitat for species dependent on it.

Presently, trees of smaller sizes than ever before are being removed and processed for timber in both thinning and harvesting operations in the Inland West. If continued and expanded, these operations could greatly reduced the risk of very large disturbances while helping achieve a greater diversity of structures across the region over time (Oliver *et al.* 1994). Recent federal policies which emphasize untouched set-asides seem more likely to increase fuel loads and stand replacement fires. The harvesting of smaller trees may be a temporary response of logging companies to the reduced timber supply from regions impacted by set-asides. Companies are paying high prices for timber and logs and incurring higher costs in the processing of small-diameter trees in order to depreciate their equipment investments rather than to lose their capital investments prematurely. Ultimately many businesses will close when substitute products---wood from elsewhere in the world, steel, aluminum, concrete, or plastic---gain in share. This business closure and substitution process is already underway; however, policy alternatives may still have a significant impact on the outcome.

Pacific Coast.

Forests of the Pacific Coast of Washington, Oregon, and northern California undergo periodic windstorms which blow over many trees. These dying and dead, overturned trees will attract insects, which will then kill more standing trees. The result is a buildup of fuel and catastrophic fires which can burn hundreds of thousands of acres within a few days. For the past few decades, the management practice of salvaging windthrown timber has prevented the fuel buildup and insect epidemics; however, the "preservation" approach of the past few years which prevents this salvage is again leading to conditions conducive to very destructive fires.

Kenai Peninsula of Alaska.

The spruce beetle has killed many trees in the forests of the Kenai Peninsula, so that now very destructive fires are threatening to burn the area. The foresters are faced with a dilemma: they are trying to prevent the fires because there are many homes on the peninsula; however, each year that they succeed leads to a larger fuel level and greater danger the following year. If salvage logging could be done here, the fuel loads could be reduced and controlled fires may be possible. (These fires may be necessary to keep the forest from turning into a grassland savannah.)

Eastern United States.

Destructive hurricanes such as Hurricane Hugo (South Carolina) and the 1938 Hurricane of New England would have resulted in catastrophic fires had not very aggressive efforts been done to salvage the dead and dying timber.

SALVAGE AND OTHER PRO-ACTIVE MANAGEMENT

The large disturbances can be avoided or mitigated by various forms of pro-active management, depending on the condition of the forest: Landscape Management, Pre-fire salvage, and Post-fire salvage. These will be discussed individually:

Landscape management.

Using scientific analysis and projection systems, we can project decades in advance how forests will grow, and when and where they will be at risk to insects, winds and/or fires and when/where they will be suitable habitat (Boyce and McNab 1994, McCarter et al. 1995). This projection allows us to manage across the landscape to reduce the need for "salvage-style" emergency activities. This approach has been detailed above and elsewhere (Oliver 1992a, b, c).

Pre-fire salvage:

Insects, wind, and general overcrowding give us further signals that fires are imminent. Some of the living and dead trees from the overly crowded stands (or downed trees) can be removed in thinnings both to reduce the susceptibility to more insects, diseases, or wind or the potential for fires and to provide timber flow, employment, and more diverse habitats.

Post-fire salvage.

Following a fire, some of the trees killed or injured in the fire can be removed to prevent insects or further rot (in the still living trees), to prevent very destructive reburns during the subsequent decades, and to provide timber flow, employment, and more diverse habitats.

EFFECTS OF SALVAGE TO THE FOREST ECOSYSTEM

There are several questions to address relative to the effects of fires and subsequent salvage:

1. What are the impacts of salvage logging on intensely burned areas?

If some trees are scorched but not killed, there may be benefits to removing some of these, in the hope that the remaining ones will grow healthy enough to avoid being killed by insects. Assuming the logged trees are killed, there are several concerns with these practices, and some potentially beneficial and some negative on-site effects. Ground based logging systems can be used on flat areas; and cable and helicopter logging can be used on slopes.

Off-site effects are primarily the costs, returns, employment, and wood flow created and will be addressed later.

On-site, there are three general concerns. Like many activities, logging with helicopters and cable systems can help each of these concerns in some ways, and adversely effect them in others. If certain mitigation's are done in conjunction with the logging, there may be some generally (but not universally) positive results. Each of the concerns will be described, followed by the effects of logging on these concerns:

1) erosion of the steep slopes. Fire tends to increase the present and future erosion possibilities in several ways:

--It immediately burns up the forest floor litter and vegetation cover, which can lead to rapid overland flow of water and subsequent gully erosion;
--It immediately creates a hydrophobic layer on the soil, which reduces soil infiltration, thus increasing overland flow and so accelerates gully erosion;
--By killing plants, it reduces evapotranspiration, and so leads to more rapidly saturated soils. These saturated soils can lead to more "rotational failures" of slopes and more surface erosion.
--Within about eight years, the roots of the dead (burned) trees will lose their strength. At that time, "soil slumping" caused by rotational failures will reach maximum probability. If the area is regenerated to growing trees, the root strength within the soil will gradually increase and the probability of soil slumping will again be reduced.

Helicopter or cable logging on steep ground, and using care with ground-based equipment on flat areas, will both fell trees and leave tops on the ground. These tops left should be beneficial in acting as barriers to overland water flow, thus reducing the gully erosion. The benefit of these tops would be especially helpful if they are intentionally left perpendicular to the slope, or otherwise placed in gullies (similar to many of the "erosion control" practices of the 1930's).

. Cable logging on steep slopes could be problematic if/where the "skid trails" parallel to the slope create channels for water movement which could turn into gullies. Mitigation measures such as putting "water bars:" on these skid trails are commonly done, and should stop the adverse effects.

Scarification of the soil during the logging may actually help break up the "hydrophobic layer" created by the fire and allow better infiltration of water into the soil, thus reducing the overland flow and subsequent gully erosion. Of course, down-hill scarification patches which instigate gullies should be avoided.

Logging will probably have little effect on the rotational failures or soil slumping, unless the slight reduction of weight and the dispersion of weight by removing the stems and leaving the tops on the ground have any effect.

If logging increases access to the site and so allows planting or otherwise regeneration which increases root strength of new trees rapidly, this may help with soil slumping.

2) Fuel buildup and reburns:

--The trees killed in the fire will eventually fall over. If, in a few years or decades, there is another fire in the same area, the downed fuel will cause the fire to burn very hot, which will exacerbate the other problems with erosion described above. In addition, this "reburn" behavior tends to reduce tree regeneration and so lead to more semi-permanent "brush fields" which are suitable for some species of animals and plants, but not others.

Logging the killed trees (or even some of the killed trees, leaving some in each diameter class as snags--such as was done after the Foothills Fire, Boise National Forest, 1992) would reduce the chance and intensity of reburns in two ways:

--By removing the tree stems, it would reduce the amount of fuel which would dry and fall to the ground and so cause the reburn to be very hot;

--It would place many of the tops close to the ground, and so cause them to decompose rapidly, thus reducing the fuel accumulation which would occur if the standing dead trees were allowed to remain.

3. Regeneration following the fires.

--I believe many burned areas are quickly, artificially seeded with grasses. Following the fires, some trees may "drop seeds" before they die. The partial shade created by the burned trees may help mitigate the heat and cold of these sites.

Logging the killed trees may adversely affect regeneration, unless it can be ensured that the trees to be removed do not have seeds, have already dropped their seeds, or can release their seeds in the downed tops after the trees are logged--or if artificial regeneration (planting) is to be done. A mitigation may be to leave standing those trees still capable of producing seeds, and log a proportion of the others.

Logging all of the trees may create adversely hot and cold microsites and so reduce the survival chances of regeneration. A mitigation measure would be to leave standing some of the trees (such as in all diameter classes, as was done on the Foothills Fire) to provide this microclimate amelioration (and to provide wildlife habitat, to be discussed).

Logging may be beneficial to regemeration if:

--The down tops create favorable, low microsites for planting or natural establishment of regeneration; or,

--The access created by the logging process allows easier access and replanting with large seedlings (as well as mitigations such as shading) which ensures more effective regeneration (assuming regeneration with trees is desired).

4. Wildlife habitat.

--The standing dead trees will provide habitat for some species, and will increase the habitat of prey for other species.

Logging some of the trees may still maintain the habitat for species using the snags, and provide down tops which can serve as dens and burrows for other species.

Logging all of the trees will provide better habitat for species not favored by any snags.

2. How does plant and animal succession for a site recovering naturally from a hard burn differ from one that has been salvage logged (assuming recommended amount of snags and down logs are left on site) and/or planted with shrubs?

The issue of "natural" must first be addressed. The occurrence of burns as "hard" are not common on all areas of a fire. Figure 2 shows the development patterns following "stand-replacement" and "minor" fires. In much of the low and mid elevations of the Inland West, frequent ground fires kept the forest relatively open--usually in a "park-like" condition. At upper elevations, fires were less frequent and the result was a stand-replacing event. These types of fires were probabilistic; however, as can be seen in Figure 3, "hard" fires did not occur naturally very much at low elevations, but were not uncommon at upper elevations.

Salvage Logging

Lower Elevations:

Salvage of some of the timber would move many aspects of the forests development from the pattern of development after a severe burn (an extreme on lower elevations) to the development pattern after a more common burn--with certain exceptions. One exception, of course, would be that there would not be the living "savannah" trees in the overstory.

Much of the lower elevations rarely had as much biomass as existed before (living) or after (dead) the fire; therefore, removing some of the timber would shift the biomass to a more naturally common amount. This reduction in snags would mean that; after the snags fell, there would be less dry fuel on the ground to support hot reburns.

Leaving all dead trees would give greater probability of hot reburns, which are often difficult to control and lead to semi-permanent brush fields since they burn up the tree seedlings and destroy the seed sources for new seeds to enter. The intensity of these burns would be relatively uncommon naturally, for reasons shown in Figure 5 and described above.

Salvaging some of the trees could lead to some mitigation of the soil erosion properties (described in Question #1, above). Since the fire was uncommonly hot under "natural" (pre-Euro-American) conditions, the mitigation would lead to the lower erosion rates more common to "natural" conditions.

Upper Elevations:

The "hard" fire was more naturally more common in the upper elevations, and recovery from it with or without some salvage logging would be naturally more common. The forests of the upper elevations initiated about 100 to 200 years ago, often after hot fires. The climate at that time was cooler (Little Ice Age) and so different species of trees may become established than would become established now--whether or not salvage logging was done.

Salvage logging (leaving some trees), therefore, would probably still keep these forests within their "natural" range of recovery patterns, but would move them less away from an unusual event than salvage logging at low elevations would do.

Planting Shrubs

Planting shrubs would increase regrowth of vegetation and may lead to less erosion. This pattern would be more similar the more common, less severe burns under "pre-Euro-American" conditions at low elevations, but not necessarily at upper elevations. Planting the shrubs may exclude trees from becoming established and so reduce the rate at which new stands would develop. Consequently regrowth of forests may be delayed unnaturally long. Regrowth to forests at upper elevations could be accelerated by planting, and grow to the savannah-like condition could be accelerated with thinning and pruning at lower elevations.

Planting the shrubs would pre-set some of the species composition of the developing stand. Without the planting, other species may invade and dominate the stand--although the theory that a set group or sequence of species invading is not considered valid.

COMPARISON OF MANAGEMENT APPROACHES WITH VALUES

89-215 O - 95 - 6

It is possible to compare salvage and other approaches to management with the different society values. The following example compares the consequences of present "commodity-based" management of the Inland West national forests with different management approaches:

The tradeoffs between values under different management approaches is substantial, as this example shows (Table 1). Determining the relative importance of each value is the policy makers' dilemma; however, this example focuses attention on the magnitudes of the tradeoffs under different management alternatives.

The results shown are based on Oliver and Lippke (1995). Other assumptions could give slightly different numbers; however, it is doubtful that the relative importance would change substantially.

Objective for Management

The overall objectives of forest management are a policy decision; however, this testimony will use several relatively robust objectives to demonstrate the tradeoffs which exist among objectives with different management approaches.

For this example, the objectives are categorized as: biodiversity and forest health, timber flow and the global environment, employment, and cost to the public.

Biodiversity and forest health can be promoted by maintaining a diversity of habitats in which species can be found and keeping a variety of stand structures so no continuity of fuel or insect-susceptible stands can lead to large disturbances.

Timber flow and the global environment are relatively complementary objectives. If wood products are not produced from forests where other ecosystem values are maintained, they will be produced from elsewhere in the world where ecosystem values are less regarded, with greater harm to the global environment.

Employment: Unemployment is a public cost, which reduces the ability to spend taxes on other environmental or social issues. Forest management produces employment through silvicultural treatments, fire fighting, timber harvesting, timber manufacturing, and extracting other values from the forest (e.g., mushrooms); jobs created by other activities are relatively few compared to the those created by timber harvesting and manufacturing (Oliver and Lippke 1995).

Costs/returns: The public's ability to pay for various ecological values through taxes competes with many other social values. This paper divides costs into two categories: costs to the federal government and costs to local governments.

Cost to the federal government: These costs can be viewed as changes in U.S.Forest Service expenses for managing national forests in different ways. In 1989 the U.S.Forest Service spent about $2.5 billion and generated revenue (primarily from timber) of about $1.1 billion. In 1993, it spent about $2.9 billion and generated revenue of about $700 million.

Costs to local governments: Local governments receive funds from national forests in lieu of taxes, based on 25% of the return from timber harvested within the local area minus certain silvicultural costs. (These are referred to as "surrogate taxes" in this paper.) Local governments also bear the costs of unemployment and benefit from increased employment.

Alternative Management Approaches

Several different management approaches for forests in the Inland West will be compared with the present management of these forests:

Present management:

Present management of national forests are roughly based on the "commodity management" approach. About 54% of the Inland West's 140 million forested acres can grow at least 20 cubic feet per acre per year, and so is considered "productive." Sixteen percent of this "productive" land is set aside as national parks, wilderness, etc. Of the remaining "productive", 36.4 million acres, are national forests. Presently, only 18% of the growth is harvested from these forests each year; therefore, roughly only 6.7 million acres are managed each year, and the remaining 29.7 million productive, unreserved acres are probably managed as "de facto" preservation.

Expanded commodity management:

If commodity management were expanded to all 36.4 million acres of productive, non-reserved forest service lands in the Inland West, timber harvest from this region would shift from the present 2 billion board feet per year to 10.9 billion board feet), but over 57% of federal forest lands there would still not be managed for timber--either because it was set aside or because it was "non productive."

Landscape management:

If "landscape management" were applied to the same 36.4 million acres, different silvicultural regimes would occur to maintain a diversity of habitats.

"Preservation management: no activities:

If all national forests in the Inland West were "preserved", harvest would be reduced from 2 billion board feet to zero, and all management would stop--except for fighting fires.

Two alternative "preservation" scenarios are also provided: "preservation with controlled fires" and "preservation with partial salvage of burned timber."

Preservation with controlled fires:

This alternative would have no timber harvest, but would include an active program of "controlled fires" to reduce catastrophic wildfires.

Preservation with partial salvage of burned timber:

This alternative would allow partial salvage of timber after it is burned. It is assumed here that 60% of the timber could be salvaged before it deteriorated. Keeping a wood harvesting infrastructure dependent on wildfires and salvaging burned timber may not be feasible, and would probably not lead to stable communities.

Comparison of Values and Management Approaches

Comparisons of impacts on the values by shifting from present management to the alternative approaches is shown in Table 1.

The costs to biodiversity, the global environment, the federal and local governments, and employment by "preservation" management are very high, compared to the alternatives. Salvage of burned timber helps mitigate some of the costs, but may be considered only a "stop-gap" measure. More pro-active "landscape management" does not yield as high values as expanded commodity management in this case (but not in other cases), but does maintain biodiversity.

The dramatic impacts on the costs are borne by the local governments. Even here, the differences in revenue to local governments by surrogate taxes are masked by the impacts on employment benefits and unemployment costs by the different management regimes. Local governments can benefit or be negatively impacted depending on federal policies.

There are additional costs and benefits not shown here. Additional costs of preservation management involve increasing the cost of wood products and reducing the buying power of the US economy by importing wood or its substitutes. The price of lumber has already increased because of harvest reductions in the Pacific Northwest but will probably not increase more; instead, more polluting substitute products such as steel studs may be used.

Summary

There may not be a management alternative which is optimum for all objectives (Table 1). The choice of how to weight each objective and which alternative to implement is the responsibility of policy makers; however, their decision will only be effective if they understand this broad range of alternatives and have a clear understanding of the consequences of the alternatives. A proactive approach to management--landscape management or, as a stop-gap measure, salvage logging, can provide many benefits at lower overall costs while still providing biodiversity and forest health.

Literature Cited

Adams, D. L. 1980. The northern Rocky Mountain region. *In* (J.W. Barrett, ed.) Regional Silviculture of the United States, Second Edition. Jon Wiley and Sons, New York. Pp. 341-389.

Agee, J. K. 1993. Fire ecology of Pacific Northwest forests. Island Press, Washington DC. 493 pp.

Botkin, D. B. 1990. Discordant harmonies: a new ecology for the twenty-first century. Oxford University Press, New York. 241 p.

Boyce, S. G. and W. H. McNab. 1994. Management of forested landscapes: simulations of three alternatives. Journal of Forestry 92:27-32.

Burk, D. A. 1970. The clearcut crisis: controversy in the Bitterroot. Jursnick Press, Great Falls, Montana. 152 pp.

Covington, W. W., and M. M. Moore. 1994. Southwestern ponderosa pine forest structure: changes since Euro-American settlement. Journal of Forestry. 92:39-47.

Daniel, T. W. 1980. The middle and southern Rocky Mountain region. In (J. W. Barrett, ed.) Regional Silviculture of the United States, Second Edition. John Wiley and Sons, New York. Pp. 377-340.

Fry, M. and N. R. Money. 1994. Biodiversity conservation in the management of utility right-of-way. Proceedings of the 15th Annual Forest Vegetation Management Conference, Redding CA. Pp. 94-103.

Johnson, C. G., R. R. Clausnitzer, P. J. Mehringer, and C. D. Oliver. 1993. Biotic and abiotic processes of eastside ecosystems: the effects of management on plants and community ecology, and on stand and landscape vegetation dynamics. In (P. F Hessburg, compiler) Eastside forest ecosystem health assessment--Volume III: Assessment. Portland, Oregon. USDA Forest Service, Pacific Northwest Research Station. pp. 35-100.

McCarter, J. B., J. Wilson, M. Wimberly, R. J. McGaughey, J. Moffett, M. S. Zens, and C. D. Oliver. 1995. A computer-based system for facilitating landscape management. *In Submission*.

O'Laughlin, J., J. G. MacCracken, D. L. Adams, S. C. Bunting, K. A. Blatner, and C. E. Keegan, III. 1993. Forest health conditions in Idaho: executive sumary. Idaho Forest, Wildlife and Range Policy Analysis Group. Report No. 11. 37 pp.

Oliver, C. D. 1992a. Enhancing biodiversity and economic productivity through a systems approach to silviculture. In The Silviculture Conference. Forestry Canada, Ottawa, Ontario. pp. 287-293.

Oliver, C. D. 1992b. A landscape approach: achieving biodiversity and economic productivity. Journal of Forestry. 90:20-25.

Oliver. C. D. 1992c. Statement before the Subcommittee on Forests, Family Farms, and Energy Committee on Agriculture, United States House of Representatives, Washington DC. March 11, 1992.

Oliver, C.D., and B. R. Lippke. 1995. Wood supply and other values and ecosystem management in Western Internal Forests. *In* Ecosystem management in Western Interior Forests, held April 18, 1994, Washington State University, Pullman, WA. Proceedings to be published.

Oliver, C. D., D. E. Ferguson, A. E. Harvey, H. S. Malany, J. M. Mandzak, and R. W. Mutch. 1994. Managing ecosystems for forest health: an approach and the effects of uses on values. Journal of Sustainable Forestry. 2(1/2):113-133.

Powell, D. S., J. L. Faulkner, D. R. Darr, Z. Zhu, and D. W. MacClearry. 1993. Forest resources of the United States, 1992. USDA Forest Service general Technical Report, RM-234. 132 pp.

Sampson, R. N., D. L. Adams, S. Hamilton, S. P. Mealey, R. Steele, and D. Van DeGraff. 1994. Assessing forest ecosystem health in the Inland West. Journal of Sustainable Forestry. 2(1/2):3-10.

Sprugel, D. G. 1991. Disturbance, equilibrium, and environmental variability: What is natural vegetation in a changing environment? Biological Conservation. 58:1-18.

Stevens, W. K. 1990. New eye on nature: the real constant in eternal turmoil. New York Times, July 31, 1990. pp. B5-6.

FIGURE 1

THE NEW YORK TIMES
SCIENCE *TUESDAY, JULY 31, 1990*

New Eye on Nature: The Real Constant Is Eternal Turmoil

The 'balance' theory may be more poetry than science.

By WILLIAM K. STEVENS

In a revision that has far-reaching implications for the way humans see the natural world and their role in it, many scientists are forsaking one of the most deeply embedded concepts of ecology: the balance of nature.

Ecologists have traditionally operated on the assumption that the normal condition of nature is a state of equilibrium, in which organisms compete and coexist in an ecological system whose workings are essentially stable. Predators and prey — moose and wolves or cheetahs and gazelles, for instance — are supposed to remain in essentially static balance. Anchovies and salmon reach a maximum population that can be sustained by their oceanic environment and remain at that level. A forest grows to a beautiful, mature climax stage that becomes its naturally permanent condition.

This concept of natural equilibrium long ruled ecological research and governed the management of such natural resources as forests and fisheries. It led to the doctrine, popular among conservationists, that nature knows best and that human intervention in it is bad by definition.

Now an accumulation of evidence has gradually led many ecologists to abandon the concept or declare it irrelevant, and others to alter it drastically. They say that nature is actually in a continuing state of disturbance and fluctuation. Change and turmoil, more than constancy and balance, is the rule. As a consequence, say many leaders in the field, textbooks will have to be rewritten and strategies of conservation and resource management will have to be rethought.

The balance-of-nature concept "makes nice poetry, but it's not such great science," said Dr. Steward T. A. Pickett, a plant ecologist at the Institute of Ecosystem Studies of the New York Botanical Garden at Millbrook, N.Y. He was a co-organizer of a symposium that explored the matter yesterday in Snowbird, Utah, at the annual meeting of the Ecological Society of America, the nation's premier organization of ecological scientists.

While the shift in thinking has not yet produced a coherent new theory to replace the old one, Dr. Pickett characterizes what is going on as "a major revision of one of our basic assumptions of how the natural world works." The developing conviction that nature is ruled more by flux and disturbance is "becoming the dominant idea," he said.

"There will always be people who will cling to old ideas," said Dr. Simon A. Levin, a Cornell University ecologist who is the incoming president of the Ecological Society. "But certainly the center of mass of thinking" among ecologists, he said, has shifted away from equilibrium and "toward the fluctuating nature of natural systems. Some scientists now

Continued on Page B6

Changing View Of Nature

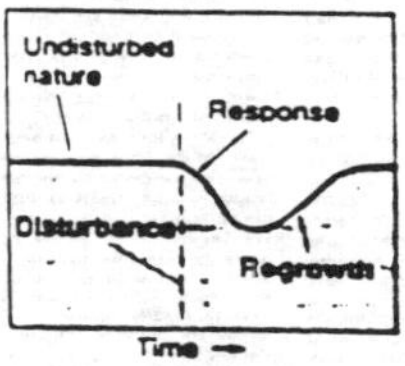

In the past, ecologists assumed that nature undisturbed was a constant state to which ecosystems and populations of animals would return after disturbances like fires.

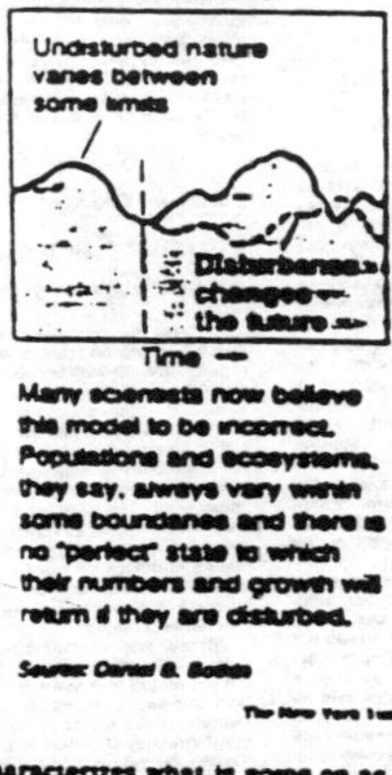

Many scientists now believe this model to be incorrect. Populations and ecosystems, they say, always vary within some boundaries and there is no "perfect" state to which their numbers and growth will return if they are disturbed.

Source: Daniel B. Botkin

The New York Times

New View of the Balance of Nature Finds the Real Constant Is Turmoil

Continued From Page 85

say that ecological communities of plants and animals are inherently unstable largely because of idiosyncratic differences in behavior among communities and individuals in them. A super-aggressive wolfpack leader, for example, can greatly increase the pack's hunting efficiency and destabilize the ecosystem — just as the death of a pack leader can promote instability by causing the pack to disperse.

But even if ecological communities do display some sort of internal equilibrium, many scientists believe, external disturbances like climatic change, year-to-year variations in weather patterns, fires, windstorms, hurricanes and disease seldom, if ever, give the communities a chance to settle into a stable state. In this view the climax forest, the neatly symmetrical predator-prey relationship and the bumper fish population become transient conditions at best, even in the absence of human intervention.

Scientists are finding this to be true on many scales of time and space, from the glacial and global to the seasonal and local, and in parts of the world long considered the most pristine and stable like the tropical rain forests of South and Central America, for instance, or the north woods of Canada and the northern United States.

In the natural landscape, "there is almost no circumstance one can find where something isn't changing the system," said Dr. George L. Jacobson Jr., who, as a paleoecologist at the University of Maine, studies ecological change as it is revealed in ancient sediments and rocks. And while there may be a tendency toward a stable equilibrium, he said, "it's never allowed to get there, so we might as well not expect it to exist."

In this developing new perspective, humans are emerging as just one of many sources of ecological disturbance that keep nature in a perpetual state of uproar. The question of whether humans should intervene in natural processes is moot, ecologists say, since humans and their near-human ancestors have been doing so for eons, and ecological systems around the world bear their indelible imprint.

The supposedly pristine rain forests of Latin America, for instance, owe some of their character to the intervention of humans who planted and transplanted trees and other plants throughout the jungle. And the supposedly unspoiled Serengeti Plain of Africa, some ecologists are convinced, owes its tremendous abundance of grazing animals at least partly to human-set fires that created savanna habitats.

The real question, ecologists say, is which sort of human interventions should be promoted and which opposed.

One of the biggest human interventions, some say, is taking place now as people pour heat-trapping chemicals, mainly carbon dioxide, into the atmosphere. Many climatologists expect that this will cause the Earth's climate to warm significantly, causing especially widespread ecological dislocation.

The temperature of the earth has shifted up and down many times in past eons, ecologists point out, and ecosystems have always adjusted. But this human intervention, scientists say, threatens to force, in a century or less, vast climatic and ecological changes that have usually taken millennia. Ecologists fear that this time, ecosystems will not adjust rapidly enough to stave off catastrophe for many species.

Moreover, some ecologists say, people are eliminating some of the diversity of habitat — and therefore of species — that other natural disruptions create and promote. "We threaten that variability because we want to manage everything like cornfields," said Dr. Julie Denslow, a tropical ecologist at Tulane University. There is, she said, "a whole camp of us" opposed to this "horrible homogenizing."

A Difficulty

Posing a Question: What Is Natural?

The new view of nature poses difficulties for conservationists and environmentalists who want to preserve things in their natural condition, scientists say, since the question now becomes: If change is constant, what is the natural state?

What, for instance, is the natural condition of the Adirondacks, where a spirited argument is going on about whether "rough" fish like suckers, shiners and chubs should be killed and removed from some ponds to make way for trout. People on one side of the argument, citing a state policy that aims to "perpetuate natural aquatic ecosystems" in the area, say that the rough fish represent the natural condition and that the ponds should be preserved in that condition. Others say that at least some rough fish are descendants of baitfish brought in by humans and that they have crowded out trout that flourished there earlier.

Is either of these alternative conditions "the" natural state? Or is the natural state the way the Adirondacks were when Europeans first arrived? Or, for that matter, the way they were in the millennia when the region was buried under an ice age glacier. Or in the succession of different forests, animals and ecosystems that followed?

"Nature can be in many conditions," said Dr. Daniel B. Botkin, an ecologist at the University of California at Santa Barbara who is a leader of the reassessment effort. Because of that, he said, conservationists and resource managers will be required to analyze a given situation more carefully than in the past and then choose which natural condition to promote rather than simply insist that humans should not upset a supposed balance of nature.

"I think he's right," said Rupert Cutler, the president of the Defenders of Wildlife, a major conservation organization. He said that the shift in thinking "suggests that the responsibility for protecting nature will require a much higher level of intense application of science than it was ever assumed to require in the past."

Empty Theory

Observations Find No Neat Balance

In its classic formulation, the balance-of-nature concept holds that an ecosystem maintains a constant equilibrium and when disturbed, it returns to its former status when the cause of the disturbance is removed.

Many scientists now say it is clear that this is not the way things work.

"We can say that's dead for most people in the scientific community," said Dr. Peter L. Chesson, a theoretical ecologist at Ohio State University who took part in yesterday's symposium along with Dr. Pickett, Dr. Jacobson, Dr. Botkin and Dr. Denslow. The other participants were Dr. Margaret B. Davis, a paleoecologist at the University of Minnesota who helped organize the symposium and Dr. Judy L. Meyer, a stream ecologist at the University of Georgia.

Many observations of the behavior of animal populations in the wild, says Dr. Botkin, do not support the assumption of neat balance predicted by traditional ecological theory. One aspect of the theory says that when a population of animals moves into an area, it grows gradually to a level of abundance at which its environment will allow it to be sustained indefinitely, and then remains at that level. Another says that predator and prey populations in a given ecosystem oscillate in numbers, with one population at a peak while the other is at a low point and vice versa, thereby creating an equilibrium over time.

But in real life, says Dr. Botkin, "when you introduce a population to a new area it goes up and then crashes, and then it doesn't remain constant. The long-term numbers vary and are much lower" than predicted by the theory. Similarly, he said, a number of studies and observations, in the laboratory as well as the wild, show that predator-prey populations do not oscillate stably and predictably. Instead, they either fluctuate wildly and unpredictably or the prey species is eliminated and the predator species dies of starvation. In one famous experiment, paramecium microbes increased rapidly. When predator microbes were introduced, they increased, too. But in the end, the paramecia were exterminated and the predators died of starvation.

Attempts to apply the classical equilibrium principle to the management of marine fisheries led to disaster, according to Dr. Botkin. For years, he said, international regulators of commercial fishing determined allowable annual catches by calculating maximum sustainable yields according to equilibrium theory. The theory was such a poor guide, Dr. Botkin said, that population after population of commercial fish suffered catastrophic declines in the 1950's and 1960's and some have not yet recovered.

Managers of fisheries are trying to move away from that strategy now, he said, by analyzing the more complicated factors that actually determine fish populations. Among these, for example, are the environmental disturbances that largely determine the size of a given year's hatching of young fish. By estimating and keeping track of these varying "year classes," managers hope to adjust catch quotas year by year and avoid wiping out an entire class.

Some scientists are not quite ready to abandon entirely the concept of an inherent tendency toward equilibrium in ecosystems. A kind of equilibrium, they say, may exist on some scales of time and space.

Scale, in fact, may be very important. While there may be enormous unbalancing disturbances and fluctuations among small populations in small ecosystems, says Dr. Pickett, the fluctuations may be dampened when the larger picture is considered, where a sort of medium or the equilibrium might apply. An animal population that fails in one environment might not do so if allowed to range over a wider area. Dr. Botkin also said it is quite possible that while a given locality's ecology would change markedly over thousands of years, there could be recurring similarities — and thus a kind of floating equilibrium — at medium-range time scales.

That, in fact, is what Dr. Chesson, the theoretician, postulates. There may, for instance, be a limited range in which an animal population fluctuates over several hundred years. An equilibrium could be calculated by taking the average of the fluctuations. But it would be a "real mistake," said Dr. Chesson, to equate this with anything "remotely like" the classical idea of the balance of nature.

Constant Change

Outside Factors Shape Ecosystems

Perhaps the most outstanding evidence favoring an ecology of constant change and disruption over one of static balance comes from studies of naturally occurring external factors that dislocate ecosystems.

For a long time, says Dr. Meyer of the University of Georgia, these outside influences were insufficiently considered. The emphasis, she said, was "on processes going on within the system," even though "what's happening is driven by what's happening outside." Ecologists, she said, "had blinders on in thinking about external controlling factors."

Climate and weather appear foremost among these factors. By studying the record laid down in ocean and lake sediments, scientists know that climate, in the words of Dr. Davis of the University of Minnesota, has been "wildly fluctuating" over the last two million years, and the shape of ecosystems with it. The fluctuations take place not only from eon to eon, but also from year to year and at every scale in between. "So you can't visualize a time in equilibrium," said Dr. Davis.

Dr. Jacobson said there is virtually no time when the overall environment stays constant for very long. "That means that the configuration of the ecosystems is always changing."

Figure 2. Stands in the Inland West generally developed after infrequent, stand-replacing disturbances (usually fires) at upper elevations (A) and after frequent, partial disturbances (ground fires) at low elevations (B). Present fire and forest health dangers in the Inland West are high because forest growth following fire exclusion at low elevations and regrowth following old fires at upper elevations have created predominantly closed forests (forests not in the stand initiation condition; Johnson *et al.* 1993).

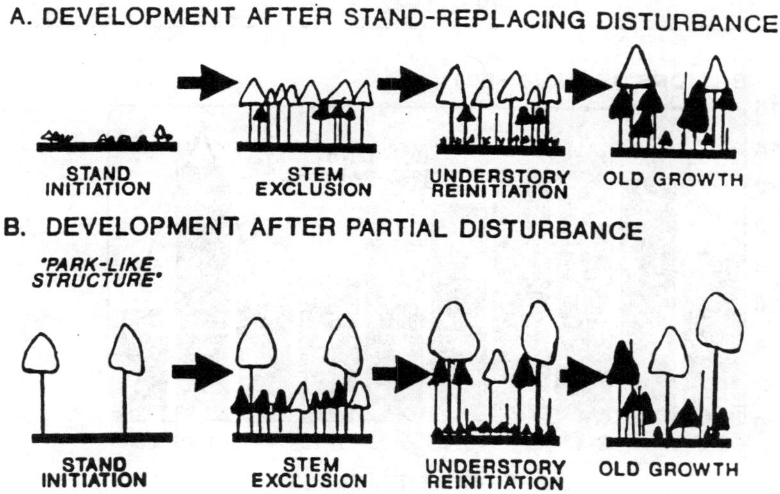

Figure 3. Change in diameter distribution of trees in the Intermountain West between 1952 (line) and 1992 (bars). Forests are increasingly composed of small diameter, crowded stands whose harvesting costs exceed their commercial timber value. Much of the timber not harvested is of small diameters; the employment created and timber value, combined, could make harvesting economically feasible (data from Powell *et al.* 1993; North and South Dakota, eastern Oregon and Washington not included).

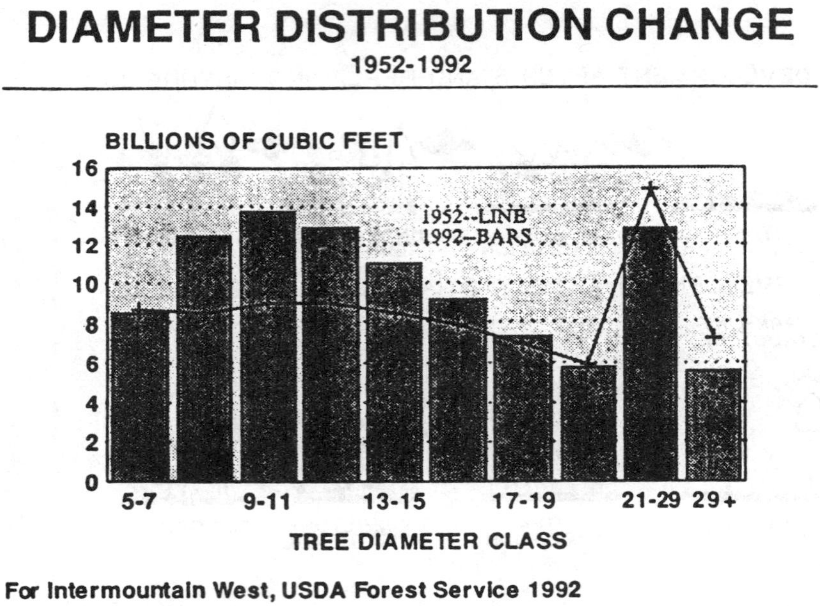

Figure 4 Net annual growth, mortality, and harvested forest tree volume (in millions of cubic feet) in the Inland West in selected years between 1952 and 1991. Stand volumes for the same area were 50 to 100 times as much as annual growth. Much of the volume is not harvested because the costs of harvesting exceed the timber value; however, if more volume is not harvested soon, the excess volume will be reduced by catastrophic wildfires at a very high public cost (data from Powell *et al.* 1993). (For conversion, one cubic foot equals approximately 5 board feet.)

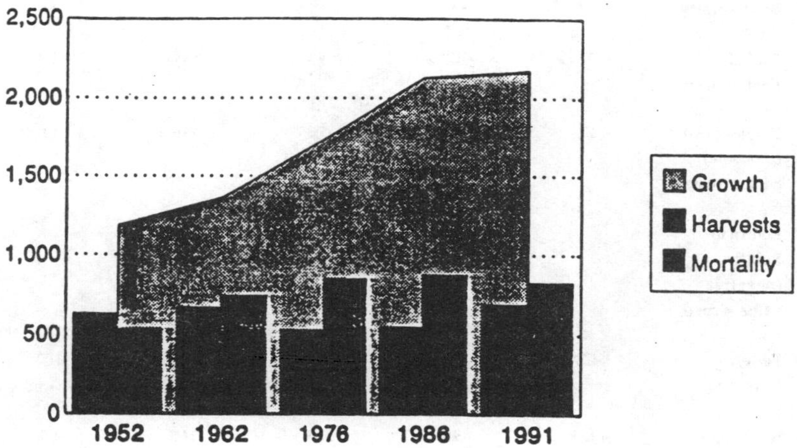

(Excludes eastern Washington & Oregon; USDA Forest Service 1982 & 1993)

Table 1. Changes in values if change from present management to alternative management approach on non-reserved, productive national forest lands in interior west (approximately 43% of federal forests in Interior West).
-- Biodiversity: "+"'s indicate better
-- Global Environment: percent change toward President Clinton's target CO2 reduction ("+" equals improvement).
-- Federal Percent Change: proportion of offset of Forest Service budget expenses.
-- Local: return ("+") or cost ("-") to local governments.

Changes in Values	Expanded Commodity	Landscape Management	Preservation	Preservation & Controlled Burn	Preservation & Salvage
Biodiversity	+[1]	+++	+[1]	++	+[1]
Global Environment	+ 18%	+ 17%	-4%	-4%	+8%
Employment (thousand person years)	72	60	-16	-16	42
Return to Public (negative value = cost)					
Federal (million)	429	228	-302	-611	-102
% Change	+17%	+9%	-12%	-24%	-4%
Local (million)	+873	+656	-266	-266	+403
Consumer Cost of Wood	Low	Low	Hi	Hi	Med

[1]The relative benefits of these three management approaches on biodiversity are uncertain; however, their benefits are less than Preservation with controlled burn (if it is possible) and much less than Landscape Mangement.

Testimony of Victor W. Kaczynski, Ph.D.

Relative to a Joint Hearing on the Timber Salvage Situation on Forest Service and BLM Lands

Before

The Subcommittee on National Parks, Forests, and Lands of the Committee on Resources

and

The Subcommittee on Resource Conservation, Research, and Forestry of the Committee on Agriculture

February 10, 1995

Room 1324, Longworth House Office Building

Qualifications: I am a practicing, certified, fisheries scientist with 25 years of professional experience with salmon issues in the Pacific Northwest. This began with my publications on chum and pink salmon while an Assistant Professor at the University of Washington. I have been a senior author on three major reports that have analyzed and described the reasons for salmon declines in northern California, Oregon and Washington States. I studied the salmon impacts of the Exxon Valdez oil spill in Alaska.

I have been a fisheries consultant to many timber companies throughout the Northwest from Alaska to California. This work studied the effects of various timber harvest and management practices on salmon habitat. I presently am the project manager of a large stream habitat survey project being conducted for forest industry companies in Oregon and advise a similar study in Washington State. Over 1,400 stream miles have been surveyed to date using state-of-the-art quantitative methods. The results of these steam habitat surveys are being used to evaluate past and present forest practices and to plan stream enhancement projects. I recently published articles on the forest industry stream surveys and their use in designing stream rehabilitation projects, and on the impact of catastrophic wildfires on streams and salmon.

Wildfire impacts on salmon stream habitat is the topic of my testimony today. Forest health is the key to the probability and severity of wildfires. Forest health will affect the area, frequency, and

intensity of wildfire. Stream habitat impacts from wildfires have not received appropriate attention. The potential for catastrophic impacts is especially high with the present situation of drought and tree species mix, densities, health, and fuel loads in lands east of the Cascade Mountains. Wildfires affect stream habitat in three ways: decreased vegetation cover, increased storm runoff, and increased sediment and debris.

Storm runoff is dynamic. It's affected by topography, precipitation characteristics, vegetation cover and evapotranspiration, and soil mantle capacity. Soil mantle capacity includes infiltration, storage and transmission of ground water. In a wildfire, vegetation cover and root systems are destroyed which leads to increased erosion and slope failure rates. The upper organic soil horizon can be destroyed which impacts infiltration and storage functions and can cause "hydrophobic" soils. Surface runoff is accelerated, peak runoff events are accelerated, and low summer flows are decreased. The net effect is stronger peaks of flood water (in the spring) and not as much water in the summer. Loss of summer flow increases summer stream temperatures and decreases stream habitat area and pool depth.

Following wildfires, streams receive a large pulse of small to large organic debris, sediment from silt to boulders, and nutrients including ammonia nitrogen. Complex chemical reactions occur in the stream and this results in a pulse of biochemical oxygen demand. The temperature of the stream can also rise dramatically. Increases of several degrees have been recorded in many wildfires. The combination of increased temperature, increased sediments, and lowered dissolved oxygen (from the BOD pulse) often causes direct fish and aquatic insect death. This occurred in the disastrous Tanner Gulch Fire in the upper Grande Ronde River in 1989. All fish and aquatic life were killed in a 36-mile stretch of the river including all adults and eggs from the endangered spring Chinook salmon population (Snake River strain), and all Chinook fry from the previous 1988 spawning. Fisheries biologists estimated that 50 percent of the fingerlings from the 1987 spawning were also killed, all that remained in that stretch of river.

Sediment and ash particles clog and irritate fish gills and this can cause direct death, or stress and vulnerability to disease, which results in death. These particles smother the spawning gravels, which decreases the flow of water through the gravels, lowering the dissolved oxygen and increasing the mortality of eggs and alevins. The upper Grande Ronde spring Chinook salmon spawning was impacted in at least 1990-1993 from these delayed sediment effects.

Vegetation cover loss was previously discussed in hydrology impacts. But this also results in the loss of canopy and shade, which increases summer stream temperatures beyond just the hydrologic temperature impact caused by loss of summer flows. And vegetation cover loss also means a temporary decrease in the input of needles, leaves and stems which are a large part of the organic food chain.

Spring Chinook salmon prefer medium sized flood plain reaches for spawning. Such habitat is especially vulnerable to wildfire impacts that occur in small forested tributary basins above these preferred flood plain reaches. This is exactly what occurred in the 1989 upper Grande Ronde River disaster. See the accompanying figure. The Tanner Gulch fire burned some 5,000 acres affecting small tributary streams directly. Two of these small tributaries experienced debris dams and then sluiced out in a rainstorm that put out the fire. The resulting flash debris flow caused the fish kill in the 36-miles reach of upper mainstream habitat.

Wildfires represent the largest single risk factor to many special status fish populations today. The stream habitat impacts that result can be larger than from any managed forest activity allowed under present forest practice rules. The current situation of poor forest health compounded by drought greatly increases the risks of wildfire. For example, in the northern half of the Wallowa-Whitman National Forest, wildfires have burned about twenty percent of the area between 1986 through 1993 (8 years). In other words, at present there is a 100-percent probability of wildfire impacting most critical fish habitat there in roughly 40 years if conditions are not changed.

Finally, one should logically ask, are the risk and impacts of prescribed burning on fish streams the same as from wildfires? The answer is an emphatic no. Professional foresters can reasonably control locations, areas of coverage, frequency, season of burns, and especially the intensity of controlled burns. The potential impacts of controlled burns on streams should be dramatically less. Prescribed burning has the potential to greatly reduce the very real risk of catastrophic impacts to fish and fish habitat from wildfires that exists today.

I have enclosed 6 summary sheets with large print that describe the main impacts that catastrophic wildfires have upon salmon streams, and I have also enclosed the figure that illustrates the vulnerability of spring Chinook habitat in many locations to wildfires. This is an example of the upper Grande Ronde River in northeast Oregon where a major population of the endangered Snake River spring Chinook salmon were severely impacted by a 1989 wildfire, and prolonged sediment impacts since then.

I sincerely hope that this information is of value to you in your deliberations.

Respectfully submitted,

V.W. Kaczynski, Ph.D.
Certified Fisheries Scientists, AFS
35022 Oliver Heights Court
St. Helens, Oregon 97051
February 7, 1995

Diagram of Upper Grande Ronde River Showing Vulnerability of Spring Chinook Habitat to Upstream Forested Tributary Wildfires

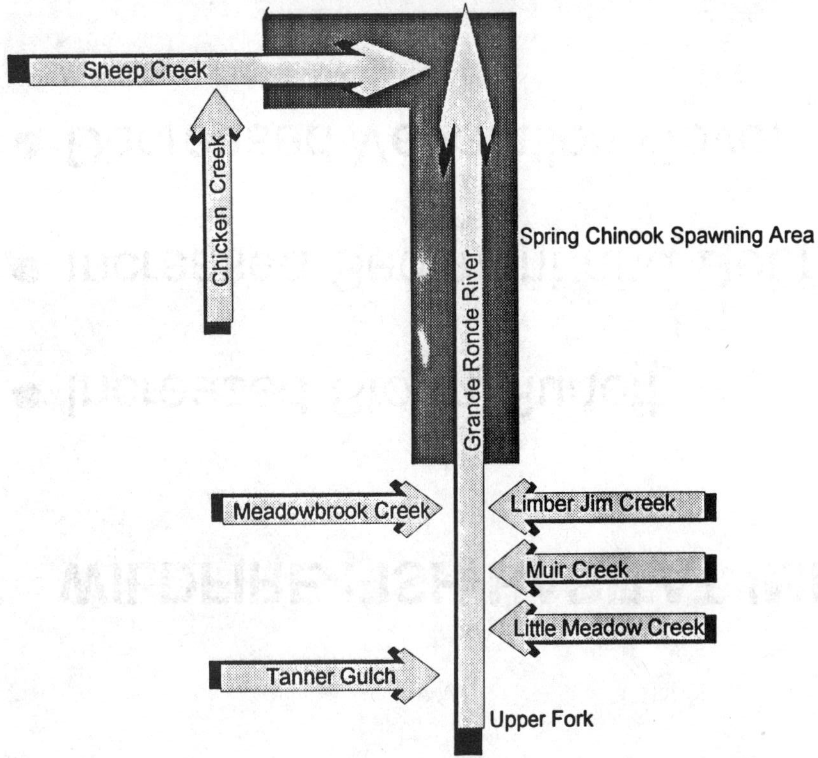

WILDFIRE-FISH HABITAT IMPACTS

- Increased Storm Runoff
- Increased Sedimentment and Debris
- Decreased Vegetation Cover

STORM RUNOFF IS DYNAMIC

- Precipitation Characteristics
- Vegetation Cover
- Soil Mantle Capacity
  - Infiltration
  - Storage
  - Transmission
- Evapotranspiration
- Topography

FIRE IMPACTS ON STORM RUNOFF

- Destroys Vegetative Cover and Root Systems
  - Increases erosion and slope failure rates

- Can Destroy Upper Organic Soil Horizon
  - Impacts infiltration and storage functions
  - May create hydrophobic soils
  - Increases rill erosion and surface runoff
  - May decrease summer flows

- Vegetation Destroyed
  - Decreases evapotranspiration losses
  - Increases stream flows, peak runoff events
  - May shorten spring runoff season

INCREASED SEDIMENT AND DEBRIS

- Pulse of Small to Large Organic Debris
- Pulse of Sediment (to boulders)
- Pulse of Nutrients Including Ammonia-Nitrogen
- Pulse of BOD

SEDIMENT AND DEBRIS IMPACTS

- Sediment Particles Can Seriously Irritate Fish Gill Tissues, Even Clog;Potential Direct Death
- Smother Spawning Gravels
- Decrease Pool Volume
- Large BOD Pulse Can Deplete DO To Lethal Levels
- Increased Nutrients Can Increase Stream Photosynthesis
- Large Pulse of Medium to Large Debris Can Increase Stream Complexity Long Term

VEGETATION LOSS IMPACTS

- Loss of Canopy and Shade

  -Increased summer stream temperatures
  -Decreased winter stream temperatures
  -Increased photosynthesis rate
  -Decreased input of leaves, needles, etc.

- May Cause Long Term LWD Recruitment Shortage

  -Potential long term stream habitat simplification

AMERICAN FORESTS

RE LEAF

TIMBER SALVAGE AND FOREST HEALTH

Testimony by

R. Neil Sampson
Executive Vice President
American Forests

before the

Committee on Natural Resources
U.S. House of Representatives

February 10, 1995

Mr. Chairman. Members of the Committee:

I am Neil Sampson, and I am here today on behalf of American Forests, a nonprofit, nonpartisan citizens conservation organization that has, since 1875, been an advocate for sound, sensible management of our Nation's forests. Our organization has been deeply involved in the forest health issue for the past several years.

I have been personally involved in such ways as chairing the National Commission on Wildfire Disasters, which rendered its report in 1994, and co-editing a book on the forest ecosystems of the Inland West that resulted from a scientific conference at Sun Valley, Idaho, in late 1993. We were deeply involved in the development of forest health legislation in the 102nd and 103rd Congresses. In October of 1994, just prior to the election, we conducted a national public opinion survey on the subjects of wildfire and forest health, and I have enclosed a summary of those results. More detailed data is available for anyone interested in learning more.

I have also enclosed with this testimony a newspaper reprint of a series that ran last fall in the Sacramento Bee. We feel this is as good a discussion of these issues as the public media produced last year, and I commend it to your attention.

At the outset, I would like to separate the discussion today into two parts. Timber salvage is one subject; forest health a very different topic. Often, these topics are combined as though they were one and the same. That is, in our view, often misleading.

Timber salvage is exactly what the term denotes -- an attempt to salvage something from a bad situation. Options are limited at that stage, and there is economic pressure to move quickly before value is lost. The result can be just about anything. Anecdotes of operations that made a lot of money and did little or no damage to the forest can be matched against those that point to salvage operations that damaged soils, did little or nothing to speed site recovery, and degraded nearby live and healthy forests in the process. The point is, you can find a story to support just about any argument you want to make. Anecdotes make a poor basis for policy formation in cases like this.

I would prefer, instead, to point to some general policy issues that I believe are worthy of note. First, while there is a real need to move quickly when valuable commodities are deteriorating, there is not a good argument for sloppy project design or careless work in the woods. That is particularly true in this time of high log values and technologies such as helicopter logging and low-impact machines. The admonition to "do no further harm" must be the first rule of engagement on these projects.

The fact that most salvage relies on sales contracts as its administrative device may increase the difficulty in obtaining good salvage projects. Bidding the highest price for the merchantable salvage creates economic incentives on the part of the contractor to get in, grab the logs, and get out. Fast and cheap. That's not a prescription for tender care of the land, nor of encouraging the non-economic work that should be done as part of a single entry to reduce fuel loadings, reduce soil erosion and sediment transport, and facilitate site recovery. A different sales device, such as an end-results contract, may be useful in some cases to change the incentives and harness incentives so that better results are realized. Legislation to authorize such a new contracting tool was considered in the last Congress, and we would encourage you to return to that topic.

There's a lot of frustration over the slow pace of Forest Service planning and implementation of salvage sale projects. Much of that frustration is misdirected, in my view. The agency's latitude to speed up the process is limited by law and regulation, and the authority of the field force to speed things up because of heavy political pressure is just about nil. Every National Forest Supervisor is caught between two irresistible forces: the local industry and people wanting to get some value from a burned forest before it is lost, and people and organizations who will appeal every plan and/or file a lawsuit to halt any action. I have talked to several Supervisors who received specific phone calls while their 1994 wildfires were still burning, warning them that any salvage proposal at all would be immediately attacked legally. Most of those have moved ahead with project plans, but the need to make them lawyer-proof adds enormously to the time and cost involved.

If the Congress feels the pace needs speeded up, it will have to change the laws that create the basis for the process that must be followed today. Those changes, done responsibly so that they do not simply open the door to widespread abuse and damage in the federal forests, are not going to be easily crafted, nor enacted without great political controversy. We have not, to be candid, identified any way to restrict citizen's access to public decisions that does not trample constitutional and legal rights. You may be able to craft a way, but it won't be easy.

Let me switch now to the topic of forest health. Advocates of timber salvage paint salvage as the first step in restoring forests. The answer to that is: Sometimes, and If. If the site is such that emergency protection and restoration is needed, and if products can be removed in a way that does not further destroy topsoils that are already damaged and weakened, and if the work is done with appropriate design and care, considerable timber can be salvaged as part of the package. Where people get concerned is when the talk focuses completely on the timber to be salvaged, and not the land treatment package that is to be achieved. When that happens, there are too many examples of salvage projects that set back forest restoration and health. Regardless of your views on the current situation, I think we must agree that grabbing quick profits at the expense of long-term soil integrity and forest health is not responsible stewardship. No responsible private owner does that, and no responsible public official should allow it to happen on public lands.

There has been a great deal of work in Congress to develop forest health legislation which is aimed at the real forest health challenge -- treating sick forests before they are damaged by intense wildfires. For those who have not done so, I commend your attention to the bills that were considered in the last two sessions of Congress. In particular, it is helpful to review the testimony received by the House Agriculture Committee in two Idaho field hearings -- in Coeur d' Alene in 1992 and in Boise in 1993. That legislative work, along with a great deal of scientific study with which we are familiar, has pointed clearly to a problem that needs Congressional attention.

The basic problem is that laws and regulations built up over the years, along with the budget decisions of past Congresses, have created a situation in which federal forest agencies cannot properly cope with changing forest conditions in the Inland West. Granted, there are forest health problems elsewhere in the country that suffer from the same lack of adaptive management ability, but the particular circumstances in the Inland West are such that the problems are most acute in that region today.

I won't go into the scientific background on that situation, but assure you that anyone interested in the subject can find plenty of reading to do. We have attached a partial list of further reading references to the back of this testimony. There are, I can assure you, more studies that emerge almost daily.

In our work with forest health legislation, we arrived at the position that, since the time, cost and delay in the federal management process is the problem, then legislation needs to find a way to cut through that. Again, that raises enormous political opposition, particularly from groups who fought for the laws and processes currently in place and do not want to see any of them weakened. In the face of that opposition, the method proposed was one where certain areas would be identified as high-risk, emergency areas, and designated as such. Within those areas, new authorities would allow faster and more flexible plan development, a pooling of available federal funds so as to allow local adaptation of available funds to the work that needed done, and an increased authority for multiple-year, end-results contracting as an added administrative tool.

The goal of the legislation was to create test areas within which "emergency room" forestry could replace the clearly-inadequate response pace of "business-as-usual" federal forestry. The approach was supported by professional foresters and industry, eager to demonstrate that they could, through good management, improve the health of forests, reduce wildfire risks, and create conditions that are better both from an environmental and an economic point of view. Opposition to the idea has been fierce, however, and while the legislation has not yet been enacted, a bill containing many of these same concepts has been introduced in the Senate by Senator Larry Craig of Idaho. We hope the House Natural Resources Committee will take up the subject soon, as well.

The bottom line is that the current situation is deplorable. In 1994, almost 4 million acres -- nearly all federal land -- was hit by wildfire. We spent around $1 billion and lost over 30 lives, to achieve horrible results on the land. Few of those fires could have been prevented by forest health projects, but some could have been made far less destructive. For every acre that experienced destructive wildfire in 1994, there are probably 5 or more that remain at high risk. Whether they burn in 1995 or 1996 is a matter of chance, weather, and other unforeseeable circumstances. But they will burn, and with the fuel loads present in many places, they will burn at destructive heat intensities. And they will cost the taxpayers billions. All of that is not conjecture -- it is a certainty.

What we urge you today is to get beyond the fight over black logs on blackened landscapes, and focus your policy attention toward the green landscapes that need treatment if they are not to suffer the same fate. The science is in place, the legislative record is a rich one, and this Congress should take constructive policy action as rapidly as possible.

For Further Reading

Agee, James K. *Fire Ecology of Pacific Northwest Forests*, Washington:Island Press, 1993, 493 pp.

American Forests, *Results from a Nationwide Survey on Forest Management*, Washington:American Forests, 1994, 9 pp. (Data summaries also available).

Monnig, Edward and James Byler, *Forest Health and Ecological Integrity in the Northern*

Rockies, FPM Report 92-7, USDA Forest Service, Northern Region, Missoula, MT, 1992, 18 pp.

Mutch, Robert W., S.F. Arno, J.K. Brown, C.E. Carlson, R.D. Ottmar and J.L. Peterson, *Forest Health in the Blue Mountains: A Management Strategy for Fire-Adapted Ecosystems,* PNW-GTR-310, USDA Forest Service PNW Research Station, Portland, OR, 1993, 14 pp.

National Commission on Wildfire Disasters, *Report of the National Commission on Wildfire Disasters,* Washington:American Forests, 1994, 30 pp.

Sacramento Bee, *Feeding the Flames* (Reprint of a multi-part special report published Nov. 27-Dec 1, 1994) Copies available from American Forests, Washington, DC.

Sampson, R. Neil and David L. Adams (eds.), *Assessing Forest Ecosystem Health in the Inland West,* Papers from the American Forests Workshop November 14-20, 1993, Sun Valley, Idaho, New York:Food Products Press, 1994, 460 pp. (Also available as *Journal of Sustainable Forestry*, Volume 2, Numbers 1/2/3/4, 1994.)

US Department of Agriculture, *Eastside Forest Ecosystem Health Assessment,* Vols 1-5, USDA Forest Service, Pacific Northwest Region, Portland, OR, 1993, 1,500 pp.

US Department of Agriculture, *Western Forest Health Initiative*, USDA Forest Service, State and Private Forestry, Washington, DC, 1994, 65 pp.

Dr. Arthur D. Partridge, Professor, Forest Disease and Insect Problems, Univ. of Idaho, and President TREAZ, Inc, Consultants, Moscow, Idaho 83843. B.S. Forestry, Univ of Maine; M.S & Ph.D. Plant Pathology, Univ. of New Hampshire.

Dr. Catherine L. Bertagnolli, Research Scientist, TREAZ, Inc., B.S. Forestry, Utah State Univ., M.S. & Ph.D., Forest Science (Pathology), Univ. of Idaho

Recently, much of which has been said and written about forest health is unsubstantiated by scientific data. Inventories and surveys are not scientific studies. The phrase "forest health," first used by a Canadian named Faull in 1930 (2.), to describe the status of disease and insect activities in forest trees, now is altered to include his idea plus everything from stand density to fuel loads, ignoring or minimizing hydrology, fisheries, wildlife, soils or positive effects of diseases and insects. It diminishes the role of past management in causing forest problems and focuses on timber production. And the resulting debate focuses on individual aspects of the issues thus exposed so that the essence is demeaned. The term itself, as employed by the major forest agencies, is impossible to define, perhaps to obscure the purposes for its resurrection. Our presentation is limited to the original "forest health."

Our brief is based on 30 years of scientific research data regarding forest diseases, forest insects and their ecosystem interactions in the Inland Pacific Northwest. During this time, we assembled and continue to assemble data from scientifically designed multiple studies that apply measurements to diseases, insects and their activities during time. We employed several procedures utilizing temporary plots and permanent, continuously monitored plots, both randomly selected and specifically selected for the presence of problems. Permanent, destructively sampled plots, confirmed by laboratory processing, temporary strip-transect plots. random and permanent overview monitoring plots, and both flyovers and visits to "problem areas" to evaluate disease and insect activities were included. Data are direct measurements or frequency statements for all vegetation, insects, diseases, etc. Records include data and drawings on multiple field cards for each plot, correlated photographs, diaries, executive check sheets, duplicate blinds for field data, transect sheets, observational notes, and audio tapes. We also critically examined the originals of agency inventory data. Analyses include chi-square associations, regression and curvilinear representations of periodic data, ordination, graphic comparisons and tabularizations.

PRESENTLY

During 1993, in the Inland Northwest, including Idaho, Montana, Oregon, Washington and Wyoming, we evaluated the conditions of 130,000 forest trees in more than 60 widespread areas. Data were assembled by experienced professional pathologists on-site and are not estimates or opinions but are summaries of measurements. These forests, currently have less than 2 clearly symptomatic trees per thousand live trees. Specifically, 0.76% of our trees are now recently killed or dying and this is not cumulative during time as described by some prognoses. As trees die, they are replaced by others. In our area, there are many more trees with symptoms of one kind or another that are not in danger of immediate mortality. In fact, many symptomatic trees live for decades or even reach old age. "Symptomatic" does not mean dying. When we measured trees on areas designated by managing agencies as "diseased," we found 15 trees per 1000 either sick or dead. That is, 1.5 % of the trees in "diseased" areas are now sick or dead. If we exclude dead trees as being indicators of past activity only, we find sick trees comprise 0.8-0.09% of those in diseased areas. Late symptomatics, easily seen and soon to die, average 0.18% of the population. Early symptomatics comprise 0.22% of the population. When we count symptomatic and dead trees at random on a forest-wide basis, we find less than 1% of the standing trees are "diseased" or "insect infested."

But none of these figures tell about the nature of the disease or insect problem in each area. We find not all diseases, particularly the often cited root diseases, are the same in either activity or progression during time. In many root diseased areas, the current level of symptomatic trees is zero, meaning the disease is not active. Thus, among 7 major root disease systems and 5 concurrent bark beetle problems in our area, one disease system, caused by Phaeolus schweinitzii, was actively killing trees and one bark beetle, Dendroctonus ponderosae, population was actively killing trees, both in very localized areas. Simply stated, we found 1 % of our plots had active root disease, 1 % had active bark beetles and 3 % had active defoliators at work. Separately, we found blister rust killing almost 10 % of the white pine trees we encountered. Loss of this magnitude is more than overcome by reproduction and increased growth in released nearby trees. Our 1994 data, yet to be thoroughly analyzed, are similar.

In general, our tests show that, during the last 4 years, we detected the lowest levels of disease and insect activity in 28 years. Diseases and insects are in balance in overall forest systems. Indeed, there are differences in activity from one place to another and, in some rare specific localities with bark beetle activity, tree mortality reached 400/1000. But when we looked at random samples of whole forest areas, instead of "problem areas," the picture changed. Then, 2% of all trees showed symptoms of imminent or recent damage including bark beetle and defoliator damage not designated as being in "problem areas." And 0.2% of the entire tree population is soon to die. These figures do not imply forests are in peril. On the contrary, when we review records of root disease activity, we find 12 trees per 100 clearly symptomatic in the years 1972-1974, a decline until 1980-1982 when 8 per 100 were symptomatic and another decline until now when less than 1 % are actively symptomatic.

In order to demonstrate trends in disease activity, we use the condition and progress of root diseases in the Northwest. These have been deemed a major problem in management. In this, and other examples, forest disease (health) is irruptively cyclic, like most biological phenomena, but the cycles do not imply doom . These records include comparative counts of diseased and healthy trees of all ages, not just "timber," along with confirmed problem diagnoses and notes of biological interactions for all forests, public and private in the Inland Northwestern United States.

Note that, on dry sites, peak periods are longer than those on mesic sites and are not depicted by the graph which includes only the mesic root-disease types emphasized in inventories. On the dry sites, periodic peaks can occur at intervals as long as 300 years. This is further conditioned by the fact that, on dry sites with spring rain, the long-term, slow-acting fungi, like Phaeolus schweinitzii, often affect young trees as well as mature ones, sometimes hindering restocking by removing seedling and pole-sized trees. Root-disease activity is not easily depicted by a single graph, but the general trend is well demonstrated above.

As you look at the cycling of root disease, notice the high levels experienced in 1972-1974. These were recognized by managing agencies at the time, but ignored until now. No emergency was declared then, but now we have declarations of and attempts at "emergency sales." When we recently visited emergency-sale areas, the mortality and late-symptomatic rates were far less than 1% of the standing timber. And, commonly we recorded high levels of recovery on these same diseased sites. After we reported this, many sales were "put on hold" because of admissions that the forest was too healthy for an emergency. And a recent document supports our assessment of forests conditions. "America's forests: 1994 Health Update. (13.), states; "Update, shows that, overall, the condition of our forests has improved significantly over the past 70 years. There have been some recent changes in tree growth and tree mortality trends, however, that bear close watching." The forest health "emergency," used in sponsoring 1992 salvage legislation seems to have disappeared and the "ecological collapse" pronounced only 3 years ago and that we publicly challenged (8.) also seems to have faded.

SOME POSITIVE EFFECTS OF DISEASES AND INSECTS

Ecology has long recognized disease and insect activities as part of the ecosystem. We emphasize only one group, root diseases, as examples in this brief. Let us, then, cite some influences or positive effects of root-disease and associated organisms in forest ecosystems, effects that if recognized can be used to improve our forests. These include:

A. Small openings in the forest canopy, created by tree death, that capture and hold winter snow, releasing it slowly because of shaded margins. This contrasts with the flooding from "rain-on snow-events" common on large openings created by seed-tree, shelterwood and clearcut systems. The same small openings are prime berry-growing areas because they retain moisture and they modify wind currents by offering an irregular profile instead of a uniform plane to the flow of air.

B. Dead trees in diseased areas which provide nest sites for woodpeckers that, in-turn, are principal native, and thoroughly adapted, agents of bark beetle control. The same trees are nesting, cache, den and shelter sites for small birds owls, squirrels, chipmunks and other wildlife and open perches for rodent-controlling raptors.

C. Dead stems on the forest floor that are "mother trees" for new forest life including trees, lichens, mosses, myriad arthropods and fungi that modify, build and improve soils. The arthropods and lichens build soils and return nitrogen to the system. This fascinating and essential microsystem is unrecognized in any study of "forest health" recently written. This and other wood on the forest floor is much more than "fuel loading." It is an essential mat for watershed development and maintenance.

D. Shrubs and small trees in the diseased areas that are winter browse and thermal protection for more forest inhabitants which are also essential forest parts. Some control insects, others are essential for seed dissemination, rodents are held in check by others and the ecological effect of all is enormous.

E. The peripheries of disease openings that provide needed "edge effects" for wildlife welfare and assure diversity. Without the "edge effect," wild game is sparse or absent.

F. The diseases and insects that remove the old, weak and unsuitable trees from a stand leaving the next generation stronger than if they did not act. This is a natural process to be nurtured not combatted.

G. The diseases and insects that return biomass to the forest system, a vital ecosystem need if long-term system balance is to be maintained. Wood-mining, continuously removing fiber without replacing its components, does not do this.

H. Some diseases and insects that play roles in ecosystems that are similar to fire: culling, thinning, removals and recycling. These roles are instrumental to successional prosperity. They are ancillary to fire in many of our forests.

I. Many insects and the fungi that cause disease are vital sources of food for birds and mammals. Armillaria spp. are preferred by humans and many wildlife and some have commercial value. Mushrooms also have therapeutic values for forest inhabitants.

J. Fungi like Perenniporia subacida that are important soil and duff modifiers playing an active role in absorbing and holding moisture. Clearcuts rarely have any operative P. subacida.

K. Root-rot fungi that:
a. assure genetic improvement by natural selection
b. return the weak and sick to the forest system in forms that other life forms use
c. create an optimal environment in rooted wood for organisms like carpenter ants that in turn aid in controlling forest pests
d. precipitate stress crops of seeds to assure reproduction following death
e. help protect soil around roots and stumps from rain impacts

f. hold water during periods of runoff. The fungi and their decays tend to be sponges. These become essential during droughts
g. help manufacture soil particles by chemical and physical activities thus providing ecosystems for subsurface organisms
h. enhance soil-particle coherence and structure to improve gas and water movement
i. make the irregular and different habitat patterns essential to wildlife and plant diversity including higher and lower life forms, all of which are active participants in dynamic ecosystem functioning
j. rot wood so that we can walk through the woods.

L. Associated bark beetles that:
a. carry stain and decay fungi assuring and accelerating biomass return to the system
b. are food sources for birds which then stop population explosions of insects
c. along with myriad other forest arthropods, are sources of nitrogen, which they capture and release for forest systems.

Positive effects are created by many other forest diseases or insects. A few include: budworms that not only remove the weak and suppressed trees but protect others in droughty times by reducing foliar water loss. Mountain pine beetle both releases understory trees and expedites the next seral stage of tree succession. Dwarf mistletoe brooms provide hiding cover for a number of birds and mammals plus nesting, loafing, and reproductive opportunities and in douglas fir cause little increment reduction until the entire tree is involved. Perception of, or sensitivity to, these benefits will become essential educational components of future forestry curricula.

None of these, or similar, effects are recognized in any statements or documents arising from the current forest health crusade, nor are multiple environmental characteristics and ecosystem cycles. How much do these positive effects contribute ? If the managing agencies have defined how much timber is destroyed, they certainly can evaluate disease and insect contributions and balance statements about "forest health." They must before we and the public will believe in their "ecosystem management" campaign !

The living forest is dynamic, cyclic, and periodic; including its component wildlife, plants, trees and disease and insects. It was 30 years ago, using this general hypothesis, that we began recording disease and insect happenings. The process involved the long-term, scientific tests reported earlier in this text. The results show some trends.

Using root disease in forest trees as a prominent example, we recorded peak symptoms of imminent death, reaching 120/1000 in 1972-1974 and another peak of 80/1000 in 1980-1982. Between these peaks , we had lows of 2/1000 in 1977 and 1993-1994. This periodicity is both non-linear and irruptive with multiple irruptive peaks. The death, caused by disease also is periodic and not steadily increasing or cumulative as erroneously portrayed in some statements.

89-215 O - 95 - 7

The trend, during time, has been towards stability. Periodicity is a normal and natural sequence of activity common to many living forest components. We expect it in animal species, in plant development and in tree growth but why not in disease and insect activity?

Also emphasized is the "spread" or potential for spread of diseases, meaning the disease moves from place to place, and this is substantially incorrect for pathogens which are natural forest components. Fungus spores may disperse but the disease does not. Endemic diseases are cyclic but rarely do they spread. Some introduced pathogens are exceptions, but even then recovery and resilience of host populations and the ecosystems overcome the invasions Expansion, not spread, of root- diseased areas is non-linear over time and, in some fungal complexes, highly irruptive. The causal fungi mostly are inherent system components Colonies with complexes dominated by the fungi Phellinus weirii, Armillaria ostoyae, or Perenniporia subacida tend to cause progressive tree mortality related to age. In such systems, tree death seemingly moves outward at maximum of 24 acres per year and a minimum of 0 acres per year but typically is irruptive for a period and lays dormant for a longer period. Those dominated by Phaeolus schweinitzii, Inonotus tomentosus, or Coniophora puteana tend to erupt suddenly in mature or overmature stands, suddenly killing many trees over large acreages. We recorded 250 acres of such activity in 300-year-old Douglas fir during 2 years, but no activity has occurred in the same area for 18 ensuing years. Because these endemic root diseases do not spread and because their causal fungi are ever-present and cosmopolitan and their activities do not follow linear progressions, it becomes essential that we relate specific causal complexes, site related characteristics and irruptive cycling to any predictions or prognoses. Data which do not include properly diagnosed complexes and ignore periodicity are useless for accurate projections. Currently, management lumps root diseases together and treats them as a singular entity progressing linearly over time (3. et al).

The more serious problems, moreover exist in areas high-graded and repeatedly disturbed by wood-mining activities, common practices in our forests. High-grading removed the best trees, genetically superior and adapted stock, and allowed unchallenged invasion by weaker species and individuals so that ever-present pathogens, natural regulators of balanced stands, took over without natural restrictions. Repeated entries into stands left soil and soil mycosystem changes that stress the ecosystem . Soil destruction and water-table disturbance by road building, improper skidding, pile burning and even chemical dumping seriously modified vegetation. The outcome is a long-term stress. And in some but not all localities, fire suppression compounded the problem. We record the most recent root-disease activity on these "managed" sites, while recovery was common on less disturbed sites.

RECOVERY

Damage is undeniably is caused by insects and disease, but if we subtract from the damage figures, the added reproduction, regrowth of released trees and natural conversions to resistant species and resistant individuals, the picture is one of recovery during time, not of severe health problems. Losses of individuals are offset by site recovery expressed as released growth activity and potential, by reproduction opportunities realized, by soil improvements as root-rot fungi return biomass rapidly, by improved mycorrhizal symbioses and by selective stocking improvement. Why is it that a balance of loss against recovery is omitted from recent documents (6.,10.,11.) portraying declining forest health? In relation to recovery, our records show natural conversions, although often slow, occur regularly. For example, many of the mature larch stands in our area are traced to areas with long standing Phellinus weirii complexes. The historic presence of white-pine-dominated stands also can be related to this complex.

Recovery, common in stands depleted by diseases or insects, is recorded in several modes.

1. Not all "symptomatic" trees die in the near future, and some survive to maturity. Symptomatic trees may take many decades to die and some reach maturity. In other cases non-symptomatic trees may suddenly succumb to root disease. In general, mature trees do not succumb until approximately 80& of the major roots have been killed. In seedlings, 15% root mortality may cause crown symptoms to develop and 30 % root mortality causes death of douglas fir and ponderosa pine seedlings.

2. Individual trees of "susceptible species" survive for decades and even for a century or more in some disease zones without ever showing symptoms. We have recorded douglas fir trees, 96-125 yrs old, in stands where Phellinus weirii was killing grand fir and rotting stumps for 30 years. Many younger survivor individuals are also prominent in some of these same root-diseased stands. We also have recorded 200-year old douglas fir in mesic-type stands declining from Phaeolus schweinitzii, and up to 400 years old in dry-site stands. Ponderosa pine have been found resisting the fungus, although present in the trees, for 300 years.

3. Mycosystem balance develops during time in root disease zones, both by development of competitive fungal colonies and by biomass return and subsequent live soil component improvements.

4. Natural conversions to site-adapted (disease-resistant, if you prefer) species and individuals are natural, but long-term, phenomena. They are normal parts of stand history. The conversion will depend on the various microorganism present, rainfall periodicity, and unknown variants. Some of these conversions, occurring naturally, but usually unrecorded because of their gradual nature are:

A. Reseeding by white pine in areas influenced strongly by Phellinus weirii. Our records show white pine up to 35 years old in such areas generally outgrowing other species in time. Six to 10 percent of these pines show symptoms of blister rust, but during time, this becomes a smaller number as the susceptible individuals drop out of the population. Twenty-five years ago 60% of the white pine were infected These data will not emerge from short term measurements on single-site measurements.

B. Removal of grand fir and douglas fir leaving larch on sites dominated by Phellinus weirii. The larch also are removed eventually, leaving pines including white, lodgepole or ponderosa depending on which is present locally. This process takes several decades to become apparent. In some cases the larch will not succumb and may remain as permanent feature. Almost pure stands generated in this away are apparent in Montana and Northern Idaho.

C. Replacement by ponderosa pine or lodgepole pine on sites with douglas fir with Phaeolus schweinitzii or Inonotus tomentosus as major biosystem components.

D. Conversions to lodgepole pine in areas with Inonotus tomentosus in spruce and subalpine fir.

E. Long-term, centuries, conversion to douglas fir in high-elevation stands with Coniophora puteana as a principal fungus invading spruce, lodgepole pine, and subalpine fir.

The consequence of such trends suggests beneficial manipulations, but these must be taken with care to examine other ecological consequences. For example, many western larch stands exist because susceptible trees were eliminated by specific disease groups and the presence of the larch suggests managing against the lost species, but the developed monoculture is apt to be an easy target for unrecognized agents. And it is possible that conversion to douglas fir in Coniophora puteana areas might be possible, but its advisability must be examined in the light of the potential loss of consequent nesting, caching and hiding benefits for wildlife or by other unweighed environmental considerations. A preference for white pine in areas dominated by Phellinus weirii might result in decimation by an unrecognized colony of Heterobasidion annosum. Nonetheless, stand manipulations can be related to the potentials for natural recovery and conversion.

It's also important to point out that diseases and insects follow a progression of stages analogous to the seral stages recognized in the ecology of higher plants except that they usually have more rapid in successional stages. i.e. years or decades instead of centuries or millennia. Properly defining and recognizing these stages is critical to manipulating the ecosystem or following it carefully and gently.

Our recovery data reflect these stages and suggest improving root-diseased areas by favoring superior natural reproduction, while interplanting with stock from local seed, to enhance the natural processes. Further disturbance in the form of "salvage" or other heavy activity is going to stress the remaining trees, further modify soil structure, remove wildlife habitats, add to water-quality problems and reverse recovery trends. Ignorance of this has led to forest problems that are less with disease and insects than they are with deteriorating soils, poor water quality, destroyed fisheries, reduced wildlife populations, reduced recreational opportunities, eliminated opportunities for future logging and general public disfavor.

In general our data imply a strong need to promote natural recovery rather than additional agitation.

These findings also emphasize a need to drastically improve procedures used in defining root disease. Disease areas should be mapped carefully using highly-trained professional expertise to examine and define all potential and actual pathogens on each site. Progressional records must become part of the inventory of such areas. But, most importantly, a sense of ecosystem dynamics, rather than impending damage needs to pervade the management philosophy. And we need others to examine the term "forest health" critically and to provide, instead of distortions and buzzwords, facts that we can use honestly and correctly.

"FOREST HEALTH" DATA BASES

Be aware that disease reports often are distorted in assessing current forest conditions. Dead trees are included in estimates so that each problem assumes a more prominent status than it should, and any tree with a rounded crown or thin top or yellowing foliage can be counted as symptomatic even though it may not die for decades if at all. Intended or not, this sort of distortion can be used to justify anything - more dollars, emergency stand entries, salvage, burning or any preordained "management objective" (1.). The, now popular, concentration on managing for root disease has precipitated activities not born out by disease histories. And even though root disease has declined in intensity during the last 10 or more years, and even though it was rarely diagnosed in inventories prior to the 1980s, and even though it peaks periodically, and even though is has been far more destructive in the past than it is now we find a sudden concentration on it as a manufactured justification to salvage. We need to embrace the fact that the causes, fungi and insects, mostly are normal parts of ecosystems subject to intelligent management but not to emergency declarations. Crash programs of the past have not worked to control any major forest problem.

The same inventory "data" now being used by the Forest Service to convince us we have severe disease and insect problems previously was used to convince us we had ample timber. Thus, was conceived the "phantom timber" (4.,5.,9.) of northern Idaho. Now we have phantom disease and it comes from the same sources.

Inventories were set up to deliver information about available timber, not to measure disease or insect activity during time, and records of this type are not part of the inventory output although the impression is given that these data are included. Inventories employ estimates of disease. They do not measure disease or insect damage or activity. Root disease severity is estimated from aerial observations of stand openings and the number of dead trees dead and dying trees with minimal ground-truthing. Disease is rated as low to severe with number from 1 to 4. They measure little or nothing. There are no counts or measurements relative to normal stands or trees. These are not measurements like those used to describe timber volume on the same sites. And the estimates include dead trees that often have been dead for decades and do not represent current mortality. Likewise, defoliation, which may be a partial or complete loss of foliage, is presented as "defoliated acres" with no indication of defoliation intensity or of the density of trees on the "defoliated acres."

Inventories are filled with errors of misdiagnosis by personnel minimally acquainted with disease or insect problems. Often these use seasonal personnel with one or two days' training in problem recognition. I even find "silviculturists" who graduated without a single professional course in pathology or entomology and it shows in their prescriptions. They do not recognize problems. We have, in the past 5 years, recorded more than 80% misdiagnoses on sale areas throughout the Northwest (7).

"Forest health" surveys, also are noted for their less frequent but ever-present misdiagnoses caused by emphases on the dramatic problems. As a consequence, they develop broad loss statements, e.g. acres of damage, board-foot loss, forests in jeopardy (3.,6.,10.,11.) but omit or forget to tell "of what?" Are these fully stocked stands, reproduction, poles, densely overstocked areas and how many trees of what size are lost, and not just attacked or discolored but killed? Many trees survive attacks. Particularly, what's the current status of each outbreak? Is this active and building, cresting, peaking and declining, or inactive? Important information, especially for the undiminished truth!

Most importantly, no information is provided regarding recovery from disease or insect attacks in any reports or statements. Without this information, "ecosystem management" is impossible.

All of this tells us that the "forest health crisis" is another paper tiger based on distortions of weak and error-filled information. There is no emergency. The whole constitutes a two-pronged crusade aimed at:

A. initiating open-ended salvage strategies. These would enable removing "dead and dying trees" which excludes little and permits cutting of almost anything depending only on the eye of the manager.

B. destroying or disabling the appeals process thus removing another democratic lever to assure the people's voice be heard.

I also call your attention to the scare-word technique; "emergency," "crisis," "imminent disaster" - used to describe disease and insect activities known to exist and ignored for decades and used at a time when scientific research shows these activities to be at a 30-year low. And even when one of their own recent brochures (13.) says " .. the condition of our forests has improved significantly over the past 70 years...."

Below, we compare the results of our summarized studies during 30 years on forests in the same areas as those covered by the inventories

And don't forget that the current forest health crusade is built on "inventories," relying on reports created from internal agency documents with little information contrary to the emergency theme. It professes statements of forest loss and mortality that are both inflated and distorted with only the productivity in terms of wood emphasized. Positive attributes of inherent fungi, insects, bacteria, birds, and myriad forest parts other than wood are ignored. The resilient or self-healing nature of forest ecosystems likewise is disregarded.

There is little argument that fisheries, watersheds and some stand compositions have undergone deterioration in the past, but there is also, conspicuously, little evidence that most disease and insect activities have changed during time. In fact, some show in fossil records for our area. They remain periodic entities, causing localized impacts at many points in time and occasional showy outbreaks that fade with time as a result of the natural resilience native to our forest biosystems. A few exotic problems like white pine blister rust and chestnut blight wreaked havoc, but even blister rust has settled into the role of occasional destroyer with an ever-evolving more resistant host population. There are insect populations that have reached similar stabilities including those of larch casebearer and spruce budworm. Without "management" interventions, these have established equipoise with their natural bird, predatory insect, virus and bacterial adversaries. This natural stability, well known to ecologists, functions to recover damage and restore normality within a range of variability over time. This RECOVERY phenomenon, you will note, is ignored by the doomsday camp of forest health practitioners. The word is subjugated or never used because recovery data (+)combined with loss data (-) will blunt the "salvage" thrust. RECOVERY, the marvelous nature of all biotic systems including most living things, forests and you!. All have built-in powers of reconstruction - thank goodness! Rejuvenation is equally as important in describing forest health as is enumeration of the number of acres or trees or affected by diseases or insects.

And so, our focus has been and will be on the biological health of forests, including the vegetation, animals, and living earth. Yes, "living earth!" One of the prime reasons why trees and vegetation are healthy or not - a healthy living earth. This is, perhaps, the most heavily impacted and most ignored aspect of our forest components. Every entry into a forest impacts the earth and some kinds of entry destroy it, particularly heavy-handed road building, careless logging and poorly controlled burning. This demands special attention because earth is the least resilient forest component, taking centuries to heal after abuse. Where are the "inventory" and "survey" data that tell us about forest soil health. Maybe we can extrapolate from information about water quality in part to express physical changes, but no data tell us about biological deterioration or recovery rates in our soils. We do know that repeated entries cause declines in wood productivity that can be related to changed physical soil attributes, and we can surmise that the extirpation of beneficial organisms like mycorrhizae in openings is likewise partly responsible for the event. But we foresters have totally excluded the prime substates from forest measurements.

Related to this, lets examine forest measurements and their contents, accuracy, frequency, and reliability. A prominent forester once asked "what's wrong with using seasonal help to do inventories." Well, because seasonally employed individuals may or may not have some forestry education or experience and often undergo as little as one days' training for disease and insect recognition prior to field work. Most have no demonstrated diagnostic capability. This is a big part of why inventories are unreliable. But look a little further at the inventory form and the codes used to enter data. Major disease and insect problems often do not appear on the code sheets, making it impossible for field personnel to record them Only "prominent problems" are included, or should that be "showy problems." And nothing about RECOVERY is included on any inventory form. Not only are inventories inaccurate, they are biased toward recording only damage and destruction. There, also, is no way to record interactional functions of the forest system. Each problem appears alone. A root disease/bark beetle interaction, common in our forests goes unnoticed or worse is recorded as two separate problems. The latter, recording two problems instead of a single interaction, results in reporting inflated numbers of both problems. If there weren't so many faults with the system, we might call this accidental, but with the faults and the need to convince funders of the enormity of problems, this seems deliberate.

And the faults don't stop here. Progressional information, that outlines the progress of a forest problem during time, as might be obtained by periodic visitations to specific sites does not exist in inventory figures and is rare in survey figures. In no case is progressional data assembled systematically on a scientific basis for decades. The public has been led to believe that progressional statistics outlining disease and insect progress has been assembled when this is not the case.

And it continues. I have personally interviewed dozens of returning college students after they worked on inventory crews. Many report superiors who discount, modify, change or distort their diagnoses, even though the student had college level training and the superior did not. Not many "professional foresters" now come equipped with college level diagnostic training and many have never taken even a basic course in entomology or pathology. My interviews tell me this distortion is not an uncommon practice.

Inventories usually also don't adequately correlate causes with the species affected which means, if management is associated with the system involved, serious errors will result.. For example, Annosus root rot in true fir would dictate entirely different regeneration systems than would the same disease in pine and ignoring this would result in regeneration failure..

How do we know all about inventories? Because, under the Freedom of

Information Act, we have examined them first hand, and because, when in the Forest Service, we worked with them in the field. And with all this background in mind, we studied original stand history figures and silvicultural prescriptions from 5 forests in the Inland Northwest including a total of 3000 plots. We studied their information at a time when EIS (Environmental Impact Statement) documents were calling root disease "severe."

To test out methods against those currently in use we have examined and analyzed data from other agencies. As an example on one forest we analyzed 1600 stand histories for their contents and accuracies and did our own, independent , on-site assessments of these data without the data being first examined.. First, the forest had pronounced annual cumulative and continuing and projected losses from root disease to be 4% per year. No periodicity, no recovery, no conversions, no regrowth, no site improvement or deterioration. An EIS (3.) said 60% of the stands have "severe root disease" The stand histories used to develop this EIS recorded 17 % of the plots had root disease with no designated cause, 59 % of the plots had little or no root disease, and only 24 % of the plots had severe root disease. Recording root disease present is much like saying trees are present. It tells nothing about problem causes, forest conditions or disease progress. This led us to look at the plots, directly on the ground, where we transected each area, and 83% of the diagnoses grossly incorrect, mainly because similar diseases were not recognized or differentiated from those present. Part of this was because the code sheets for the inventories lack provision to record 5 root disease systems common to the area, meaning that it was impossible for field personnel to record some even if they could recognize them. More can be attributed to improperly trained or even untrained field personnel

Table 1. A field analysis of root disease diagnosis on 860 inventory plots.

DIAGNOSIS	NO OF PLOTS	NOT DIAGNOSED OR MISDIAGNOSED	CAUSE
ROOT DISEASE	266	17%	NONE
FUNGUS A	722	81%	Armillaria
FUNGUS B	582	40%	P. weirii
FUNGUS C	38	60%	P.schweinitzii
FUNGUS D	0	!00%	H. annosum
FUNGUS E	0	100%	P. subacida
FUNGUS F	0	100%	I. tomentosus

* numbers in this table will not add as expected, because some areas had multiple root-disease fungi

Incorrect or incomplete diagnosis of causes, as illustrated here, means improper management procedures will be implemented, particularly planting. You can't recommend resistant species when you don't know what organisms are present.

We also found the inventories 53% inaccurate in problem evaluation. That is, the forest health problems reported as bad and worsening are not only inaccurately portrayed by the information used but were greatly inflated. Using the same inventories and Forest Service severity ratings for root disease, as an example, we found the average severity, from their data, to be "1." Severe, according to their rating is "4." Even their own data contradict the statements of "severe root disease" issued to the press in 1989 (12.).

• Remember too that the evaluations of problems, in "inventories" or "surveys," is guesswork. Disease and insect activity is not measured. It is "estimated," using questionable criteria including stand openings, dead standing trees and "symptomatic" trees. A dead tree can stand for decades, a symptomatic tree can live for a lifetime and openings in a forest can be the results of myriad forces. Couple this with the observers' training, commonly summer help, and the result is gross inaccuracy.

The history of surveys is similar. In surveys of several national forests 46% of the trees diagnosed as having dwarf mistletoe had, instead, elytroderma witches brooms, lophodermium brooms or brooms caused by other agents. And in these records, as in others, recording only mistletoe on dead trees as the cause, ignores the possibility that another agent was the actual cause. Much mistletoe mortality has been, thusly, overstated. Combined causes rarely are recorded in either inventories or surveys.

Also remember, too, that inventories were designed, not to evaluate ecosystem components, but to measure the amount of timber available. While timber volume is accurately portrayed by these inventories, diseases and insect activities are mere afterthoughts not accurately defined. Calling such information "scientific" is a stretch of the truth.

The consequence of using such information is little more than fraudulent misrepresentation of actual forest conditions. These data contain no scientifically valid measurements or time-based trend information as implied by statements that forest health is on the decline..

The important point to be made is that we cannot accurately diagnose and then predict and recommend on landscape or watershed-wide bases. Diversity is just as common among disease and insect systems as it is among vascular plant habitat types.

It, also, is not possible to assess "forest health" anywhere when you exclude its components from your data bases. Ecosystem management means evaluating all factors contributing to the system. Yet, in management plans, the Forest Service lumps all root disease together diseases and treating them as one for management purposes. Eight major biotic systems in our forests lumped together all the same ? Why not then lump all tree species together ? Is this how we will see "ecosystems" managed ?

Also, you will find no place in Forest Service inventories or in subsequent documents where recovery of forests is included or discussed. In other words, only death and destruction are recognized. There is no way to include, recognize or evaluate the offsetting effects of healthy trends, recovery, improvement, restoration, correction or renewal in forests. These words are never used in the declarations of impending disaster, even though we hear reference to ecosystem management which certainly includes forest recovery. Is this, principally, because including active recovery would discredit the espoused "impending disaster?" Living systems all have built-in abilities to respond to attacks and often overcome adversities, but management blindly ignores these abilities. Consequently, reports of poor and declining forest health also ignore this fact and severely distort conditions as they actually exist. Part of this is because of inadvertence, but part can be attributed to the need and drive to obtain funding from the Congress. While we need to be watchful of our forest conditions, we do not need to exaggerate and distort for fear that later, if an emergency truly develops, ears will be deaf to the real need.

It's also noteworthy that the principal agency that will benefit from the "forest health" bills is the same agency providing the information used to formulate the legislation. No external, neutral review! More importantly, the proposed legislations have repeatedly attempted to circumvent or destroy the appeals process. It is only this appeals process that caused the agencies to change in the recent past. Good or bad, it is effective in a democratic society. Furthermore, the record of emergency programs, administered through the agencies is appalling.

IN THE PAST

First we had an enormous, nationwide, "Ribes eradication program for blister rust control." peaking in the 1950's and fading in 1960's. Many thousands of workers, housed in the hundreds at tent cities throughout out western forests, pulled out this alternate host for white pine blister rust. A special research station was built at Deception Creek in the Coeur d Alene National Forest for white pine research alone What is the result of all these millions of dollars spent on blister rust ? No recognizable impact on the disease in our forests.

Then, in the late 1950s and early 1960s the then division of Forest Disease and Insect Management (FIDM, now FPM) of the Forest Service promoted painting or spraying white pine with antibiotics. Actidione and Phytoactin were applied to hundreds of thousands of acres. The effect ? The chemicals hid symptoms temporarily but had no effect on the disease and actidione made many workers very ill.

In the 1950s oak wilt control was to be accomplished, in the Midwest, by cutting "buffer zones" around "disease centers;" a 50-foot clearcut surrounded each such area. The result ? The disease escaped the buffer and it was discovered that more timber was lost by cutting the buffers than the disease destroyed. Explore this if you like. A 50 foot increase in the size of a 200-foot circle adds 177% more area to the cut. Note too, that "salvage," as this is called, includes the dead material and the green wood from the buffer strip and it is sold at a fraction of the market price.

This same process has been applied to "controlling " root disease with similar findings. And let's not forget that the "thinning to improve forest health" now being promoted on television and in newspapers also can cause root disease activation and expansion. Like wise partial cuts and clearcuts do nothing to control root disease and are associated with increased damage over time.

In another scenario, lindane was sprayed on beetle-infested trees, during the mid to late 1970's, to control mountain pine beetles. The result ? The oil base, used to carry lindane, did more damage to the trees than the beetles.

The history of spraying for spruce budworm, a longstanding effort, follows a similar but more complex pattern. First begun in the eastern United States and southeastern Canada, it was found to maintain insect populations at levels higher than without the spray and over extended time periods. The periodicity of normal population dynamics was altered and damage by the insect was not controlled. Simultaneously, the spray chemicals destroyed other biotic components of the system, particularly predators and parasites, modifying the ecosystem drastically and causing numerous wildlife problems. Once the predators were thus removed, the insect populations grew virtually unrestricted and outbreaks like those in the Blue Mountains of Oregon during the 1980's and 1990's became rallying cries for the forest health crusaders. Once the spraying stopped, these forests recovered

Crash programs like these, designed to overcome an "emergency," have been extremely costly failures. None has significantly affected disease or insect problems in any forest.

Why isn't all of this recorded in the literature ? Because negative results, failures, rarely are reported and because of the attendant embarrassment.

This leads to our major concerns with "forest health emergencies." That is, the use of these statements in building new legislation. In some proposed national legislation the managing agencies are given carte blanche to "salvage dead and dying trees." In the proposals this would occur without permitting the appeal process to operate. Eliminating the appeals processs is a subject for extensive debate on its own but more importantly, the term "dying" can be interpreted to mean anything alive. Such language, in a law, will permit the continued, unrestricted tree cutting of the past. And without appeals, removing all dead trees would permit destruction of vital nesting sites for wildlife and biomass returns. We strongly believe the true purpose of the "forest health" reports is to garner support for salvage bills that protect the industry, not the environment. Even this protection will be short-lived as our remaining timber is mined and loggers no longer have a livelihood. The true problems of forest health lie in unhealthy streams and river, unhealthy wildlife populations, and disappearing fish populations, unhealthy recreational opportunities, unhealthy local economies based on timber alone, and unhealthy circumstances when harvests are done and companies move. Let's design legislation to deal with the real forest problems, not the invented ones.

No direct, scientific evidence or clear loss figures have been presented by the managing agencies to convincingly indicate a health emergency in our northwestern forests.

FOR THE FUTURE

If, indeed, overall forest condition is a real concern of the managing agencies, we expect the emphasis to shift from quota fulfillment to human and ecosystem preferences. A preference for those uses that assure a dynamic, ever improving forest, as nature does by selecting superior trees, and an emphasis on the small communities and loggers living close to each forest. A sales preference given to small, local loggers, even if its done at a dollar loss to the agency, will in the end preserve important human resources and provide a gentle means to recover selected dead trees from the scattered locations where they develop. And we who have a concern for forest treatments expect involvement at all levels on an equal basis. The logger, the mill owner, the hunter, the berry picker, the environmentalist, the wildlifer, the fisherman, water users, recreationalists. Leave any of us out of it or restrict our access to causing change, even if it's done accidentally, and be assured of conflict. Put us together on an equal basis for all uses and users and we can have both working ecosystems and sustainable forest outputs. And damn the politics of "forest health" for that's all it is!

Testimony of Dr. Arthur Partridge
Joint Hearing of House Agriculture and Resources Subcommittees
February 10, 1995
Page 18

Figures.

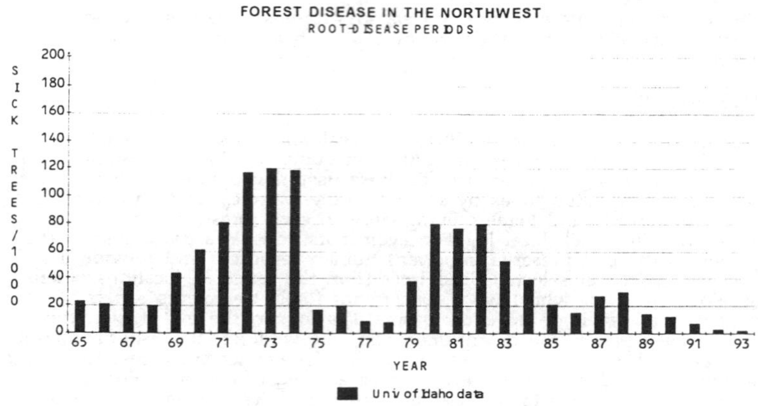

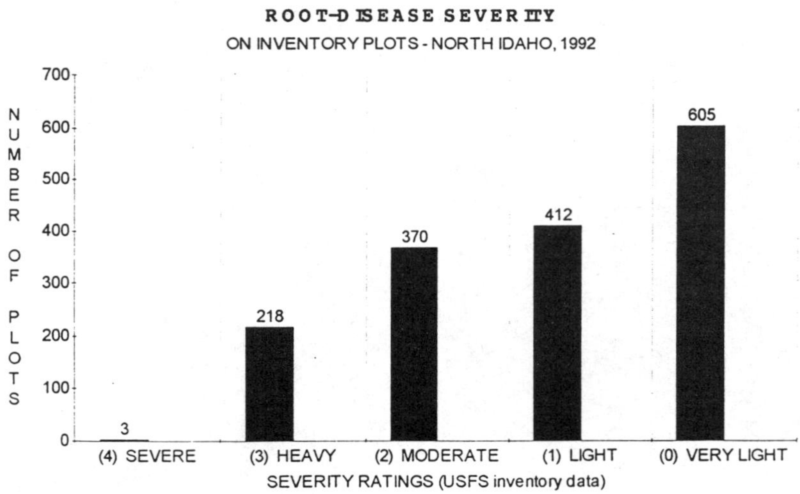

CITATIONS

1. Aplet, G. 1992. Forest health: Ecological crises or timber driven hype ? Transitions. 5 (10 & 11): 14-17.

2. Faull, J.H. 1930. The health of the forests. Illustrated Canadian Forest and Outdoors. March 1930. pp.1-4.

3. Horizon Forest Resource Area. Final Environmental Impact Statement. 1991. Idaho Panhandle National Forests, Fernan Ranger District. Coeur d' Alene, Idaho.

4. House Subcommittee on Interior Appropriations. Feb 27, 1992. Testimony. " Phantom Trees."

5. Lewiston Morning Tribune. 1992. Cruisin Truth. 21 June 1992.

6. O'Laughlin, et al. 1993. Forest health conditions in Idaho. Idaho Forest, Wildlife and Range Policy Analysis Group, Report No. 11. 244 pp.

7. Partridge, A.D. & C.L. Bertagnolli. 1992. Using root rot to justify overcutting. Transitions. 5 10&11): 48-53.

8. Partridge, A.D. & C.L. Bertagnolli.1993. Forest Health: Pathogens and pests - Engines that drive succession. Inner Voice 5, March/April 1993.

9. "Salvage" issue. 1993. Transitions. Jan & Feb, 1993.

10. Sampson, R.N. & D.L. Adams, Eds. 1993. Assessing forest ecosystem health in the Inland Northwest. The Forest Policy Center, American Forests, Wash, D.C. 101 pp.

11. Sampson, R.N. & D.L. Adams, Eds. 1994. Assessing forest ecosystem health in the Inland West. The Haworth Press, Inc., N.Y. 461pp.

12. Spokesman Review. 1989. Root Rot Invasion. June 11, 1989.

13. U. S. Dept. Agric., Forest Service. America's forests: 1944 health update. U.S. Dept. Agric., Forest Service. Agriculture Information Bulletin 696. 20 pp.

STATEMENT OF ROY GROSSEN

Mr. Chairman and Members of the Committee,

My name is Roy Grossen and I reside in Council, Idaho. I am Mayor for the City of Council and President of North West Timber Workers Resource Council. I work in a sawmill in Council which will be permanently closed down March 31, 1995. The closure will put 56 employees out of work due to the lack of available timber in a county where the total labor force is only 1,800 people. The loss of 56 jobs in our local area is devastating. Our County will lose 30% of its tax base. The local hospital and the railroad will close as the result of the shutdown of the mill where I work.

Changing economic conditions have created uncertain times in other small communities in America, but I believe the situation faced by rural communities in our region is unprecedented because it was created entirely by the failed policies and land management programs of our federal government. The Boise Cascade sawmill where I work is only one example of a series of mill closures in the inland west brought on by the shutdown of federal timber management programs in the region. Our neighbors to the north in Grangeville, Idaho lost nearly 200 jobs just two months ago when a highly efficient, modern sawmill was forced to close due to lack of timber supply. This mill, like the one where I work, is virtually surrounded by timberlands owned almost exclusively be the federal government.

In Joseph, Oregon another sawmill closed in May of last year with over 100 logging mill jobs lost. Again, this mill was surrounded by national forest lands, federal forests which were producing little or no timber sales. All of these sawmills could and should be running today. They should be in operation to provide employment opportunities and support for our rural communities. But these mills also ought to be working at full capacity to process the tremendous volumes of dead and dying and burned timber that surrounds each and every one of the communities I previously mentioned. The irony is that each of the three sawmill closures I have referred to sits next to national forest lands that have been overrun with insects and disease. Not only have these lands not been properly thinned and managed to maintain healthy timber stands, but as these forest have decayed there has been little or no action to salvage the dead and dying timber before it succumbs to rot or fire.

The bureaucratic gridlock that has stopped land managers from properly managing our region's federal forests has been brought on in large part by the avalanche of frivolous appeals by special interest groups and the impact of federal environmental laws like the Endangered Species Act. The Endangered Species Act and accompanying recovery plans for species like our region's Snake River Chinook Salmon, has been used by extremist groups to shut down the timber industry in the inland west. Although every credible analysis of Idaho's salmon populations has shown that stream habitat has little or nothing to do with the specie's decline, the Endangered Species Act has still been readily available to groups whose sole mission is to stop all logging on federal lands. These groups have not only used species like the salmon to stop the harvest of dead and dying timber, many have also publicly cheered as catastrophic fires burned up our public forests. The same people who believe that all logging is inherently bad also say that all forest fires are a benefit to nature and to our society. Their rational is not only flawed, it is cruel to those of us who depend on timber from federal lands to support our families.

The actions of these groups have been devastating to myself and my fellow workers at the mill in Council. And the forest environment is suffering as a result of their forced lock-down on public land as well. Because of under-harvest and lack of active-management, growth on the tow national forests closest to my home in Council has declined dramatically. In fact, recent studies by the U.S. Forest Service have shown that timberlands on the Payette and Boise National Forests are actually dying faster than they are growing. In other words, for each board foot of timber growing on these forests each year, 1 and 1/2 to 2 board feet is dying!

The result of such substantial decline in productivity was very predictable. Prior to the summer of 1994 a group of independent scientists under the banner of the American Forests issued a report saying that if swift action were not taken to salvage dead and dying timber on the forests in southwest Idaho, the risk of catastrophic wildfires would continue to rise.

During the past summer wildfires burned across 3.7 million acres of timberlands in the western U.S. These fires not only consumed huge tracts of dead and diseased timber on the national forests near my home, they also burned through overstocked, decaying stands in

Washington, Oregon, Montana and every other state in the west. In addition to destroying over 1 billion dollars of commercial timber value, the fires also had devastating impacts on soils, streams and wildlife habitat. An analysis of the huge fires on the Boise National Forest shows that scientists expect erosion on the burned lands to increase from 1/10 of a ton per acre to about 23 tons per acre! It will take hundreds of years to replace these lost soils, and it may take generations for streams to recover from the landslides and massive slope erosion which occurred already.

Just listen to this quote from the Boise River Wildfire Recovery Draft Environmental Impact Statement, "As a result of a light to moderate intensity storm on September 29, 1994, several acres within the Bear River, Crooked River, Rabbit Creek and Thorn Creek subwatersheds experienced severe soil erosion and subsequent sedimentation. Numerous small debris torrents/mud slides occurred. Three of these blocked the North Fork Boise River Road #327. One passed over this road and blocked two-thirds of the North Fork Boise River With a mud slide. In addition, several miles of roads had culverts plugged and numerous debris flows blocked the road surface."

The fires that burn as the result of poor land management on national forests in the west aren't economically or environmentally friendly! They destroy critical wildlife habitat, burn streamside areas so hot that they kill fish and create catastrophic erosion that clogs trout and salmon spawning streams with silt and debris. In addition to consuming at least 5 billion board feet of timber, forest fires in the western U.S. in 1994 cost taxpayers nearly a billion dollars in firefighting expenses and resulted in 26 fire fighters losing their lives.

What will happen on these burned timber lands now that the fires have been extinguished? I believe that less than 1% of the 5 billion feet of burned timber will ultimately be offered for sale because the U.S. Forest Service is completely hamstrung by federal laws, rules and regulations. Why will such a small volume of timber be offered for logging? Probably the biggest single reason is the change in the administration appeals regulations that was implemented by the Clinton Administration in 1993. Prior to 1993, U.S. Forest Service Supervisors could order salvage sales exempt from the endless stream of appeals that challenge the harvest of this dead and dying timber. Since then, under the Clinton Administration, regulations have changed allowing over 100 days for filing and review of paper challenges to Forest Service salvage efforts. Keep in mind that in the forested mountains near my home a 100 day delay can take you right out of this summer's logging season and right into winter. Because of deep winter snowpacks on our mountainous terrain we're prevented from accessing many of these timber sales in the winter months. Consequently the 100 day appeal delay can result in logging being postponed a full year in some cases. In other words, the resource is wasted, and by using the appeals process as a delay tactic the opponents of logging have achieved their objective. They successfully prevent logging even though in nearly every case their appeals are found to have no merit whatsoever.

The solutions to our current dilemma are obvious. First, the U.S. Forest Service must be directed to identify timber stands on America's National Forests that are dead or at risk to disease and infestation. The Forest Service, then, must be authorized and directed to use expedited and simplified timber sale preparations. This may require changes to the current national Environmental Policy Act, but it likely can be accomplished by directing simple changes and exemptions to current rules and regulations. Finally we must see swift and common-sense reforms made to the Endangered Species Act. All timber, grazing and mining operations on every national forest in my region are currently facing the threat of a federal court injunction which could stop all of these activities and the preparation efforts for the salvage of burned timber, instantly. This injunction, now stayed by the federal courts until March 15, was brought on by an obscure legal action filed under the Endangered Species Act by the Idaho Chapter of the Wilderness Society and the Pacific Rivers Council.

The opportunities for using the Endangered Species Act, in its current form, as a weapon to stop land management activities on federal land are endless. Without substantial reform this law will continue to stymie land managers who attempt to deal with the forest health crisis in our region. Ironically, rather than protecting the species the law is designed to protect, species such as Chinook salmon are threatened by the fires and subsequent habitat damage that result from failure to properly manage our federal timber stands. In other words, in Idaho, the law is probably hurting sensitive and endangered species more than it is helping them.

If we see reforms to the Endangered Species Act and changes to the appeals process and other administrative rules which guide fedral land managers in their preparations of timber salvage we have a chance to recover the value of the timber burned in the recent fires. These changes are also absolutely critical if these same land managers are to protect other dead and decaying stands of timber from the same catastrophic fate. In forests throughout our region we see up to 400 trees per acre where scientists tell us that only 40 or 50 should grow under natural conditions. Without immediate attention from Congress and the Administration, these timber stands will continue to invite fire and continue to threaten the health of the ecosystems in our region.

The Forest Service's commitment to implement ecosystem management in the west is a hollow promise unless they are given the tools to restore the vast acreages of decaying timber in our region's forest. Without your help, the goal of improving and protecting our forest environment won't be achieved. Rather we will continue to follow the current trend of forest decline and destruction by fire. Our communities will continue to lose jobs and public revenues. And families in towns just like Council, Idaho will continue to face the trauma of unemployment and dislocation.

Please implement the reforms I have discussed here this morning. This Congress can write a better Endangered Species Act that protects animals and people. It can pass legislation that will exempt sales of dead and dying timber from the administrative appeals process. And the Congress can help us take care of our forests by directing and funding our federal land managers to do the right job out on the ground and in the woods. Please help us take care of our forests and our families and maintain the only way of life we know.

Thank you for your consideration in this matter.

Roy Grossen
P.O. Box 226
Council, Idaho 83612
208-253-6482

STATEMENT OF PATRICK CONNELL

Mr. Chairman, my name is Patrick Connell. I am Vice President for Resource Operations for Rocky Mountain Log Homes. Our business is located near Hamilton, Montana. We are locally owned and have grown from a backyard operation to the premier Western manufacturer of solid wood log homes. Together with our affiliate, Pioneer Log Homes, we employee over 100 workers. I am also here representing the Independent Forest Products Association and their 100 member companies.

I am testifying because I am concerned about the torturously slow progress being made on the salvage of the forests which burned last year. I would like Congress to pass legislation that removes all procedural road blocks which delay the salvage efforts. Without such legislation, I believe less than 5 % of the timber which burned this summer will reach the market.

Millions of Acres of Burned and Dead Timber

This past summer, million of acres of dead, dying, and healthy forests burned in this country. Somewhere around 4 million acres burned, many of them in the interior Western forests of California, Washington, Oregon, Idaho, Montana, Wyoming, Utah, and Colorado. After 80 years of keeping fires out of these forests, combined with a nearly decade long drought, these fires came as no surprise.

What may come as a surprise to many Americans is that we have millions upon millions more acres of overstocked, dead and dying forests that are poised to suffer the same fate. The strategy of setting aside forests from management and then chasing after insect and disease problems, while hoping against hope that we do not have a bad fire year is wrongheaded and a prescription for disaster. If Congress does not straighten out the convoluted environmental laws and regulations which keep federal land managers from proactively addressing overstocking in our federal forests, and at the same time send a clear unfettered message to federal land managers to clean up their dysfunctional management style, millions more acres will suffer the same fate as our Western forests suffered this past year.

The forest on federal lands, in most Western states, are out of balance with nature. By precluding fire and, over the last ten years, precluding land managers from aggressively sanitizing disease and insect infested stands, we have conditions that have never been experienced in the Western forests. Vast acreages are choked with understories of dense, disease prone, shade intolerant species like Western White fir. When these trees are stressed by drought, insects, or disease, they become fuel ladders to the large old growth species land managers are currently protecting from harvest. A fire in these stands will likely kill the very trees the federal land managers are attempting to save.

Congress only has to look at the forests which burned this summer in Idaho and Washington to understand how this occurs. Congress should be looking at eastern Oregon and the Sierra Mountains in California to understand what is likely to occur those areas in the next few years.

Legislation Needed to Deal With the Forest Health Crisis

Congress must pass comprehensive forest health legislation to ensure the remaining Western forests are not destroyed through benign neglect. Such legislation should direct federal land managers to make forest health the number one priority. It should direct federal land managers to manage all federal lands. The strategy of setting aside areas and precluding active forest management is not working. We cannot manage stand density on 30 % of the land, leaving roadless areas to die, and expect forest health problems will stay out of sight and mind. When insects, disease, and fire come, they will impact all acres without any adherence to the geo-political boundaries we draw on maps. Mr. Chairman, the forest health conditions in the West are such that we are going to have a succession of fire seasons that are as severe, or more so, than what we experienced in 1994.

A Billion Dollars Spent on Fires Suppression -- Hundreds of Millions of Dollars in Revenues Foregone

In 1988, the Forest Service estimated it spent over one billion dollars to fight the fires in and around Yellowstone Park. In 1994, they spent nearly that much fighting fires in Idaho,

Washington, Oregon, California, and Montana. In both instances, the wood burned in these events was worth hundreds of millions of dollars. In 1988, very little of the volume burned was salvaged. Preservationists understand that by delaying the salvage efforts by only a year or two, they can preclude entry in these areas. When the wood is not harvested within a year or two, it rapidly loses commercial value. We are concerned that the federal land managers salvage efforts this year will be too little, too late.

Although the Clinton Administration says it wants to make salvage a priority, their recent proposed budget for FY 1996 tells a different story. In a year when 4 to 6 billion board feet of timber burned, the Clinton Administration is requesting funds to harvest only 3.7 billion board feet of timber nationally. To put that in perspective, in FY 1995 they requested funding for the harvest of 4.075 billion board feet. Prior to 1993, the Forest Service routinely sold between 9 and 11 billion board feet annually. If the Administration recognizes the forest health crisis, then why didn't they reflect that in their budget requests?

After spending an estimated one billion dollars suppressing these fires, it is criminal for the land management agencies to impose an impossibly long implementation process, which will forego hundreds of millions of dollars of potential returns from the harvest of these dead trees. Millions of dollars will be foregone if salvage of this material does not occur this summer. As Congress struggles with balancing budgets, please realize our federal land management agencies are walking away from hundreds of millions of dollars of revenues because an unworkable process has been imposed on them. On the Payette National Forest in Idaho, a forest I am familiar with, they estimate that over 1.2 billion board feet burned. At $150\MBF, a very attainable price if salvage could occur this summer, $180 million in revenues would be produced. The counties in the area would stand to receive $45 million. But that is not going to occur. The Payette recently announced that it hopes to salvage 200 to 259 MMBF. If recent history repeats itself, less than 10 % of the volume which burned in the West will be salvaged before it loses most of its commercial value. If Congress could pass legislation and motivate the land management agencies to salvage the burned, dead and dying timber in a timely fashion, it could generate an estimated $750,000,00.00[1] Can this country afford to salvage only 10 to 20 percent of the material which burns each year?

Preservationists Rhetoric is Just That -- Rhetoric

You will hear from others that the salvage of these forests will do more harm than the fires. I want to assure you, as a person who spent my summer in the midst of the largest single forest fires in Idaho's recent history, that those statements are not based on fact or reality.

Our company has purchased many salvage sales from the Forest Service in the last six years in Regions One, Two and Four. We hold salvage sale contracts on several forests in Montana and Idaho, including sales on the Payette National Forest. One of our salvage sales (Hendricks Creek), a sale of material killed by Spruce Bark Beetle, was almost completely burned by the 280,000 acre Corral fires when it blew up in late September.

Even if you have no feelings for the commercial value of the trees that were burned in these fires, and care only about the deer, elk, salmon and other creatures, you too must conclude that these fires produce a habitat crisis for all species which lived in or near these forests.

Animals are not the only things which suffer when these forests are ravaged by fire. Near our Hendricks Creek salvage sale is a small creek called Cloochman Creek. Cloochman Creek was a Class One fisheries stream and is the headwaters of the Payette River. As a result of the fire, Cloochman Creek is devastated. The overstory, which shaded the creek and the fish and aquatic insects which live in this creek, is gone. So too, for all practical purposes, is the Class One designation.

---

1 Based on $150\MBF for 5 billion board feet of timber which is estimated to have burned in the summer of 1994.

After the fire, I visited a small spring near our sale area. It is a primary headwaters spring for the Payette River. What we saw was a cesspool of ash and burned wood. The spring is no longer a clear pool where wildlife can come to drink. The best way I can describe it is having to drink out of a used ashtray. It is totally gummed up and contaminated by ash. Previous to the fire, there was a 75 foot buffer strip protecting the spring from the impact of man. It was fire, Mr. Chairman, not logging or other activities that destroyed this spring.

ESA Consultation is Partially Responsible for the Size of the Fires This Summer

As you may know, the Payette, and several other National Forests in Oregon, Washington and Idaho are prime habitat for Snake River Sockeye salmon and Summer Run Chinook salmon. Both of these runs have been found to be endangered under the Endangered Species Act. As a result, the Forest Service must consult with the National Marine Fisheries Service before carrying out any projects which might affect the salmon. In the case of this summer's fires, the interaction between the Payette National Forest and the National Marine Fisheries Service is insightful.

When the fire broke out on the Payette, the Forest Supervisor directed his staff to contact NMFS and request an emergency consultation to learn how the NMFS wanted the Forest Service to behave in fighting fires within endangered salmon habitat. In what can only be called the "closest cooperation", NMFS first questioned the authority of the Payette National Forest wildlife biologist to request an emergency consultation. The Forest Supervisor then wrote a letter telling NMFS that his biologist was authorized by him to negotiate an emergency consultation.

At this point, NMFS then had the gall to question whether or not the fires constituted an emergency. Eventually, the Forest Service convinced NMFS personnel that an emergency did in fact exist and NMFS worked up its concerns and limitations on fire fighting. Eight days after the initial request, the Forest Service received their marching orders from NMFS. Those orders directed that bulldozers and other heavy track equipment could not be used to fight fire in anadromous fish habitat.

It is almost inconceivable, if your goal is to put the fires out, not to utilize heavy equipment in fighting fires in the West. It is one of the most cost effective, productive methods of fighting fire, when the terrain allows use of such equipment. No amount of hand crews can compete with even the smallest bulldozers. The consultation stipulation by NMFS is, in my mind, criminal. Hundreds of millions of tax payer dollars could have been saved. Thousands of acres of forest might have been saved from these fires. Mr. Chairman, over 300,000 acres of the Payette National Forest burned this past summer. Nearly one third of the entire area within the forest boundary was ravaged by these fires. Had bulldozers been available to the fire fighting teams, I believe may of these acres would not have burned.

In my mind, these fires will do more adverse damage to the fisheries than if the fire fighters had bulldozed 10,000 acres of fire line. There is simply no comparison between what these fires did and the limited amount of damage firelines constructed by bulldozers might have produced. NMFS should face stiff Congressional oversight for their callous disregard for the damage these fires did, for their callous disregard for the expense required for fire suppression, and for their obnoxious attitude toward the Forest Service in questioning whether or not an emergency existed.

Mr. Chairman, I also believe your Committees should hold oversight hearings related to how fire suppression is being carried out, as well as whether or not the Fish & Wildlife Service and the National Marine Fisheries Service Endangered Species Act consultation processes are even-handed and productive when faced with millions of acres of fire damaged timber that needs to be salvaged.

NMFS Consultation Process is Administered in an Uneven Manner

During the fires last summer, I was constantly in and out of our Hendricks Creek salvage sale before the Corral Fire burned through the sale area in September. During that time, I became aware of a road project to reconstruct a road and a parking lot for the Brundage Ski Area near McCall, Idaho. This project was approved by NMFS, through its consultation process, and was implemented during the last fire season. The road construction for the Brundage Ski Area parking lot is within an anadromous fisheries. Construction occurred concurrent to this summer's fire suppression efforts in the next drainage to the north. NMFS allowed the use of heavy equipment for this project, which placed a fair amount of silt and dirt in the stream which ran near the parking lot. At the same time, NMFS would not allow the Forest Service to use bulldozers and other heavy track type equipment to fight the fire. I do not understand how NMFS can defend this decision, but the results are plainly clear. Due to the minimal impact suppression tactics (MIST), which were developed by the Forest Service and NMFS, and the no bulldozer in anadromous fish habitat consultation from NMFS, the equipment and expertise of local Idaho loggers was virtually ignored.

On the very morning that fire ravaged our Hendricks Creek salvage sale, I had a logger with $2 million worth of bulldozers and other heavy equipment just 15 minutes away from the fireline. Rather than use this equipment to build a fire line and potentially stop the fire before it reached our sale, the Forest Service directed that the equipment be evacuated. I believe the order from NMFS to fight the Idaho fires without bulldozers was responsible for this wrongheaded decision and the NMFS consultation requirements were absurd. I understand the need to protect salmon habitat, but letting fires burn the habitat will not protect the salmon.

Conclusion

Mr. Chairman, I urge your committee to develop legislation which will allow the timely salvage of dead, dying and burned timber. I hope you understand the need to direct our federal land managers to treat the lands we entrusted to them with more respect. As a taxpayer, I view the resources on those lands as having value. I want those values protected and when untimely catastrophes occur, like they always will, I want those land managers to salvage the perishable commodities in a manner which captures as much value as possible.

Finally, Mr. Chairman, even though this hearing is focused on salvage, I hope you will focus sufficient attention on the National Marine Fisheries Service so that they do not make wrongheaded decisions like the one they made on the Payette National Forest this past year. I have seen what bulldozer firelines can do and I have seen what fire running wild can do -- I will take aggressive fire management any day. I believe most forest creatures would tell you the same.

Mr. Chairman, I appreciate the opportunity to testify and I would be happy to provide you any backup information you might request. I ask that my testimony be entered into the record for this hearing.

STATEMENT OF D.R. JOHNSON

I want to extend my thanks to both Chairman for holding this very important hearing. The issue of timber salvage is timely and needs to be addressed immediately by Congress. I cannot speak on this issue from a National aspect, but I think, what we in Oregon, call the Eastside Forests, are representative of the problems we are all facing in the timber industry when it comes to the harvest of salvage timber.

First, let me give you some background. I have a family owned mill in Prairie City, Oregon. Our mill employs over 200 people, and in a small area like ours it is the soul of the economy. Oregon has led the world in timber production for years and we pride ourselves for harvesting timber and maintaining the healthiest forests in the world. In the past few years, timber production has come to a virtual halt which has crippled our industry and put thousands of hard working Oregonians out of work.

We want to continue to provide real jobs, with good pay. If something is not done soon we will lose good jobs, a solid tax base, and a community.

I want to briefly make five major points:

First, the harvest of salvage timber and the immediate reforestation of an area is a plus for the environment. This is a win-win situation. This will slow the spread of disease, lower the fire danger, and start the process for improving forest health.

Second, the system for offering timber sales is broken. The Forest Service and the Bureau of Land Management cannot move quickly enough to offer salvage timber sales. When you place all the requirements of planning screens, many self imposed, such as PAC fish considerations and current NEPA compliance standards, along with the Endangered Species Act's heavy hand - - - sales cannot and do not get offered --- and if they do, they end up in court.

I know the issues surrounding timber sales are complex. But we should not stand by and let the resource go to waste. It is a crime, to let dead and dying trees go to waste when there is a shortage of lumber for our mills to supply the nation.
That salvage timber puts dollars in our employees pockets, and provides funds for the Treasury.

Third, the window of opportunity is now open to make meaningful use of the salvage timber resource. Between six and 24 months is the timeframe. Any program not producing timber within that timeframe will do no good. We need relief from the current system for offering timber sales or nothing can or will be accomplished.

Fourth, we need to set the goals for salvage timber sales Forest by Forest, or BLM District by District. Those goals can then be tracked by those of us closest to the resource. Currently there is no accountability and each Forest seems to set its own standards and limits on what can or cannot be done. Any bill coming out of Congress must give specific goals and place accountability. If that does not happen we will end up with another massive program, with no one really in charge, and with no meaningful results.

Fifth, I encourage the Subcommittees to dig deep and find out just how much salvage volume is really out there. The volume numbers, provided by the agencies, that I have reviewed totally underestimate what I know exists in the Forests in my area. For example, the Forest Service says there is only 30 million board feet on the Malheur National Forest. I think that number is much closer to 200 million board feet and I have attached to my testimony data that make that point. A great deal of salvage timber resources are being placed off-limits by letting the agencies continue business as usual. The Committees needs to clear away all the chaff and find out what is really there. I think everyone will be surprised. That is why my fourth point of assigning targets is so important.

In closing, I want to again like to extent my thanks to all who helped make this hearing possible and encourage you to move with utmost haste to get a reasonable piece of legislation passed. By doing nothing a great deal of timber resources will be lost. Your efforts are on the right track and all of us who make our daily living in the forest products industry stand willing to help in any way possible.

Thank you and I would be happy to respond to any questions you may have at the appropriate time.

Testimony by Robert Lindsay to the House Committee on Agriculture and Committee on Natural Resources in joint hearing.
10 February 1995

Mr. Chairmen and members of the committees. I am Robert Lindsay, a Forest Resource Consultant from Eugene, Oregon. I am here today to detail for you the increasing complexity of salvaging dead and dying material from our national forests.

An excellent example of this complexity is the comparison of two forest fires on the Willamette National Forest. In September 1988, the Shady Beach Fire burned 9,163 acres on the Rigdon Ranger District. In October 1991, the Warner Creek Fire burned 8,973 acres on the Oakridge Ranger District. The two fires are about six air miles apart. The suppression cost for the Shady Beach Fire was 14.5 million dollars and the suppression cost for the Warner Creek Fire was 11 million dollars. I have been closely involved in the recovery efforts for both fires. I was a member of the Environmental Analysis Team for the Shady Beach Fire and on the Public Participation Group for the Warner Creek Fire. I spent extensive time on the ground working with the USFS, environmental groups, OSHA and other interested parties on both projects.

The Shady Beach Fire contained a total of 166 million board feet of dead and dying timber. The EIS was completed and timber sales prepared and sold, and harvest operations of 131 million board feet (80% of damaged timber) of timber begun in July of 1989, only 10 months after the fire. The sale value of salvage material was 36 million dollars. Local governments received 9.4 million dollars in lieu of tax payments and an estimated 1179 jobs were supported by the material from the fire area. The sales paid for reforestation of the fire area, other rehabilitation work and returned a sizable amount of money to the federal treasury. Currently 95+% of the fire area meets or exceeds reforestation standards and other environmental damage has been ameliorated.

The Warner Creek fire contains 180 million board feet of dead and dying timber. Today some 40 months after the fire, the Environmental Impact Statement is being challenged in court and no salvage sales or operations are occurring. A large percentage of the timber on this fire is true fir and other species which deteriorate rapidly following fire damage. This material is still there today, rotting away, with much of it no longer merchantable for anything except paper chips.

Why the dramatic difference in recovery operations for the two areas? The difference is in land allocations, the spotted owl, court challenges and injunctions, Option 9 and constantly changing rules and regulations concerning forest management.

Shady Beach was composed primarily of land allocated for timber production with an existing network of roads. The Environmental Analysis was completed on an accelerated schedule, the Environmental Analysis team included representatives from industry, environmental groups, and the Oregon State Fish and Wildlife Department. It complied with all environmental requirement of the soon to be implemented 1990 Willamette National Forest Management Plan. It retained wildlife trees, maintained buffers on all streams, required logging systems which did not disturb the soil, addressed the growing spotted owl controversy, monitored stream temperatures and sedimentation, and many of the other features which have since become the buzzwords of forest management. The USFS exempted the project from administrative appeals. I feel because of the inclusion of all parties on the EA team, no court challenges were filed. Salvage operations, reforestation and mitigation projects were basically completed by fall of 1991.

Warner Creek occurred in October of 1991 after release of the Spotted Owl Management FEIS, which was found inadequate by the federal courts in May 1992. In July of 1993 the "Forest Ecosystem Management: An Ecological, Economic and Social Assessment"; Report of the Forest Ecosystem Management Assessment Team (Femat) was released. July 1993 saw the release of the Draft Supplemental Environmental Impact Statement on Management of Habitat for Late-Successional and Old Growth Forest Related Species within the Range of the Spotted Owl. Most of the fire area had been designated as a Habitat Conservation Area (HCA). Warner Creek was the first major fire to occur within an HCA. There were no guide lines, rules, regulations or policies in place to guide the EA team in its efforts. There was constant change and shift in direction.

The official purpose of the project was to recover spotted owl habitat affected by the fire. But the process was hampered by constant review and change by the Northern Spotted Owl Oversight Team, the Oversight Steering Committee, the Interagency Northern Spotted Owl Conservation Group, the Regional Ecosystem Office, the Regional Interagency Executive Committee as well as consultation with the United States Fish and Wildlife Service.

Thus the EIS and recovery process for Warner Creek stands at 40 months and still counting. The FEIS has been challenged in Federal Court. The FEIS proposes to harvest nine (9) million board feet (only 5%) of the 180 million board feet of timber dead or dying on Warner Creek. The economic feasibility of that harvest is very questionable. Under the most optimistic scenario, the USFS could recover some 3 million dollars from these salvage sales.

Of this amount, the county would receive $800,000 in lieu of tax payments and 81 jobs could be supported. But remember the Federal Government has already spent 11 million dollars in suppression costs and one million dollars plus for the EIS and other work. The legal cost of the appeal, and costs of reforestation and other environmental work is still to be tallied. The bottom economic line is the taxpayers are spending some 10 million dollars on the area, while an estimated 30 million dollars worth of timber is left to rot.

An even more important issue is what is the long term prognosis for the area impacted by the fire? Will it be Spotted Owl habitat faster by letting the timber rot? Will the area be at low risk of additional fires? I strongly believe the answer to these questions is NO!

Immediate salvage and reforestation would have returned the area to productive status within a short period of time. Yes, mother nature will reforest the area but on her time table. Depending upon seed conditions, moisture and weather factors , this could take from 3 or 4 to 10 or 20 years; that is, if another fire does not occur within the area. If we look at fire history within the Pacific Northwest most major fires reburned several times prior to establishment of a new healthy forest. The amount of dead and down material at Warner Creek is ripe for additional fires. The area is in one of the high lightning strike areas of the Willamette National Forest.

This a brief description of two fire salvage and recovery projects on the Willamette National Forest. But the current requirements for completion of a EIS or EA for any forest activity is a minimum of two years from the time someone decides something should be done until the FEIS of Decision Notice is signed. Then, sale layout, contract preparation, sale advertisement, and contract award usually adds another year before actual harvest operations begin. This may be tolerable for a green timber sale. But this is totally intolerable for salvage operations! Many tree species like pine, true firs, hemlock and others deteriorate rapidly following fire, diseases, or insect mortality. This material becomes of very low or no value after a three or four year delay.

Congress must streamline and expedite the rehabilitation process so our forests can rapidly be returned to productive status and valuable forest products can be salvaged in a timely manner.

Thank you for the opportunity to testify today. I will be happy to answer any questions you may have.

89-215 O - 95 - 8

TESTIMONY OF DONALD E. OLSON

I. Introduction

Thank you, Mr. Chairmen and members of the Subcommittees, for the opportunity to testify today. I am Don Olson, President of Kaibab Forest Products Company, headquartered in Phoenix, Arizona. In addition to representing our company, I am here to represent the forest industry in the Southwest, where I serve as chairman of the Region 3 Management Committee. The committee is made up of the principles of the forest products companies in the Southwest Region, representing the timber purchasers on issues affecting federal land management and timber supply.

I am also representing the American Forest & Paper Association as chairman of AF&PA's Public Forestry Board of Directors. AF&PA is the national trade association of the forest, pulp, paper, paperboard, and wood products industry. We represent approximately 450 member companies which grow, harvest and process wood and wood fiber; manufacture pulp, paper and paperboard products from both virgin and recovered fiber; and produce solid wood products. The association is also the umbrella for more than 60 affiliate member associations that reach out to more than 10,000 companies. The association represents an industry which accounts for more than seven percent of total U.S. manufacturing output. It directly employs about 1.4 million people and ranks among the top 10 manufacturing employers in 46 states. Like Kaibab Forest Products Company, AF&PA has many members who are wholly or partially dependant on timber from the national forests and other federal lands.

II. Forest Health is Seriously Declining in the National Forests of the Southwest

Numerous studies have been conducted in Arizona, New Mexico, and Utah which document how the forests of this region have become overcrowded, resulting in declining health and sustainability of forest conditions. Forest insects and diseases are increasing well above normal levels, and as dwarf mistletoe and bark beetle infestations increase, tree densities increase and woody fuel loads become explosive, the risk of catastrophic wildfire occurrences also becomes much greater.

So far in the Southwest we have been relatively lucky. Our last major wildfire in this region was the Dude Fire on the Tonto National Forest in Arizona. In June 1990, over 24 thousand acres burned at a cost of $12 million and six lives. Approximately 36 million board feet of timber was lost, and due to Forest Service delays very little of it was salvaged. The Dude Fire was unusual by historical standards, since the crowded forest conditions, with extremely high fuel loads, created an unnatural stand replacing fire of high intensity unlike any previously recorded in the region. After the fire, most of the killed trees were not even salvageable, and in many areas the intense heat had sterilized the soil causing sheet erosion after the summer rains and losing two to three inches of valuable topsoil. Unfortunately, the conditions that led up to the fire are not unique -- Forest Service and Northern Arizona University scientists predict that vast acres of the Southwestern forests are now likely to be destroyed by high intensity stand replacing fires . . . they say it is not a question of "if," but rather "when."

Future versions of the Dude Fire can and should be prevented, but it requires taking action at a time when the Forest Service seems unable to do so. The agency is caught in a gridlock of conflicting management and environmental laws, implementing regulations, and administrative policies, and an atmosphere in which it is now popular to appeal and litigate harvesting decisions at every turn. In addition, appropriated funds for the Forest Service have been reduced every year, and the Forest Service reinvention process has resulted in a critical loss of experienced personnel. As a result, and unnecessarily, we have lost thousands of acres of forest vegetation and wildlife habitat. Today as mills close permanently, we are losing the very infrastructure that is needed to salvage the dying timber, improve the conditions of the overcrowded stands, and provide timber products for the nation before they burn up in smoke. After this infrastructure is gone, the jobs critical to the survival and maintenance of our rural communities and cultures are also lost.

In the Southwest, researchers have conducted several studies and documented changes in the forest conditions since European settlement began. They have used early photographs, anecdotal accounts, inventories and other scientific studies to conclude that the forests prior to settlement were savannah like, open, with more grasses, seeps, springs, and increased stream flows, and different wildlife habitat conditions than exist today. (Source: Covington and Moore, *Changes in Forest Conditions and Multiresource Yields from Ponderosa Pine Forests since European Settlement*.)

In a study of the Bar M Canyon watershed in Arizona, Covington and Moore found that the early conditions averaged 23 trees per acre where today there are as many as 850 trees per acre. They estimated the following accompanying changes:

- a 92% reduction in herbage production
- a 31% reduction in stream flow
- a 730% increase in forest floor fuels
- a 1700% increase in sawtimber volume (in board feet)
- a significant decrease in scenic beauty
- a shift from conditions favoring species that thrive in open savannah conditions (antelope, elk, turkey, bluebirds and grasshoppers) to species that favor dense forests (spotted owl, porcupine, and tassel-eared squirrel)
- decreased vigor and increased mortality of all trees, but especially older trees
- increased forest canopy closure and development of fuel ladders, plus accumulation of ground fuels, resulting in high crown fire hazards.

Clearly, these unnatural trends, which are representative of Southwestern forests, will continue if the forests are not thinned out -- either by insects, disease and wildfire (which will result in much greater losses than would be desired), or by human activity (by logging and precommercial thinning).

Kaibab Forest Products Company has been a leader in developing innovative stewardship methods for conducting, under strict contractual conditions, a wide variety of activities that go well beyond the harvesting of forest products to help the Forest Service achieve sustainable ecosystem conditions and lead to improved forest health. To date, we have successfully completed two land service contracts on the Dixie National Forest and are well into our third on the North Kaibab National Forest. These last two projects were authorized by the Interior Appropriations Committee on a test basis in 1991. Under these contracts we have conducted thinnings, salvage, tree planting, prescribed burning, stream restoration, wildlife habitat improvement, and created fuel breaks. We have also completed a number of recreation projects, including trail construction. We have also conducted surveys and are doing monitoring of various conditions as required by the contracts.

Through these activities, we have been directly involved in helping to improve the conditions on the Dixie and North Kaibab National Forests. At the same time, we have been able to provide our mills with needed timber, conduct the activities at a lower net cost to the Federal Treasury, and we have helped the Forest Service achieve the goals as set forth in the land and resource management plans. However, these efforts have been very small scale compared to what is needed. Our rural communities and mills cannot survive on the small volume of work generated by the few timber and service contracts that the Forest Service has issued in the last three years. This very low level of activity has caused further increases in the amount of fires, insect killed trees and salvage that we are experiencing today.

III. A Lack of Timber Supplies is Eliminating the Forest Products Infrastructure in the Southwest.

As recently as the beginning of the 1990s, Kaibab Forest Products Company was operating three very efficient operations in the Southwest, employing a total of 500 people, all in small rural towns. Since that time we have had to reduce shifts and even eliminate two of our mills. Now we have only one very small mill with 70 employees operating in Southern Utah. On February 1st, we had to permanently close our Fredonia, Arizona mill due to a severe decline in available supplies of timber from the Forest Service. This is notwithstanding the fact that forest growth greatly exceeds historic harvest levels, and the forests of the Southwest are experiencing a tremendous increase in the numbers and density of trees and a serious decline in forest ecosystem health that would best be solved by an active forest management and timber harvesting program.

The Fredonia mill is only the most recent of many facility curtailments and closures throughout the Southwest. For example, over the past ninety years, thirteen wood and paper mills, owned by six different firms, have operated in Arizona. The earliest facility was established in 1908, three facilities were established in the 1930s, and four more (including Kaibab's Fredonia and Payson plants) were built in the 1950s. Of these, all eight were still operating in 1991 with a total of 1,965 employees. In addition, by this time the White Mountain Fort Apache tribe had established a facility in 1963 which was operating with 423 employees, and another small facility was built (by Peterson Logging in 1983) with 16 workers. Total employment in the state in August 1991 was 1,965, as shown on the attached chart. (Source: Region 3 Management Committee.)

Except for the White Mountain Fort Apache facility, these mills have always been totally dependent upon timber supplies from the National Forests. Like other mills in the Southwest, we have essentially no alternative sources of timber supply -- no corporate timberlands, very little state or county sources, and very little nonindustrial private lands. Only the White Mountain Fort Apache Reservation has a source of timber from tribal lands.

During this period the forest products industry responded to the need for harvesting and made the investments that built several rural communities. The forests of the Southwest were at the same time producing more and more trees and fibre. Between 1962 and 1986, forested acreage on all lands within the region increased by 5 percent, total tree volume increased by 13 percent, and standing volume on the national forests increased by 21 percent. This increase occurred even while industry used 16 percent of the volume that was present at the beginning of the 25-year period. The increase also does not include the growth in volume that occurred on reserved areas, such as wilderness. During the same period, the acreage in reserved areas was increased by over 2 million acres, or 232 percent. (Source: U.S.D.A. Forest Service, Southwestern Region, *Changing Conditions in Southwestern Forests and Implications on Land Stewardship*.)

In recent years, the Forest Service has sold slightly more than 300 million board feet per year, on average. The annual allowable sale quantity, or the amount planned for sale through the forest plans in Region 3, was more than 400 million board feet. When these plans are projected over the long term, the forests can sustain a long term annual yield of more than 800 million board feet. (Source: U.S.D.A. Forest Service, *Status of Timber Data from Forest Plans,* 1993 and 1995.)

Despite this fact, the total volume of timber sold by the Forest Service in Region 3 has declined steadily since 1986 (at 446.8 million board feet) to a low of only 119 million board feet in 1994. This volume includes pulpwood, firewood and other products. The volume of sawtimber sold, shown on the accompanying chart and historically representing the biggest portion of the total sales, has declined since 1989 from 348 million board feet to a low of less than 50 million board feet. These starvation levels of volume will not sustain the sawmills in the region. (Source: U.S.D.A. Forest Service, *Region Three Sawtimber Program*.)

This drastic drop in the timber sale program has resulted in the curtailment of shifts and complete closure of mills in Arizona and throughout the region since 1990. By July 1994, three of the Arizona mills (Payson, Flagstaff and Williams) were closed and dismantled; last week we closed our Fredonia mill, as I have already pointed out; and every surviving mill (with the lone exception of a very small SBA operation) has been operating at reduced levels for at least two years. I am certain there will be more permanent mill closures. In addition, Stone Container has announced that they will no longer utilize any roundwood and sawmill residual fibers at their Snowflake paper mill by the summer of 1996 due to the shortage of federal timber sales. (See: *Arizona Forest Products Industry Crewing Report*.)

Our critics may claim that the forest industry is not progressive, that we cannot change with the times, yet nothing can be further than the truth. In the Southwest, the industry has spent many millions of dollars to improve our facilities in recent years. Kaibab Forest Products Company alone has invested millions to ensure our mills could process the smaller logs the Forest Service now prefers to sell, and we are not unique. Most mills now can profitably process logs from 6-inch diameter trees, a product that is common when the Forest Service utilizes thinning prescriptions to improve its overstocked forest stands. In addition, with a viable industry in place, we can quickly adjust to salvage the dead and dying timber when it is necessary following a fire or insect epidemic, provided that the Forest Service responds in kind.

All of our investments are for naught if the Forest Service cannot sell sufficient amounts of timber to maintain the quality of our forests and the viability of our mills. By whittling its timber program down to nothing, the Forest Service will be unable to address the increasing level of forest health problems and to prevent the continued decline in forest quality. Furthermore, by focusing primarily on current salvage needs and by ignoring the preventative measures that are necessary (and more cost effective), the forests in the Southwest will only get worse and the agency will be completely unable to address the growing severity of the problem.

IV. Effects on the Local Communities are Devastating.

The North Kaibab Ranger District of the Kaibab National Forest is a unique forested plateau of about 240,000 acres. Net annual growth is nearly 100 million board feet per year. But for the last four years, the Forest Service has sold less than 12 million board feet each year. Our Fredonia mill relied on timber from the North Kaibab for almost 50 years, and with the forest's very high sustainable growth rate our mill should have been able to thrive well into the 21st century. But the mill cannot survive on only 12 million board feet a year and even this low volume has become very uncertain. With the February 1 closing of the mill, 200 employees are losing their jobs. Instead of well paying jobs with good benefits -- in Northern Arizona and Southern Utah these were among the best jobs to be had -- many of these workers will now have to join the unemployment rolls. The economic costs to the government are high -- in income taxes foregone, increased social services and unemployment costs, and the lost economic base for the local community. In fact, upon the announcement of our impending mill closure, the Mayor of Fredonia expressed great concern that he did not know how the small town of Fredonia will survive.

While we have been forced to "downsize," the Kaibab forest continues to grow, needing thinning and salvage. Why has this been allowed to happen?

V. Conflicts between Conflicting Laws and Regulátions, including Endangered Species Issues, have been a Significant Factor in Hindering Proper Forest Management.

Changing direction for the management of wildlife habitat has had a major influence on Forest Service policies for timber production and other land management activities in the Southwest. Since the 1990, the Forest Service has spent millions of dollars studying the habitat needs of the Northern goshawk, a bird that is common in our Southwestern forests. In 1992 this work culminated with the Agency's publication of management guidelines for the goshawk which were broadly supported by the scientific community. These guidelines followed a broad, ecosystem-based approach and they addressed the habitat needs of some 14 different species. The guidelines called for specific silvicultural (timber management) treatments to improve forest conditions for the goshawk and its prey, and those treatments were consistent with what ecologists tell us are necessary to improve the health of our overcrowded Southwestern forests.

When the Mexican spotted owl was listed as a "threatened" species under the Endangered Species Act in 1993, the goshawk management direction was replaced by a completely different approach. Due largely to the controversy over management of the Northern spotted owl in the Pacific Northwest, the agency adopted new guidelines for management of Mexican spotted owl habitat which precluded timber management activities over much of the Southwest. This occurred even on the North Kaibab despite the fact that there have been no verified sightings of the Mexican owl on the entire North Kaibab plateau.

The management guidelines for the owl are completely at odds with the needs of the goshawk, not to mention the need to address other forest health concerns. Nonetheless, the listing of the owl has forced us into our present situation -- disagreement over the proper approach to managing habitat for species with conflicting needs; creating a simple argument against harvesting timber (it might hurt the owl, even though it doesn't live here!) which is used by appellants who oppose timber harvesting for any reason; and a timber program which has fallen to near zero and turned our industry into the only truly threatened species in the Southwestern forests. In fact, we are now the one that is likely to become extinct. Once we are gone, what business would make the substantial investments needed to rebuild, given the risk that raw materials from the public lands may not be available?

Conflict over habitat management has not been the only problem. In Region 3, nearly every timber sale planned for sale has been appealed. To my knowledge, nearly every single agency decision has been upheld on appeal. Appellants have also gone to the courts, litigating timber sale decisions, the forest plans, and numerous other agency decisions.

VI. Region 3 is Representative of a Much Bigger Problem which is Evident throughout the West and the Entire Nation.

While I have used Kaibab's experience in the Southwest as one example, unfortunately there are many others. As our industry is forced out of business in regions where we are highly dependent on federal timber supplies, we lose the ability to respond to future forest management needs. In the meantime, we have vast acreages of forest land with dead and dying timber as a result of the past summer's wildfires and epidemic infestations of insects and disease. These lands need treatment today, to salvage what is already dead and dying, and to improve conditions as a preventative measure against future catastrophes.

I would like to provide one more example: In Northern California, there is two billion board feet of standing dead timber on National Forest lands right now. Due to the effects of a prolonged drought, recent fires, and the lack of adequate timber management activities in recent years, the mortality continues today. Nonetheless, the Forest Service's planned timber sale program for FY 1995 includes only 250 million board feet of green sales, 350 million board feet of salvage, and 70 million board feet of carryover volume from the 1994 program. Even if the salvage volume were doubled, it would not begin to meet our needs.

For FY 1996, I understand the Forest Service program for the entire nation includes only 1.5 billion board feet of salvage -- not enough to remove that which is standing dead and salvageable in California today! But by 1996, if we haven't already taken aggressive action, only half of the two billion board feet that is now dead will still have enough value left to support a timber operation.

VII. Conclusion

There is a forest health crisis in our nation today, and the national forests of the Southwest provide only one example. Other witnesses will describe the severity of the situation throughout the West. But the Southwest is unique in one respect -- throughout the region the national forests provide the sole source (not just the "primary" or a "major" source) of timber for the forest products industry. We should not have to be here today asking for a few scraps of salvage to tide us over, hoping that somehow we will all come to our senses and go about the business of sustaining our very valuable forest resources and ecosystems.

In the Southwest, our industry has operated for more than 60 years at a level sustainable over the long term, and we have done more than provide jobs and revenues to the local and federal treasuries. Kaibab Forest Products Company has taken pride in being good corporate citizens, and we have taken the lead in developing innovative approaches for improving the management of our federal lands.

I must emphasize, however, that the problem is truly national in scope. As serious as the problem has been in the Southwest, we must remember that every region of the country is currently affected by forest health problems. For example, in the Southeast, 14 million acres of Southern pine had outbreaks of the Southern pine beetle in 1992. The Virginia outbreak of 1993 was the most severe in recorded history, killing over five million trees. Other insects and diseases are increasing in importance. For example, oak decline has intensified as many of the hardwood forests in the Southern U.S. approach maturity and face recurrent episodes of drought. Dogwood anthracnose, the hemlock wooly adelgid and the gypsy moth continue to spread.

In the Northeast, the gypsy moth has defoliated millions of acres of forest. With repeated defoliations in many areas, much of the timber has been killed. Dogwood anthracnose continues to spread in the Northeast, and oak wilt has been an increasing problem in the Midwest. Throughout the Northeast and Central region, Dutch elm disease has developed a more aggressive strain which is killing trees that survived the initial spread of the disease. Butternut canker has now spread to a level that threatens the survival of the butternut tree.

I know you are aware that in 1994, 3.7 million acres of forest land burned, with fire suppression costs amounting to more than one billion dollars. Twenty six firefighters lost there lives. The cost to the Nation in a single year has been tremendous.

Every region of the country has proven the common need for aggressive hands-on forest management. Letting nature take its course has proven foolhardy economically, environmentally, and in the human sense, tragically. For a problem this widespread, the solution must be national in scope.

Despite our industry's excellent record, the government's lack of direction and oversight for managing our federal lands over the long term failure and to adequately address our immediate salvage needs in the short term is forcing our industry out of business and only worsening the state of our forests. If we do not maintain a viable, responsible forest products industry by providing timber at sustainable and reliable levels, we will lose the very infrastructure that is needed to utilize our resources rather than leave them to die, go up in smoke, and create hazards for our own communities.

Your committees have the opportunity to restore the needed leadership and bring sense back to our legal system. We need thorough oversight and reform of the conflicting laws which govern the management of our federal lands. We need better accountability and leadership in our federal agencies. And while oversight and development of appropriate legislative solutions may take some time, we need immediate action to enable the Forest Service to attend quickly to our most urgent forest health and salvage needs.

Thank you for your interest in this critical issue. I appreciate the opportunity to testify and I would be happy to answer any questions you have.

CHANGES IN FOREST CONDITIONS AND MULTIRESOURCE YIELDS FROM PONDEROSA PINE FORESTS SINCE EUROPEAN SETTLEMENT

EXECUTIVE SUMMARY

The goal of this research was to determine changes since European settlement in forest conditions and resource yields for a southwestern ponderosa pine watershed. Based on early photographs, anecdotal accounts, and several studies in southwestern ponderosa pine, our hypothesis was that presettlement forests were much more open than they are today, and thus that herbage production, stream flow, wildlife habitat, etc., would have been substantially different under the natural disturbance regime of periodic (2-10 years) surface fires. This report presents quantitative estimates of these changes.

Methods consisted of first measuring the density and age of trees, stumps, and snags on sample plots to determine current tree density as well as density before livestock grazing and fire exclusion (circa 1870). Then, we used a multiresource simulation model to simulate changes from 1867 to 1987, as well as from 1987-2027.

We mapped all trees on eight 0.25-hectare plots and all presettlement trees on sixty-two 0.25-hectare plots.

We found that presettlement tree density was approximately 56 trees per hectare (23 trees per acre). This average of 56 presettlement trees per hectare is based on a total of 984 presettlement trees sampled, of which 50% were living, 43% were stumps and 6% were snags. This presettlement tree density stands in stark contrast to the current density of approximately 2100 trees per hectare (850 trees per acre) of predominantly small diameter trees. This increase in tree density is estimated to have caused:

1. a reduction of 92% in herbage production
2. a reduction of 31% in stream flow
3. an increase of 730% in forest floor fuel loading
4. an increase of 1700% in sawtimber volume (bd ft)
5. a decrease from 115 to -8 in scenic beauty index
6. a shift in wildlife habitat from one favorin species more successful under savannah conditions (e.g., pronghorn antelope, elk, turkey, bluebirds, grasshoppers) to one favoring species more successful under dense forest conditions (e.g., pygmy nuthatch, spotted owl, porcupine, and tassle-eared squirrels).

This increased tree density may also result in decreased vigor and increased mortality of all trees, but especially those in the oldest age classes. Finally, the increased canopy closure, vertical fuel continuity (fuel ladder), and ground fuel loads result in high crown fire hazard, which was probably extremely rare and localized under natural conditions.

Simulations through the year 2027 (160 years after livestock grazing and fire-exclusion), indicate that, in the highly unlikely absence of thinning either by natural agents (wildfire, insects, disease) or human activity, these trends will continue.

Two key management implications emerge. On sites with high post-settlement tree density, common throughout the southwestern ponderosa pine type, it is unlikely that trees of presettlement origin will survive beyond 2025. Because of rapidly declining vigor and large phloem volume, these trees are prime candidates for bark beetle infestation or other lethal biological agents. In addition, high forest floor loads coupled with a continuous fuel ladder make it highly probable that crown fire will occur, killing virtually all trees within a burned area. A central conclusion is that to preserve these ancient trees and avoid major conflagrations, environmentally sound methods of reducing both tree densities and fuel loading must be developed and implemented immediately.

Arizona Forest Products Industry Crewing Report

Community	Firm	Year Established	Employees Aug '91	Nov '92	July '93	July '94	Jan '95
White River	Fort Apache	1963	423	460	310	310	293
* Fredonia	Kaibab	1951	234	218	179	189	175
Payson	Kaibab	1952	74	55	5	0	0
Winslow	Peterson Logging	1983	16	16	16	0	0
Heber	Precision Pine	1932	197	90	29	54	59
Williams	Precision Pine	1974	73	20	31	0	0
Winslow	Precision Pine	1952	119	90	64	80	82
Snowflake	Precision Pine	1985				28	36
Eager/Springerville	Precision Pine	1993				23	18
Nutrioso	Reidhead Lumber	1939	33	33	33	38	38
Eager	Stone Forest	1934	317	115	107	99	125
Flagstaff	Stone Forest	1908	418	101	20	5	3
** Snowflake	Stone Forest	1957	575	575	556	535	545
			2477	1773	1350	1341	1354

* Fredonia is in the process of totally shutting down - no employees after June 1, 1995.

** The paper mill will convert to 100% recycle sometime in 1996.

1/23/95

REGION THREE

SAWTIMBER PROGRAM

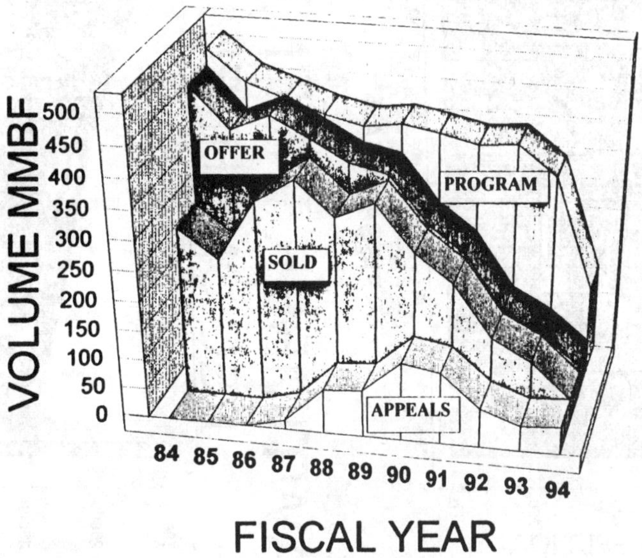

GROWTH VS HARVEST
REGION THREE

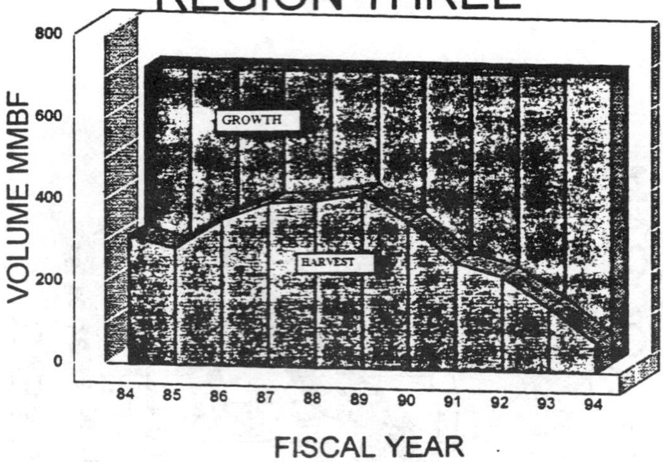

SAWTIMBER INVENTORY
REGION THREE

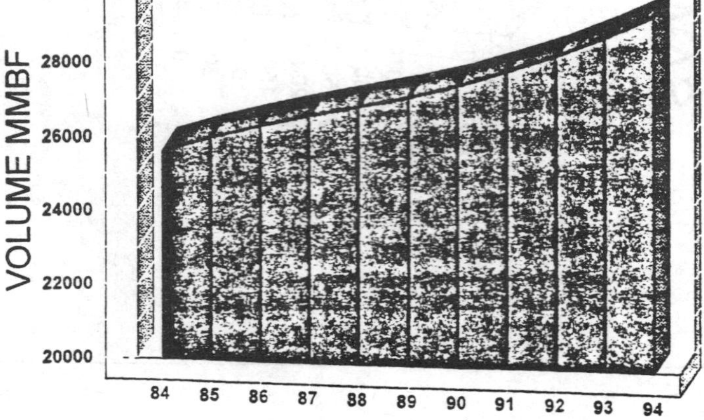

Testimony of Rita Carlson
Vice President of Natural Resources and Public Lands
of the Alliance for America
before the
House Resources Subcommittee on National Parks, Forests, and Lands
February 10, 1995

Mr. Chairman, my name is Rita Carlson. I live in Lewiston, Idaho, am an employee of Potlatch Corporation, a member of UPIU 712 and Vice President of Natural Resources and Public Lands for the nationwide grassroots network, The Alliance for America. Today I represent my fellow workers from Lewiston and the Alliance for America. Thank you for hearing my testimony.

During this hearing I'm sure you will hear from a host of forest scientists that will tell you about the problems facing forests in the West. I'm sure you will hear from professional land managers who will tell you about the many options available for addressing forest health, such as salvage logging, commercial thinning, controlled burning, and others. You will probably also hear from some who claim that the best way to manage the forests is to let nature have its way. I'm sure you will listen closely to what these scientists have to say and will then attempt to make good policy decisions to deal with the problem.

I am not a scientist. If I'm an expert on anything, it is on the impact that failing forest policy, failing forest health, and failing forest product companies have on individuals, families and communities of the Intermountain West.

This expertise has been gained through my personal involvement in a number of grassroots organizations that have formed in order to deal with environmental policy gone wrong. This expertise is a product of witnessing the pain felt by thousands in timber-dependent communities that are reeling from years of broken promises by federal land managers.

In my testimony today, I will attempt to put a human face on the issue of forest health and encourage you to keep that face in mind as you discuss ways to untangle the mess our forests are in.

Throughout the forests whose health is in trouble live hundreds of thousands of people who have built lives, families, homes and towns in and around our national forests. During the last 100 years, this forest-resource-providing heritage has matured and we now can boast of being the most efficient, safe and environmentally sensitive wood providers in the world.

Many areas of the Intermountain West have whole communities that planned their futures around the promise of a sustainable supply of raw wood products from the national forest system. The forest planning process of the 1970s and 1980s promised these people that we would protect the many values we enjoy in the forest -- such as water quality, wildlife and aesthetics -- while managing to produce products we use as a society. The federal government promised that the forests we are dependent upon would continue to be managed for "the most good for the most people." These promises have been broken.

The forest planning process that spent 10 years gathering input from the public, and then made those promises, seems to have been scrapped. Forest management gridlock, analysis paralysis, and out-of-control litigation is now keeping the foresters and the forest workers from managing the forest for "the most good for the most people." It is now clear that in our towns these broken promises threaten both our economic and environmental futures.

Economically, these broken promises have been, and continue to be, severe. The first to pay the price of these broken promises are the people close to the forest - people like Errol Roberts of Joseph, Oregon. Errol used to work for the Boise Cascade mill in Joseph. That mill closed last summer. The community of Joseph has now lost all of its mills. The Boise Cascade mill was one of three that has closed in the last several months, thus eliminating employment and primary support for 160 families. Included among them were Errol's brother (a 24-year employee) and dozens more who had spent all or most of their working lives at that mill.

Joseph is in Wallow County, which now has the highest unemployment in the state, hovering between 15 and 20 percent. For those who lost their jobs, the six-month period of unemployment compensation is now running out. Job prospects in Joseph are virtually nonexistent, unless the unemployed want to join the ranks of the seasonal workers who were called in last summer to battle the 100,000 acre fire that roasted the dead and dying forest land around the community.

The social services that exist in cities to supply a safety net for people who are at the end of their rope do not exist in rural areas. The social services that do exist are ill-equipped for the massive collapse of the timber industry in the area.

Certainly, some areas in rural America have broader economic bases that can absorb some job losses. But, most of the towns being hit with forest industry closures in the Intermountain West are small towns with no time, and little opportunity, to diversify their economies. They have no options or immediate hope to offer their people.

Dr. Bob Lee of the University of Washington has long warned the state and federal governments that many rural care-giving services are woefully unprepared for the human wave that has been generated by a collapse of the national forest sale program. He and others have warned that in our communities we can expect to see a rise in the social ills that always go hand-in-hand with unemployment. He and others have warned of increases in the abuse of drugs, alcohol, spouses and children, and increases in heart attacks and suicides. We are now learning that Dr. Lee and the others are right.

In Libby, Montana, the local women's crisis hotline has seen a 300 percent increase in usage since the beginning of mill closures 18 months ago. A recent headline in the Libby paper indicated that the food pantries were running dry and that, according to the county service officials, "we don't know what to do - we have families living in their cars in campgrounds."

These proud people that are paying the price of failed policy are frustrated by the situation they find themselves in because it all seems so unnecessary. Were they losing their jobs because the forests they love had been mismanaged to the point that it was time to (if you will), "pay the piper?" then they would have to accept their fate. And, accept it they would.

However, these same people live in, work, and play in the forest and see the shape that it is in. They understand that decades of fire suppression, along with rampant disease and insect infestations, have built a powder keg in the forests they love. They know that without management, nature will again try to get rid of some of the fuel by burning millions of acres of the forest, just ad it did last summer.

From their homes, these unemployed men and women can see millions of acres of forest that are prepared or preparing to burn like those that burned last summer.

They stand in unemployment lines and, with more than a little frustration and disgust, glance at the hillsides that should be managed to improve the health of the forest, employ them and help to feed their families.

The environmental cost of not managing for the health of our forests is also a painful frustration for our rural areas. As we hike through the forest and see the unnatural fuel load lying on the ground, we know that when the fires come they will burn too hot to allow new growth for decades to come.

We know that if we were allowed to help manage the forest for the good of all, many of our favorite areas for hunting, hiking, berry-picking, camping and fishing could be saved. We know that, without some move by Congress, it is just a matter of time before we will have to live through another summer of dismay in which our future, our forest's future, and our childrens' forests' future, go up in smoke.

The forest families that I represent ask this Congress to step into the debate over forest health and offer a ray of common sense and hope.

5

We ask that Congress not abandon management of our resources to nature in a misguided effort to re-create some picture of the past that has never existed.

We ask that you consider the importance of our resource providing culture when determining how best to bring our national forests back to health.

We as that our "vision" of the future of forest resource management be used in determining "what is best" for the lands we depend upon. A copy of our ion Document is included in my testimony for the record.

Also, for the record, I offer this pile of letters from those who will be impacted by your decisions. There are more than 600 of them here.

Finally, for the record, I ask that the video of the Fredonia mill closing in Fredonia, Arizona, be included in the Congressional Record. If you want to see what a loss of a way of life is like, I encourage each of you to watch this video.

For those of us that have lost our jobs, this debate is too late. The rest of us are ready, willing and able to help you plan and implement forest policies that will restore our forests back to health. But, we don't have much time and neither do our forests.

Rita Carlson
February 10, 1995

NORTH LAKE TAHOE FIRE PROTECTION DISTRICT

Post Office Box 385
Crystal Bay, Nevada 89402
(702) 831-0351 • FAX (702) 831-2072
Loren E. Enstad - Fire Chief

February 8, 1995

Report to the House of Representatives, Committee on Resources

Introduction:

My name is Gerald L. Adams, and I am the Fire Marshal of the North Lake Tahoe Fire Protection District, which is located on the north shore of Lake Tahoe in the state of Nevada. My community is known as Incline Village, Crystal Bay.

It is a community that is recognized for it's scenic, and forested natural beauty.

The problem:

It must be clear in my presentation today that my knowledge of the forest health issues are directly related to the Lake Tahoe Basin region, and the Sierra Front range. Although the wildfire and forest health issues, are generally the same across the western United States, and even in the hardwood forests of the eastern portions of the U.S. In my studies of the wildfire problems, I have found that it generally relates to how we have managed these forests, or not managed them. Our past management practices, and primarily our "fire exclusion" policy, the interruption of one of the natural processes, is our reason for the decline in forest health, and our natural resources. In some cases we have even "protected or preserved our natural resources to death", such as the Tahoe Basin.

We need to place ourselves in perspective to the forest systems that we are attempting to manage and understand that we're dealing with a "human caused problem", not a nature caused problem. We need to understand that these natural systems, such as the Tahoe Basin were, and are, fire dependent, and have evolved over hundreds of thousands of years on that management process, and we, a small speck in time, have interrupted that natural process by moving into, and building structures in these "fire type environment's". If we do not allow the natural fire process to manage the fuels in our neighborhoods, and around our communities, than we must develop alternatives that mimic that natural process. Those alternatives are various fuels management options, such as **removal, reduction, or replacement** i.e. from selective timber harvesting, to prescribed burning.

My belief, and the basis of my communities fuels management program, has been and continues to be, that a balance between the management of the fire dependent fuels, and the fire protection needs of the community, can be accomplished.

This reduction in fuels, or the modification of fuels has demonstrated, that these actions are effective in reducing the risk of wildfires successfully in other communities that have faced wildfire situations. Additionally my community understands that we will never be able to 100% exclude the fire risk, but we can reduce the impacts of naturally occurring fires, in our fire dependent environment that we have chosen to live in, recognizing that life in general is not risk free.

The Incline Village Crystal Bay, Defensible Space program:

To be brief I will keep this short. In 1986 as the Fire Marshal of our community, I recognized the fuels problem that my community faced. My fire agency had successfully kept or contained all of our wildland fires to under 1/4 of an acre, for more than 20 years. Our fuels were becoming more dense, over grown, and harder to suppress, and dryer summers were becoming the norm. Generally "fire exclusion" in our community was well into it's 80th year.

In understanding we had a serious wildfire threat, and attempting to look at what could become a solution to our fuels problem, kind of from a risk analysis standpoint, we looked at it from the three common fire components of the wildland fire situation, i.e. what could be changed, or modified? The three components are;
(1) **Topography,** (2) **Weather,** (3) and **Fuels.** and being that fuels are the only thing that could be modified, that's where we began or effort.

It needs to be stated that I unsuccessfully for about a year and a half made an effort on my own, to develop a fuels reduction program, within the community. In 1987-88 a cooperative effort within the community was developed. This began with a joining of common goals with the University of Nevada, Cooperative Extension Office, and my Fire Prevention Office, this was the beginning of a community, and eventually a regional cooperative effort.

This entailed, both California, and Nevada state forestry agencies, the U.S.F.S. Lake Tahoe Basin Management Unit, the Tahoe Regional Planning Agency, our General Improvement District, private land owners, and citizens, our business community, Chamber of Commerce, Board of Realtors, Service Clubs, The regional Sierra Front Wildfire Cooperators, (a multi local state, and federal fire agencies), and numerous others. The logic of a needed cooperative effort, was that wildfires do not respect political, or private boundaries. Wildfire is every one's problem.

In 1988 a "pilot project " of fuels modification, and removal, was granted, by the Tahoe Regional Planning Agency, the approving agency, and the General Improvement District, who is responsible for the land. In the spring of 1989, with the assistance of the Nevada Div. Of Forestry hand crews, 480 live and dead trees, were removed, as well as some brush reductions, on a total 20 acres.

Our objective was to show that fire protection concerns, as well as environmental concerns, could both be met in a "fuels reduction" program.

The Tahoe Regional Planning Agency, (T.R.P.A.) was very pleased, and if a grade value could be placed upon the work , we would have received an "A+". Our objective was to be conservative in our removal process, and it was commented on, that we could have removed more of the tree stand than we had.

Our fuels reduction approach, has and still operates from the conservative mode, and it has worked well in the continuing programs developed through the years. Our first 20 acre program in 1988-89, gave us the stepping stone, to the next 20 acres, which began in 1990. Our next step was a much greater project.

In the summer of 1991, with approvals from the T.R.P.A., and approvals from "our taxpayers" during numerous public hearings within our community, approximately 1 million dollars of the communities tax dollars were expended to remove the diseased and dying tree's within 750 acres of the communities most hazardous drainage's. This selective timber removal operation, was accomplished by the use of a helicopter. Approximately 18,000 tree's were removed, with only 5% being live green. Fuels reduction on the ground, ladder fuel and brush reductions were also accomplished. This reduction and removal process, left our department with 11,000 slash piles to burn through the winter of 91-92. With the cooperation of our Counties Air Quality Board, and good wind conditions, we were able to burn approximately 8,000 piles in that winter season. The remainder were finished up the next winter.

Our community is approximately 9,000 acres, with approximately 7,500 buildings, from high-rise casino's to very large single family dwellings. Our General Improvement District is responsible for 1,100 acres of land, with currently 95% of that public land having had the fuels reduced, and maintained on a on going basis. Regarding the private lands, approximately 45% have had some or all of the fuels reduction accomplished. The U.S.F.S. has 680+ sensitive urban lots with in our community, in a cooperative effort with our department, and Nevada Div. of Forestry, 650 of those lots have had fuels reduction accomplished. In the community overall, we have made a good start, but still have a ways to go. Next year we will begin "prescribed burning" as one of the options to on going maintenance of the fuels, in our drainage's. One of our on going management options, is to return fire into the ecosystem.

Our fuels reduction program, is called the Incline Village Crystal Bay Defensible Space program, and has become a model within our region, and in Northern California, as well.

The wildland urban interface:

The wildland urban interface problem is not new, the Native Americans experienced wildfires, and in some cases utilized fire as a tool, before European man began to settle America.

Our recognition of the urban interface problem on a national level became apparent almost three decades ago, with the publication of a National Fire Protection Association, wildland urban interface problem recognition, where 1400 homes were lost. The years that followed continued to address the wildfire issues, as they increased, and in some years they decreased. But "the 1987 fire siege of California" began the fires of the future quotes, which have become more notable since.

As humans move into these fire dependent environments, which currently is on the increase, we as the public servants are not educating them on the risks associated with, where they build their houses, or we fail to provide adequate planning for fire occurrences in the development stages of their homes. This creates primary problems for the Fire Ground, or Incident Commanders, of the U.S.F.S. and B.L.M., land management agencies, as well as in agencies similar to ours.

The critical factor becomes apparent, with limited resources, you either protect the natural resources, or protect the lives and property, of people that have moved into the wildland urban interface areas. Some times the small fires become the large fires, and we lose both, with an alarming increase in the natural resource losses, and a continuing escalation in the amount of lives lost. It has become a no win situation for the Incident Commanders.

The Costs:

The 1994 fire season is a good example, of the types of fires that we are seeing more often each fire season. In 1994 literally millions of acres of natural resources were lost, or in natural terms, you could say evolved through a natural cycle. And by no means should we discount the loss of 33 fire fighters lives, attempting to protect those resources, other peoples lives, and property. When all the bills are in, I have been told that the national suppression bill will reach **approximately 1 billion dollars,** and that will not include the dollars expended at the state levels.

In the suppression efforts, the fire service agencies attempted to protect natural habitats, that may, or may not, have provided cover for endangered plants or animal species, however where these losses occurred, and in human terms, these forest systems were drastically modified, or changed, and will not return to what it was, way beyond our life times. These are the results of our past management practices, and I believe we need to evaluate all the costs associated with the way we are currently doing business, and ask ourselves "can we do it better a different way", and what are the underlying costs to our natural resources?

The wildfires are becoming more advanced in fire behavior, with the suppression costs escalating, while at the same time we are seeing reductions in the budgets for fire fighting manpower, and resources.

We have had armies, and air forces of firefighters at these large complex fires, and we have had to attempt to burn them out of fuel or wait for the weather patterns to change. These are the same proven tactics that we have used for decades, and they still work, it's just that the fire behavior is more radical, because of the tremendous buildup of unmanaged fuels. We still need to continue to fund our suppression activities, but we also at the same time need to begin addressing the unmanaged fuels, with allocated dollars, that will eventually maybe balance the suppression expenditures.

I researched one fire in 1992, that was very close to the Lake Tahoe Basin. I did so because of the similar fuel types. This example is only one of many that could be evaluated for cost comparisons, of pre-suppression work vs. fuels management or fuels reduction, before the fire.

The El Dorado National Forest, the Cleveland Fire, September 1992, 12:04 PM. High winds, low humidity, steep terrain, and heavy concentrations of forest fuels with extremely low fuel moisture content, contributed to problems with long range spotting. Final size of fire 24,500 acres.

The National Fire Protection Association (N.F.P.A.) Journal November/December 1993, edition, lists the Cleveland fire as the nations largest loss wildland fire 1992. (Michael J. Sullivan, Fire Analysis and Research Div. (617) 984-7484)

The recorded loss is totaled at $245,525,000. which does not include the 16.5 million dollars in suppression costs, and the loss of two lives (air tanker pilots).

The break down is as follows:

41 homes and structures		$ 3,500,000.00
private/timber stand losses		230,000,000.00
marketable bio-mass		1,000,000.00
re vegetation/slope stabilization		2,000,000.00
Pacific Gas & Electric, utilities		7,000,000.00
Sacramento Utilities Dist. (SMUD)		175,000.00
Caltrans, roads, signs, infrastructure		250,000.00
D.C Air Tanker		1,000,000.00
(missing item)		400,000.00

	Total:	$245,525,000.00

Additionally there were 72 injuries with no recorded costs associated to them. These losses plus the suppression costs, average out to approximately **$10,700.00 per acre.** Our communities average highest cost since 1988 including our helicopter operation has averaged **$800.00** pre acre.

In these days of cutbacks, budget reductions, and doing more for less, can we afford these "Fires of the future"? Shouldn't we be reviewing the past to learn and better define a strategy for the future, looking for the best approach for the protection of lives, reducing the escalating costs in property damage, and attempting to reduce the wildfire impacts to our natural resources.

Other items of importance:

1. If we are to manage our natural resources, from a ecosystem management strategy, then the use of Prescribed fire needs to be discussed, where it conflicts with the Air Quality Standards, the PM 10 standards. There is a constant battle between local, state, and federal agencies in this area.

2. First let me make myself clear, I personally think we need to manage our forests, but I also believe that the management can be accomplished in a more gentle manner. I feel that there is a risk in doing something in the forests, and a risk in doing nothing, such as attempting to preserve a living system. When managing the forest I feel that the end objective should be in leaving the lightest footprint as possible, when the job is done.

3. Local state and federal agency, cooperative efforts must be established, to effectively manage any landscape. It doesn't make sense to manage fuels to a so called property line, or jurisdiction, and stop. The fire won't! Large scale management operations should develop cooperative efforts with numerous landowners, in the total landscape.

4. Some how there has to be a way to encourage other markets or use's of forest products. There has to be some use of the small diameter product. It is generally what came off our project, because of the dense stand configuration, and the shaded crowns. This seems to be the case in other forests. On our projects, we couldn't even give the mulch away for free, yet the landscape contractors in Reno Nevada were paying to have mulch shipped from Oregon, at 35 dollars a cubic yard. This was a time of drought, when zero-cape landscaping was being promoted.

Respectfully

Gerald L. Adams, Fire Marshal

STATEMENT OF

THE NATIONAL ASSOCIATION OF HOME BUILDERS

Chairman Allard, Chairman Hansen and Members of the Subcommittees:

I am Jim Irvine, a home builder from Portland, Oregon, and the 1995 President of the National Association of Home Builders, otherwise known as NAHB. On behalf of the 180,000 members of NAHB, I would like to express my appreciation for the opportunity to address the issue of Forest Health. Our forests are a great resource, and their health is critical to the ability of future generations to enjoy their majesty and derive benefit from that which they have to offer. Indeed, the health of our nation's forests, both now and in the future, is an area of great interest for NAHB as we are the single largest end user of forest products in this country.

Background

New home construction and remodeling and repair of homes account for more than two-thirds of all lumber consumed in the United States each year. The rest is used for non-residential construction and manufacturing. So as you can see, the home builders and, most importantly, home buyers of this country depend a great deal on a steady, predictable supply of good quality lumber at reasonable prices. As you know, over the past couple of years, lumber prices have been extremely volatile, with an underlying trend upward. This is extremely problematic for the home building industry, as there is a significant impact on housing activity as a consequence of higher prices. And, while many have questioned our continuing focus on this issue,

claiming prices have stabilized, consider the following: In March of 1994 prices hit $486 per 1000 board feet, then dropped to $356 by April 29. They jumped again to $431 on June 3, and dropped to $351 on September 23. On November 4, prices jumped to $413, and have since subsided to $378 where they now stand. I can tell you from personal experience that this is extremely frustrating. Our desire is to offer the lowest possible price to our customers, but instead we continue to be forced to account for sudden spikes in lumber prices.

Lumber prices have a profound impact on housing affordability. For every $50 increase in the price of lumber, the cost of building an average (2,000 s.f., $120,000) home rises by approximately $1,000. Just this seemingly small increase forces approximately 20,000 people out of the housing market. Sadly it is primarily first-time home buyers who make up this market share. Furthermore, the impact this has on the economy is substantial. Not only are 20,000 less people able to invest in their future by purchasing a home, but for every home that is not built, approximately two real estate industry jobs are not realized.

Mr. Chairman, our mission as home builders is to provide decent, affordable housing to the people of our communities. This price volatility has, and continues to, significantly hinder our ability to do that.

It is a well-recognized fact that without a healthy housing industry, we cannot have a healthy economy. Indeed, housing has led this nation out of every recession since World War II. Unfortunately, with interest rates having moved sharply upward, the ability of housing to drive today's economy is jeopardized as fewer people are able to afford a home. Add to that fluxuating lumber prices and an overall upward trend, and the situation is exacerbated.

Cause of Lumber Price Volatility

Many have argued that the cause of rising lumber prices is not due to a reduction in timber supply, but rather an increased demand for lumber, both domestically and abroad. Naturally demand does play a role in lumber prices, and exports have an impact, but to attribute lumber price volatility to these factors is erroneous, if not ludicrous.

There is one, and only one, primary reason for the volatility in lumber prices: the dramatic decrease in timber supply from public lands. It is the one factor that has shown significant and consistent change. Indeed, lumber consumption and lumber exports have remained constant over the past five years. Timber harvests from private lands and lumber imports have actually increased, which generally would mean greater price stability. Instead, prices have fluxuated wildly, reaching a record high of $506 at the beginning of 1994. The decrease in Forest Service timber sales from the entire country tells the story -- they have dropped from over 10 billion board feet in Fiscal Year 1991 to an estimated 4.2 billion board feet for Fiscal Year 1995.

Moreover, if the Administration's plan is enacted, they will drop even further in FY '96, as the proposed budget calls for sales levels of only 3.7 billion board feet.

What does this have to do with the subject of today's hearing? A great deal. Most significantly, the fact that each year, billions of board feet of salvage timber that could be turned into quality lumber lies rotting on federal lands. Indeed, it seems abundantly clear that at our fingertips lies an opportunity to at least make a substantial dent in the timber supply problem -- both in the short term and the long term. Yet, environmental extremists continue to squawk, the Administration continues to balk, even in the face of an Option 9 that has not lived up to its billing, and the timber continues to rot.

Mr. Chairman, this must change. We must take advantage of this opportunity, and aggressively undertake forest health procedures such as salvage sales and targeted thinning to provide some desperately needed relief to the decimated timber pipeline.

While forest health activities will provide assistance in the area of timber supply, they have important benefits on other fronts as well. I would like to address two of them, as I believe this will strengthen the argument for increasing these activities. They are protecting the environment and the improving the situation with the federal budget.

Environmental Protection

Last summer, due to the fact that salvage was not adequately cleared and effective thinning practices could not be undertaken, 67,000 wildfires scorched over four million acres of prime forestland. They burned with such intensity that soil, watershed, and plant conditions were unnaturally altered. Untold numbers of animals which resided in those forests undoubtedly perished in those fires. All of this occurred as a result of misguided policies and actions allegedly meant to protect the environment. Mr. Chairman, living in the Northwest I have seen the results of those fires -- the endless acres of black, barren earth -- and " environmental protection" is not a term that leaps to mind. I must say that if find it extremely puzzling that organizations and decision-makers whose avowed mission is to protect the environment would pursue policies that put such vast tracts of it at risk.

While tragic, last year's forest fires may have taught us a painful, but important lesson: a strictly "hands-off" approach to forest management is simply not in the best interest of the environment. You will hear that our forests and the species they supported thrived until the white man tread upon this land. You will hear that they even thrived into modern times when timber conglomerates began to turn them into purely profit-making resources. Indeed, you will hear that the health of our nation's forests is on the precipice of disaster, and that unless we drop our saws and walk out now they may be ruined forever.

These are impassioned appeals, Mr. Chairman, but they are totally misdirected. I would like to refer to a publication that NAHB has produced called "The Truth About America's Forests," and would like to submit it for the record. The publication draws from U.S. Forest Service statistics which tell us not that the health of our forests is declining, but exactly the opposite. In fact, between 1952 and 1992, the average timber volume per acre of our national forests has increased by fully one-third. Furthermore, more trees are growing in the nation's forests now than at any time since 1900. This is a direct result of the fact that with each passing decade, silvicultural and overall forest management techniques have improved. A significant component of that has been salvage timber treatment and more effective thinning techniques. That is, until recently.

In a similar vein, in the past, stands of trees were overcrowded, and therefore unhealthy, as too many trees competed for sunlight, soil nutrients, and moisture. As forests grew more dense, and the forest ceiling closed in, undergrowth supporting a myriad of species would disappear. Fortunately, modern forestry efforts have served to bring substantial improvement to this situation.

A good indication of this improvement is the increased abundancy of animal species dependent on the forests. Salvage clearing, forest thinning, and an increase in the acreage of managed forests promoted the growth of vegetation that supports

89-215 O - 95 - 9

a great variety of animals. I submit to you examples of four animals that tend to reside in forestlands. From 1930 to 1990:

- The Whitetail Deer population has grown from approximately 1 million to over 15 million;
- The Wild Turkey population has grown from approximately 100,000 to nearly 4 million;
- The Pronghorn Antelope population has grown from approximately 10,000 to over 500,000; and
- The Elk population has grown from approximately 50,000 to over 500,000.

Mr. Chairman, it is my impression that we have been led to believe that any time man comes into contact with the environment, it can only lead to its ultimate demise. The facts show that this is simply not the case.

Certainly we cannot be so arrogant as to believe that we can, or should, attempt to alter the course of Mother Nature. However, as we have seen in many cases, a helping hand can pay off in long-term benefits.

Federal Budget

I'd like to now turn to the impact forest health efforts can have on the federal budget. One of the criticisms of stepping up the salvage timber program is that we simply cannot afford it. Indeed, as it was this year, the salvage timber program is often the target of budget cuts within the President's budget. Mr. Chairman, I propose to you today that we cannot afford not to increase salvage sales.

As I have stated, removing dead and dying timber and incorporating advanced thinning techniques is critical to preventing forest fires such as those we witnessed last summer. Unfortunately, as a result of the inability of the Forest Service to perform these tasks, it spent nearly $1 billion fighting those fires. Add to that the lost potential revenue from the forests, the costs of rehabilitating the burned areas and performing wildlife and watershed restoration, which will reach into the hundreds of millions, and we begin to see the impact of not funding forest health programs.

Taking this a step further, the salvage timber program is a net revenue producer. The Salvage Timber Trust Fund, which was established to provide the seed money for the initiation of the salvage program, has been fully reimbursed and continues to run a net surplus. The Trust Fund is one of the most healthy components of the Forest Service Timber Sale Program, and should be expanded to take advantage of the tremendous potential that exists in our national forests.

And, Mr. Chairman, the potential truly <u>is</u> tremendous. U.S. Forest Service statistics indicate that historically only the surface has been scratched in terms of undertaking forest health efforts on the timberlands that have been affected by fire or insect damage.

Each year from 1987 through 1991, the most recent year analyzed, on average 10.6 billion acres of national forestland was damaged by fire or insects. Of that amount, an average of 1.83 billion acres, or only 17%, were treated. This means that in each of those years an average of 8.77 billion acres of our forestland that required forest health treatments rotted rather than being put to productive use. This is extremely frustrating for home builders, and certainly for home buyers, who pay the price for the lack of timber production from our national forests.

I would like to talk about this potential in a different light, and look at it from a home building perspective. I have heard estimates that last year approximately 5 billion board feet of dead and dying timber sat on our national forest floors. It is extremely disheartening to me when I think about the potential for housing that simply rotted away. Consider that it takes approximately 10,000 board feet of timber to build an average home. Therefore, the wood that rotted away last year could have produced enough lumber to build <u>500,000</u> homes. If this were not disconcerting enough, consider that due to the fact that this salvage did not get cleared, we lost

<u>another</u> 3.5 billion board feet of standing timber to the fires! All told then, the ramifications of the Forest Service's inability to conduct forest health practices has cost us timber that could have built <u>850,000</u> homes!

On a smaller scale, even the ability of the Forest Service to achieve maximum results in current salvage programs could truly make a difference. Consider that for FY '95 the Forest Service estimates that it will only be able to retrieve roughly 656 million board feet of lumber. However, they have noted that if the appropriate determinations are made, and the environmental impact statements indicate they can go forward, and their funding were to go far enough, they could retrieve 1.493 billion board feet of salvage timber this fiscal year. This is a difference of 837 million board feet. Therefore, the difference between what the Forest Service will most likely do, and what they feasibly <u>could</u> do, could build 83,700 homes.

Mr. Chairman, the potential is there, we simply must tap into it. To do otherwise is a disservice to forest protection as well as to our national economy.

Conclusion

NAHB supports any effort to provide for short-term salvage timber sales, whether it is an effort to streamline approval of the sales by replacing lengthy Environmental Impact Statement (EIS) with environmental assessments, or the adoption of sufficiency language to insulate these sales from the constant legal

challenges they have faced. At the very least, Congress should rethink the need for EIS's on salvage sales, considering the fact that dead and dying timber is unusable within 12-18 months.

Also, NAHB supports any efforts to increase forest health activities over the long term. Maintaining and improving the health of our nation's forests is a national obligation and is truly paramount to the ability of home builders to provide affordable housing.

Mr. Chairman, it is critical that we look at forest health as an investment. It is an investment that will result in minimized costs down the road. It is an investment in our heritage and in our future. It is an investment that will bring long term gains to the treasury. It is an investment that will help boost the economy through more stable lumber prices, and therefore more stable housing prices.

Thank you for this opportunity to testify. I look forward to any questions you might have.

####

WWF

CONGRESSIONAL TESTIMONY BEFORE THE RESOURCES COMMITTEE: SUBCOMMITTEE ON NATIONAL PARKS AND FORESTS

Presented by Dr. Dominick A. DellaSala, Senior Forest Ecologist, World Wildlife Fund, on 10 February 1995

I would like to thank the chairman and members of the committee for inviting me to testify this morning. As a doctor of forest ecology, I lived and worked for 8 years in the Pacific Northwest, investigating the impacts of logging operations, including thinning and salvage, on fish and wildlife. I understand that although this hearing was originally intended to address forest health, the members of this committee would prefer testimony focusing on salvage and thinning. While I am quite qualified to do that, I think it is imperative that members of this committee understand that thinning and salvage are merely components of forest health in general, and can only be dealt within that context. Because of the interconnectedness of forest functions, thinning and salvage cannot be dealt with independently.

While I realize that this hearing was conceived of in the aftermath of the tragic effects of last year's fires in the inland northwest, thinning and salvage practices alone will not prevent forest fires, or control the spread of forest diseases. While we agree that there is opportunity to use thinning and salvage to boost local economies, such activities must be conducted within the framework of NEPA and scientific assessments currently underway in the region. Similarly, it is imperative that these appropriate safeguards be taken to ensure that economic gains are also sustainable and not just short term.

World Wildlife Fund
1250 Twenty-Fourth St., NW Washington, DC 20037-1175 USA
Tel: (202) 293-4800 Telex: 64505 PANDA FAX: (202) 293-9211
Incorporating The Conservation Foundation. Affiliated with World Wide Fund for Nature.

In addition, having worked on salvage effects, I realize that there are opportunities to remove some trees damaged by fire through salvage. However, salvage operations should be conducted outside roadless areas and late-successional forests (forests older than 200 years and undisturbed by logging), and should leave large, older trees untouched. This is because large trees are resistant to fires and therefore act as natural fire breaks, are often resistant to disease, and provide essential habitat for species that feed on destructive insects. Salvage operations must also utilize appropriate logging techniques that minimize soil damage. If we continue to cause soils to run off into streams, we will not only destroy salmon spawning beds, but reduce the ability of forests to recover from logging. Lastly, while some level of salvage may be acceptable, maintaining adequate amounts of coarse woody debris is essential for cycling nutrients back into soils, and providing structural habitat for many insect eating species that will help reduce costly insect outbreaks. The Forest Service has some scientifically credible guidelines in place for leaving trees within salvage areas to reduce these impacts.

While thinning and salvage may appear to reduce the intensity and frequency of fires, or insect outbreaks, there is no agreement from the scientific community that this in fact is true, particularly during periods of drought like last year. On the contrary, there is evidence that extensive thinning, salvage, and spraying with insecticides diminishes the ability of a forest to respond to insect outbreaks. Many species (ants, wasps, bats, birds) feed on destructive insects and are more effective and economical at keeping these insects in check than is pesticide application. Most of these species live in late-successional forests, further supporting the position that those areas should not be logged or salvaged.

Having worked on numerous thinning projects, it is my professional opinion that thinning will result in even greater forest health problems and fire risks over the long-term. Thinning can dry out the forest understory and increase fuels by leaving behind the slash created by thinning. Road building to access areas for thinning also increases fire risks. In fact, many of last year's fires were caused by careless people having access to fire prone areas through the already extensive road network crisscrossing our national forests.

In closing, I am not advocating that thinning and salvage be prohibited on federal lands. However, it is vital that roadless areas and late-successional forests be exempt from these activities - these few remaining natural areas are absolutely critical in maintaining salmon populations on which local communities are economically dependent. We urge the committee to resist the temptation to use salvage and thinning as a primary means of increasing the dollars generated from our nation's forests and for achieving forest health objectives. The committee should instead concentrate on logging practices that will protect remaining late-successional forests and restoring salmon populations both of which are essential for keeping the inland northwest forests healthy, functional, and prosperous for future generations.

I would like to note that there is strong public support for restoring salmon populations in the region for economic reasons. A recent study by "Save Our Salmon (a northwest conglomeration of environmental and fisheries organizations) indicated that restoring Chinook Salmon in the Columbia River basin would generate $349 million in additional revenues and return fishing jobs to the region.

I have provided more extensive information in support of my testimony and I welcome any questions you might have. Thank you for your interest.

THE WILDLIFE SOCIETY
5410 Grosvenor Lane • Bethesda, MD 20814-2197
Tel: (301) 897-9770 • Fax: (301) 530-2471

TESTIMONY OF THOMAS M. FRANKLIN

WILDLIFE POLICY DIRECTOR OF THE WILDLIFE SOCIETY

BEFORE THE

RESOURCES SUBCOMMITTEE ON NATIONAL PARKS, FORESTS AND LANDS

AND THE AGRICULTURE SUBCOMMITTEE ON RESOURCES CONSERVATION, RESEARCH AND FORESTRY

OF THE

U.S. HOUSE OF REPRESENTATIVES

10 FEBRUARY 1995

Mr. Chairmen and Members of the Subcommittees, my name is Thomas M. Franklin. I am a Certified Wildlife Biologist and Wildlife Policy Director of The Wildlife Society. The Wildlife Society is the association of professional wildlife biologists and managers dedicated to excellence in wildlife stewardship through science and education. I was pleased to be invited to speak to you today about salvage timber sales in the American West and their implications for wildlife and wildlife habitat. My testimony will include a summary of a report from an independent panel of scientists that carefully studied eastside forests in Oregon and Washington states. I will conclude my comments with some observations and recommendations from The Wildlife Society.

A panel of ecologists from five scientific societies recently conducted a study that found the remaining old forests east of the Cascade Crest in Oregon and Washington more fragmented than at any time since European settlement; leaving native fish populations severely depleted and watersheds extensively degraded. The scientists concluded that the findings point to poor health of entire landscapes, not just of forests.

The national forests east of the Cascade crest are as ecologically important as the westside forests addressed in the President's 1993 Northwest Forest conference. Yet no synthesis of scientific information about the Eastside was available. To begin to fill this void, several members of Congress requested our societies to establish a panel of scientists to review the status of all Eastside forests and their associated resources.

The panel's report, **Interim Protection for Late-Successional Forests, Fisheries, and Watersheds: National Forests East of the Cascade Crest, Oregon and Washington**, analyses current conditions in 10 national forests east of the Cascades. It covers forest resources, resident and migratory fishes, aquatic systems and wildlife. The findings demonstrate the diversity of habitats, species, and histories in these national forests and make clear that comprehensive interdisciplinary approaches to landscape management are essential to halt degradation of Eastside resources.

Concerns about management of forests throughout the West have risen with the wildfires of 1994. Some scientists, resources managers, and citizens are calling for immediate intervention through logging to improve forest health. To alleviate these threats, many are advocating widespread salvage (removal of dead and dying wood) and thinning (cutting small live trees), with inadequate analysis.

However, the Eastside Forests Scientific Society Panel's report concludes that such narrowly conceived approaches to forest management are inadequate for protecting forest resources, whether water, fish, timber, or wildlife. Salvage and thinning may benefit some dense tree stands, but these techniques may at the same time increase risk to forest resources other than timber.

The panel, comprised of members of The Wildlife Society, American Fisheries Society, American Ornithologists' Union, The Ecological Society of America, the Sierra Biodiversity Institute and the Society for Conservation Biology, gives 12 recommendations for protecting eastside landscapes. The panel emphasizes that its recommendations should be in effect only until a long-term management strategy, cooperatively developed, can be put in place. These recommendations target areas containing the ecological building blocks for restoring and sustaining the health of the entire Eastside.

The panel's recommendations fall into five categories:

1. Protect remaining late-successional/old-growth forests; large old trees, and dominant ponderosa pines.
2. Protect aquatic diversity areas, roadless regions, and stream corridors.
3. Limit timber harvest on steep slopes, fragile soils, and unique or vulnerable sites.
4. Create multi-organizational teams with broad expertise to develop long-term management plans

for all eastside national forests.

5. Set up a monitoring program to track eastside landscape conditions for the long term.

With specific reference to salvage logging, the panel found that salvage cuts that remove a substantial proportion of standing, downed, or potential future coarse woody debris are detrimental to most old forest organisms. The value and effect of salvage cuts in general, and for any forest patch in particular, need to be investigated and evaluated. They recommend limiting salvage cuts only to specific, carefully managed situations where old growth is present. The panel's interim recommendations also urged the establishment of a panel with broad expertise to develop long-term management guidelines for securing the ability of eastside forests to resist drought, crown fires, and catastrophic outbreaks of insects and pathogens. The scientists stated: "Fire prevention and early logging practices have altered some late successional/old growth (LS/OG) systems, making them vulnerable to drought, insects, and fire. Salvage and thinning are two legitimate techniques--but not the only ones--for lowering the risk from such disturbances. Lack of consensus and past abuses, in which large healthy trees were cut in the guise of salvage, lead us to recommend a comprehensive study of this issue. Scientists disagree over how to define the goals of salvage and thinning and how to select areas where salvage or thinning is required. At issue is the purpose of removing dead material: for ecological or economic enrichment? for short-or long-term return? No consensus exists on silvicultural practices for minimizing the effects of drought, fire, insects, and pathogens; or the conditions that warrant managing LS/OG to reduce risk of catastrophic loss; or on the levels of treatment that reduce risk without compromising ecological values. Sustaining regional resources and their use depends on

89-215 O - 95 - 10

enlightened and comprehensive approaches to protecting forest health.

Such approaches should include assessment of forest health and development of ecologically sound techniques for restoring unhealthy stands. In particular, stands should be identified where excessive understory fuel has accumulated (overstocked stands) or where fire prevention or selective logging of big, valuable trees has altered stand structure. They suggest that (1) controlled burning be done or natural fires be allowed to burn where fuel levels are low enough to avoid runaway fire; (2) selective logging be restricted to thinning from below in overstocked stands; and (3) dominant and codominant trees not be cut in the guise of improving forest health."

Independent of the Eastside Forests Scientific Society Panel report, The Wildlife Society wishes to offer some observations and suggestions concerning timber salvage sales. Much of the concern of wildlife professionals is due to the focus on dead trees instead of the forest. They wish to capture the dead standing timber while it is still valuable, and the consequences of opening more road access, and effects on other resources are not getting the attention they deserve. There seems to be little concern for wildlife or fish resources among those who support aggressive salvage operations. Their focus is only on how the burned stands are vulnerable to fire, how much timber volume has been lost, and how something needs to be done about it immediately. The problem with forest health is not new. It was recognized nearly 30 years ago, but the Forest Service has done little to address the problem. Only now, they say that we have a crisis that requires extraordinary actions to resolve.

Wildlife professionals have several important questions that should be answered before salvage sales are expanded. How much attention has the Forest Service given to analyzing the effects of salvage on fish and wildlife? What emphasis is placed on roadless areas? With regard to forest regeneration, are salvage sales going to be done on the best tree growing sites or where the biggest trees exist? They are not necessarily the same places. Also, have salvage sales been effectively coordinated with state fish and wildlife agencies?

The Wildlife Society does not oppose salvaging some of the dead standing trees in areas where access already occurs, on sites where opportunities to regenerate forests are best, where fish and wildlife values, including cover, may be enhanced, and where watershed damage is most likely to be minimal. However, sufficient dead standing trees of varied size classes need to be retained as these snags are extremely valuable for wildlife. We oppose salvage sales that open up road access, are on poor timber growing sites, and do not adequately consider fish and wildlife and watershed values. We are concerned that many forest biologists provide input that is not incorporated in salvage sales. We strongly recommend that state fish and wildlife agencies be involved actively in the salvage sale process.

The Forest Service apparently believes that it has support for extending salvage sales, but it should not ignore the consequences of its activities. The Forest Service and Congress would do well to listen carefully to the concerns of professional biologists. If they listen, carefully analyze the possible effects of their actions, and follow existing environmental laws, perhaps some of the conflicts that resulted from ignoring biologists' warnings in the "spotted owl forests" in westside forests can be avoided.

The Forest Service is moving ahead with post-fire rehabilitation and timber salvage sales without a long-term plan for restoring forest health, protecting riparian habitat, providing connectivity for wildlife habitat, protecting old growth, and managing roadless areas. Actions are being driven by each year's fires. We recognize the dilemma they face with the threat of wildfires, but are concerned that the Forest Service may be foregoing long-term options for fish and wildlife conservation and ecosystem health. Salvage timber sales should be limited to previously roaded areas where they can do the most good at regenerating the forest while protecting old growth and restoring the ecological integrity of selected watersheds.

Thank you.

George E. Brown

REMARKS PREPARED FOR PRESENTATION BY REPRESENTATIVE GEORGE E. BROWN, JR. STATEMENT BEFORE THE SUBCOMMITTEE ON RESOURCE CONSERVATION, RESEARCH, AND FORESTRY AND THE SUBCOMMITTEE ON NATIONAL PARKS, FORESTS, AND LANDS

OVERSIGHT ON FOREST HEALTH AND EMERGENCY SALVAGE SALES

Mr. Chairman, I thank you for the opportunity to say a few words about this issue of "forest health" and the role that salvage logging has played in contributing to forest health problems.

Our forests are indeed beset by many problems: watershed damage, dying trees, soil erosion, over-grazing, wildlife facing extinction. But to declare that "salvage sales" will be a panacea for these problems is foolish and short-sighted. In so doing we are prescribing the wrong treatment for a real problem. Most of the attention in this forest health issue is being paid to fire, disease and insect damage, rather than to some of the more serious problems such as soil erosion and habitat destruction. Perhaps it's because fire, insects and disease are commodity damaging and don't allow for a maximization of timber production. However, they are also naturally occurring and are necessary and beneficial to a healthy ecosystem. The others, which are results of our "management", most certainly are not.

Forest Health is the health of soil, water and air. Defining Forest Health as tree vigor is inconsistent with Ecosystem Management. There *is* a forest health problem in the West but its solution is long term protection and recovery of healthy water, soil and air. Emergency salvage sales and other "quick fixes" have little hope of achieving the objectives of forest health.

I find it very interesting that within the last few years, as restrictions on clearcutting and other ecologically damaging practices have been implemented, the timber industry and some members of Congress have discovered that there is a "crisis" of "forest health" problems. Even more interesting is their solution to this crisis: road-building and logging.

1987 and 1988 saw intense fire seasons across the West, far worse than what we have seen in recent years. And yet this period was at the height of clearcutting, logging, roadbuilding, and all of the management practices endorsed by the timber industry. Wildfires over the past few years have burned no more lands overall than during many other times in the past century. But now, fire, disease and insect damage, all natural and *important* functions of forest health, are being spoken of as symptoms of forest health problems.

Apparently the situation is so dire that industry and some congressional salvage proposals recommend suspension of Endangered Species Act (ESA) and The National Environmental Protection Act (NEPA) procedures to quickly deal with this "crisis". The mentality being that we must cut the trees *immediately* in order to save them. The solution of bypassing ESA and NEPA procedures and giving the managing agencies carte blanch to salvage dead and dying trees is not an appropriate one. Furthermore, a "dying" tree could be interpreted to mean anything alive. And with the appeals process eliminated, such language, in law, would basically permit unrestricted tree cutting.

Decades of fire suppression has indeed allowed some sections of the National Forests to grow thicker and more flammable than would have otherwise occurred. However, dense stands combined with brush and logging slash that have been unable to burn naturally pose a fire hazard that salvage logging will not solve. Even if salvage logging removed every dead tree, or if logging greatly thinned many forests, wildfires would still burn every year when heat, winds and fires combine. Some of the West's largest fires burned intensively through large areas already roaded and logged.

Since salvage sales are "sales" they generally focus on removing commercially valuable timber. Large trees are selected for removal, while smaller, non-merchantable trees along with debris, and logging slash are left on site. The larger removed trees are the least flammable fuels, while the smaller ones and especially the logging slash are the most flammable. The removal of large, live trees, snags and logs deprive the area of important shade and moisture reservoirs, making these sites hotter and drier. Add to that the dense stocks of even-aged firs that are often replanted for timber production and the sites are actually filled with a greater concentration of fuel.

Fire hazards and fuel loading are usually defined by "tons per acre" of dead material. This is a very misleading and inaccurate way to determine the fire hazard of a forest. For example, if an area has about 20 tons per acre of dead and down material, it is usually classified as a fire hazard. However, if this 20 tons per acre is in the form of just one huge dead tree per acre, either standing or down, there is very little fire danger. If that same 20 tons per acre was in the form of slash and debris scattered all over the forest floor then there is a fire hazard. Fire could easily ignite, spread, and build enough heat to ignite the living trees; but logging isn't going to solve the problem. Logging actually makes the fire danger worse. Taking an upright tree, even a dead tree with its branches high above the ground, and feeling it, branching it, hauling out the main trunk and leaving the top and all the branches on the ground makes a much more flammable situation than before logging.

Even though selective cutting in some areas is desirable, it is not always economical. The Congressional Research Service estimated that "thinning" just 10 percent of western national forests would cost $3.5 billion. Any true remedy for dangerous fire potential would have to include: taking out, logging, and/or burning out openings in many of the hundreds of thousands of acres of "tree farms" which, if left in place, could ignite and spread fire very fast; removing or control burning the lower elevation chaparral which acts like kindling; hand piling of natural and post-logging slash; and removal of non-commercial sized crowded thickets such as small white fir. All of these measures are very expensive. The salvage logging that takes place is not about clearing the forest of potentially dangerous fire kindling and ensuring forest health, but about taking the big, valuable trees. I have seen some of the areas in the Sierra that have been "thinned". The site usually looks like a clearcut with the big, profitable trees taken and the thin, little trees left.

Additionally, roads need to be built to do a "salvage" sale. According to fire officials, there are three leading causes of fire: men, women and children. Building roads into roadless areas to conduct salvage logging is not going to reduce the risk of future fires as it is only opening up the area to future human disturbance. Road building and salvage sales will not solve the overall problems. Only a sound, long-term ecosystem management approach will be effective.

Another important element that needs to be considered in this debate is the significant role that fire plays in forest health. We should not view a burned forest as a waste or a destruction. Fire produces an array of vital nutrient stimuli, chemical and biological soil changes, and plant successions that logging does not provide. Some trees, such as the Giant Sequoia, depend upon recurring fires for their own regeneration.

Fire-killed trees are very important to the regeneration of a burned forest and are a vital part of watershed and stream recovery. The dead trees, both standing and down, also provide critical habitat for many forest animals. When large snags and logs are removed, the area is exposed to greater sunlight. This affects the whole underground ecosystem of flora and fauna that are critical for making nutrients available to tree roots.

Yellowstone National Park, which the Park Service "let burn" in the 1988 fire, has today, according to scientific opinion, fully recovered. As an ecosystem it is even healthier and more diverse than before the fire. There was very little human intervention in the aftermath of the fire. The Park Service allowed time and nature to heal the forest.

In conclusion, I believe that any decisions to increase the use of salvage logging in our National Forests should be based on a scientific consensus that it has been effective in controlling fire and that it is of benefit to the forest ecosystem. I do not believe that under any circumstances we should allow the NEPA and public appeal processes, which are there to help protect against mismanagement and abuse, to be by-passed. It took years of poor management to create the unhealthy conditions in some of our forests. It will take years of sound, ecosystem management to restore those areas to health. The quick fix, emergency approaches being advocated have not worked in the past and are not appropriate now.

STATEMENT OF CONGRESSWOMAN JENNIFER DUNN
SUBCOMMITTEE ON NATIONAL PARKS, FORESTS AND LANDS
FEBRUARY 10, 1995

GOOD MORNING MR. CHAIRMAN. THANK YOU FOR THE OPPORTUNITY TO COME BEFORE YOUR COMMITTEE TO SHARE MY CONCERNS ON THE ISSUE OF FOREST HEALTH IN MY STATE OF WASHINGTON.

LAST YEAR'S DEVASTATING FIRES IN THE STATE OF WASHINGTON BURNED AN ESTIMATED ONE BILLION BOARD FEET OF TIMBER. I REMEMBER FLYING HOME TO WASHINGTON AND HAVING THE CLEAR BLUE SKY AT 40,000 FEET CLOUDED WITH SMOKE FROM THESE FIRES . WHILE THE LARGEST OF THESE FIRES BURNED IN AREAS COVERED BY PRESIDENT CLINTON'S FOREST PLAN, I WAS IN CONTACT WITH OLD FRIENDS WHO WERE TRYING TO PROTECT THEIR ORCHARDS FROM FIRES BURNING LESS THAN A QUARTER OF A MILE AWAY FROM THEIR LAND.

BECAUSE OF THE FLAWED FOREST POLICIES OF THE CLINTON ADMINISTRATION, THE FOREST SERVICE NOW PLANS TO SALVAGE LESS THAT 10 PERCENT OF THAT BURNED TIMBER AND MUCH OF THAT VOLUME WILL NOT BE OFFERED FOR SALE UNTIL LATER THIS YEAR.

THE MANAGEMENT DIRECTION OF PRESIDENT CLINTON'S PRESERVATION PLAN CALLS FOR MILLIONS OF ACRES TO BE LOCKED UP AND LEFT TO THE UNPREDICTABILITY OF MOTHER NATURE. THIS FAILED POLICY WASTES A VALUABLE RESOURCE THAT COULD EMPLOY THOUSANDS OF HARD-WORKING AMERICANS AND PROVIDE WOOD AND PAPER PRODUCTS FOR AMERICAN CONSUMERS, AND THEREFORE BRING MONEY INTO THE FEDERAL TREASURY.

PAGE 2

THERE IS ALSO AN ENVIRONMENTAL TRAGEDY ASSOCIATED WITH THIS FAILED POLICY. BY NOT REMOVING A SIGNIFICANT AMOUNT OF THE FIRE-KILLED TIMBER, IT INCREASES THE HIGH LIKELIHOOD THAT THE AREA WILL BURN AGAIN IN THE VERY NEAR FUTURE. SUCH A REBURN WOULD DESTROY MORE VALUABLE FOREST RESOURCES, WILDLIFE HABITAT AND PLACE HUMAN LIVES AND PROPERTY AT RISK.

IN CONCLUSION, WE NEED TO PASS LEGISLATION THAT EXPEDITES SALVAGE EFFORTS AND ESTABLISHES A NEW FOREST MANAGEMENT POLICY WHICH PUTS FOREST HEALTH AHEAD OF FOREST PRESERVATION. IT IS OF UTMOST IMPORTANCE THAT ANY LEGISLATION CONTAIN SUFFICIENCY LANGUAGE TO REDUCE OR ELIMINATE FRIVOLOUS BARRIERS TO THE PERMITTING PROCESS.

MR CHAIRMAN, I ASK THAT AN ARTICLE ENTITLED "WESTERN FOREST HEALTH INITIATIVE WATERED DOWN" FROM THE NEWSLETTER "FORESTRY FORUM" BE ENTERED INTO THE RECORD. THIS ARTICLE UNDERSCORES THE PROBLEMS THAT HAVE PLAGUED THIS ADMINISTRATION BECAUSE IT REFUSES TO SUPPORT SOUND SCIENTIFIC RECOMMENDATIONS EVEN FROM THEIR OWN AGENCIES.

THANK YOU MR. CHAIRMAN.

FORESTRY FORUM

Vol. IX, No. 3 February 3, 1995

New Rules Proposed for State and Private Lands

DNR Releases DEIS for Owls and Murrelets

The Washington Department of Natural Resources has issued a two volume draft environmental impact statement describing new rules to protect spotted owls and marbled murrelets on state and private lands. The rules are part of a comprehensive habitat conservation planning process the DNR has undertaken.

he rules would reinstate the infamous spotted owl circles in special emphasis areas (SOSEAs). The alternatives range from six SOSEAs to fifteen SOSEAs throughout western Washington. The no-action alternative would have no specific protection for spotted owls or murrelets.

The comment deadline is March 17, 1995. Hearings will be held in March in Olympia, Aberdeen, Bellingham and Ellensburg. NFA will coordinate the development of a comprehensive review of the planned rules. */Ralph Saperstein*

Western Forest Health Initiative Watered Down

Oregon Proposal Too Aggressive

The Western Forest Health Initiative, released by tthe Forest Service last month, appears to have ignored the recommendations of the first team that was chartered with preparing a report. The administration's plan calls for 330 forest health restoration projects covering about 1 million acres over the next two years. This is one-fifth of the 5 million acres recommended by the agency team that prepared the recommendations last fall.

In addition, the team recommended that obstacles such as appeals and conflicting laws be looked at closely. The team's findings stated that "the existing approach to NEPA is cumbersome and difficult to implement. Limitations in using categorical exclusions causes delays in forest health project implementation. The revised appeal regulations...also appear to many to be causing forest health and fire recovery projects to be delayed." The administration's plan does not address these issues at all.

You may recall that last fall the Forest Service convened a team of agency personnel to develop recommendations on forest health issues. This team, later to be known as Phase I, prepared a report and

What's Hot

Printed on recycled paper

presented it to the Chief and Agriculture Undersecretary Jim Lyons. However, this Phase I report never saw the light of day until it was recently leaked. Instead, a Phase II team was assembled that developed the final, watered down plan that the administration released in December.

It would seem that if the administration is serious about addressing forest health issues, it should start by listening to the experts--those that work on the ground and understand the mechanics the best. This latest development not only casts doubt on the administration's intentions, but it is a very costly and risky gamble with the nation's national forests. */Chuck Burley*

Lyons and Thomas Threaten Environmentalists

Support Forest Plan or Else

Undersecretary of Agriculture Jim Lyons and Forest Service Chief Jack Ward Thomas met with the Ancient Forest Alliance last month to warn them about opposing implementation of the President's Plan. According to a report of the meeting obtained by NFA, the Alliance was "given a stern lecture by Undersecretary Lyons."

Lyons cautioned that environmentalists must support the President's Plan or the "administration would be unable to fend off ...efforts by the Republican leadership to dismantle or rewrite environmental laws."

The report noted that, "(t)he Alliance was also treated to a grim threat from the Chief that timber sales would move forward despite costs, burned areas would be salvaged to produce volume, and roadless areas would remain part of the timber base." The Chief also stated, that the Forest Service "is not doing anything anymore, only planning and analyzing."

On the subject of salvage in the Columbia Basin Thomas said, "I promise to move aggressively. There are jobs to be gained, material to be used, it's hard to make an argument against it. We intend to move on this." */Ralph Saperstein*

Governor Kitzhaber Visits Eastside

Last week, Governor Kitzhaber and Paula Burgess, the Governor's Natural Resources Advisor, visited central Oregon. Industry representatives met with the Governor and Ms. Burgess at Ochoco Lumber Company's headquarters for one hour. The Governor started by stating that his objectives included bridging the gap between rural and urban communities and getting timber in the pipeline. Kitzhaber then asked what the obstacles were to eastside timber sales.

The discussion that followed focused on eastside screens, consultation, appeals, salvage, salmon, and other issues affecting timber supply. In addition, representatives from secondary manufacturing made it very clear to the Governor that they too are being hard hit by the timber supply crunch.

Overall the meeting was very informative. The timing was also fortuitous because the Governor was leaving for Washington, D.C. soon after the

FORESTRY FORUM
is the bi-weekly newsletter of the
Northwest Forestry Association
1500 S.W. First, Suite 770
Portland, Oregon 97201
(503) 222-9505
(503) 222-3255 - fax

Jim Geisinger, *Publisher*
Ralph Saperstein, *Editor*
Cindi Barrett, *Assistant Editor*
Tina Thomas, *Finance Manager*

Contributors:
Chris West, (503) 222-9505
Chuck Burley, (503) 389-2306
Bob Dick, (206) 352-3910
Ross Mickey, (503) 342-1892

The Resources Agency of California

Pete Wilson
Governor

Douglas P. Wheeler
Secretary

California Conservation Corps • Department of Boating & Waterways • Department of Conservation
Department of Fish & Game • Department of Forestry & Fire Protection • Department of Parks & Recreation • Department of Water Resources

TESTIMONY OF TERRY BARLIN GORTON
ASSISTANT SECRETARY FOR RESOURCES
FOR FORESTRY AND RURAL ECONOMIC DEVELOPMENT
STATE OF CALIFORNIA

BEFORE THE

SUBCOMMITTEE ON NATIONAL PARKS, FORESTS, AND LANDS
COMMITTEE ON RESOURCES

AND THE

SUBCOMMITTEE ON RESOURCE CONSERVATION, RESEARCH, AND FORESTRY
COMMITTEE ON AGRICULTURE
U.S. HOUSE OF REPRESENTATIVES
WASHINGTON, D.C.

PREVENTING CALIFORNIA WILDFIRE DISASTERS, AND SALVAGING TIMBER ON FEDERAL FOREST LANDS DISTRESSED BY INSECTS, DISEASE, AND FIRES WOULD IMPROVE FOREST HEALTH AND CREATE JOBS FOR TIMBER WORKERS

February 10, 1995

Mr. Chairman and members of the Subcommittees, thank you for this opportunity to present testimony on behalf of Governor Wilson about the threat and effects of wildfire, and the importance of salvaging burned, dead, and diseased timber on federal lands in California.

I will describe the conditions that have created and worsened the situation. I then will outline remedies that the State of California advocates or is undertaking with the federal government, and our recommendations for congressional action.

The Resources Building Sacramento, CA 95814 (916) 653-5656 FAX (916) 653-8102

California Coastal Commission • California Tahoe Conservancy • Colorado River Board of California
Energy Resources, Conservation & Development Commission • San Francisco Bay Conservation & Development Commission
State Coastal Conservancy • State Lands Commission • State Reclamation Board

The Nature of Fire in California

Unique weather, vegetation, landscapes, and other ecological elements make California a natural setting for seasonal wildfires. Fires ignited by lightning or human activity have occurred regularly across the mountains and valleys for thousands of years, greatly influencing the distribution and condition of grassland, desert, shrub land, and forest ecosystems.

In prior centuries, California's forests were less dense and more diverse than they are today. When fires occurred, many of them burned "cooler" than modern-day fires and were less likely to climb into tall old-growth timber or cause long-term damage to the forest floor and topsoil. Such fires burned the "understory" - the brush and smaller trees - but generally did not reach the crowns of taller trees, and spared most of the mature timber.

The periodic occurrence of fire also tended to limit the size, frequency, and intensity of succeeding fires. As a result, the historical forest pattern was a mosaic of patches that had burned at different times. These regularly occurring, regenerating fires served the ecosystem of California well in times when relatively few humans were present.

Causes of the Current Fire Threat

Today, forest conditions have changed, resulting in two major causes of California's current, severe fire threat:

- the inclination prevalent through most of the 20th century to view fire as an unequivocal foe to be fought and prevented under all circumstances, and

- the growing tendency of people to live on forest and wild lands.

(1) Viewing Fire as a Foe

Historically, Native Americans in California successfully used fire to manage the land, and such practices have continued on a smaller scale to the present. However, as humans widely explored the interior of California and began to reside in forests and wildlands, the threat of fire posed an increasing risk to life and property. The instinctive response was - and now the general legal requirement is - to attempt to suppress fire whenever and wherever it occurs. For the purpose of safety, there was and is no alternative to fighting fires when they burn, and the skill and bravery of the men and women engaged in dangerous hand-to-hand combat with flames has been necessary to save the lives and property of countless Californians.

As a result, the governmental approach to the fire threat historically has been to respond to the outbreak of fire and make on-the-ground firefighting a priority. The creation and the success of Smokey Bear and his maxim - "Only you can prevent forest fires" - is indicative of government's effort to raise public involvement in fire prevention for the past half century. However, this message has been largely limited to influencing individuals' conduct within the forests and to ensuring that accidents do not happen. Government has not widely advocated or pursued broader preventive activities such as fuels management.

The modern inclination to suppress all fires as rapidly as

possible has created its own problem. Over time, regular fire suppression has resulted in fewer fires. However, whereas most fires used to be small and low in intensity, they are now higher in intensity, though less frequent. By preventing smaller fires, forests and other wildlands grow unhindered for greater periods of time, resulting in the accumulation of a larger fuel load.

<u>The Fuel Load</u>

Trees and underbrush that historically burned naturally and regularly intentionally have been kept from burning for decades, accumulating as fuel for future fires. When these fires occur, and are fed by the increased fuel, they become larger and more destructive than they otherwise might have been.

Dead and downed trees cause much of the fuel load on forest and wild lands, though an overstocked inventory of healthy trees creates an even bigger fuel hazard. Most dead and dying trees are the victims of drought, insect infestation, and disease due to high tree densities - conditions caused or worsened by a lack of consistent fuels management. Debris left after logging also contributes to the problem.

In the case of living trees, fire suppression allows greater numbers of young trees to survive past the seedling stage and increases the density at higher levels than would likely occur without fire suppression. Younger trees, in turn, must compete for water and become more susceptible to attack from pests. These smaller trees become 'ladder fuels' that carry fires from the forest floor to the top of canopies or 'crowns' where fires spread quickly and intensely.

The U.S. Fish and Wildlife Service recently announced a proposed rule under Section 4(d) of the Endangered Species Act lifting incidental take prohibitions on specified non-federal lands in California and Washington habitat of the threatened Northern Spotted Owl. In so doing, the Service recognized that wildfire poses a significant risk to owl habitat and, therefore, the viability of the species. This represents a positive step.

(2) The Increasing Wildland/Urban Interface

All across California, the wildland/urban interface and mix is increasing. More Californians - retirees, vacationers, commuters and telecommuters - are living in and around the state's forests and other wildlands than at any time in our history. Today we are travelling farther and deeper into the forests to live and be away from urban centers and settled rural areas. Never before have so many people been distributed so widely throughout fire-prone areas. For example, population growth in some Sierra Nevada counties has been close to twice the state average in recent years, and projected rates of growth are among the highest in the state.

Further, many new interface dwellers possess insufficient understanding of the role that fire plays in an ecosystem or of the natural risks of living within wildlands and, thus, often do not use fireproof materials in the construction of buildings or provide adequate clearance from vegetation for their houses. This places more lives and structures at risk from fire.

Fires that historically could and would have been allowed to burn naturally with little threat to humans now pose a major threat to people and property. Fire agencies no longer have the option of letting fires burn with the knowledge that they will likely burn themselves out without posing a risk to lives and homes. Protection services are now needed in these remote locations, greatly complicating firefighting efforts and requiring additional physical and fiscal resources.

California's New Fire Strategies

The State of California recognizes that our vast and biologically diverse resources must be managed in an integrated, preventive manner that fully acknowledges that fire will, and under certain circumstances should, occur across California. The amount of fuel available to burn must be reduced, and tens of thousands of acres of forests and other wildlands should be treated annually.

Responding to this need, California is making a subtle, but fundamental, transition in the way we regard and manage the threat and occurrence of wildfires. At the same time, public policy regarding fire in forests and other wildlands is evolving in a manner that is socially, environmentally, fiscally, and economically beneficial.

Governmental agencies responsible for fire protection and natural resource management are increasingly recognizing that fire is a naturally occurring component of broad ecosystems, that wildfires are best prevented and fought through long-term fuels management and other anticipatory actions, and that the citizens of California have an essential role in realizing more effective fire protection in our state. Fire no longer is viewed as primarily a seasonal phenomenon to be combatted on the occasions and at the sites where it occurs. Instead, the emerging consensus is that fire must be managed as a component of forest and ecosystem health and that the risk of wildfire varies in the different forests and regions of the state. Thus, wildfire prevention must be integrated into and supported by other natural resource programs and policies.

The advantages of this modified approach to fire management and fire prevention include increased safety for citizens and their property, greater protection of biological diversity including threatened and endangered species, improved air quality, and reduced and more effective public expenditures.

The California Fire Strategy Team

In June 1994, the California Resources Agency initiated the establishment of the cooperative, interagency California Fire Strategy Team in order to assess the severe fire season then emerging, enhance and further the many continuing efforts to mitigate California's fire risk, and develop strategies to make greater use of limited fiscal resources for fire suppression and protection.

The Fire Strategy Team is composed of representatives of the state (including the California Resources Agency, Department of Forestry and Fire Protection, Board of Forestry, Department of

Fish and Game, Department of Parks and Recreation, California Conservation Corps, Office of Emergency Services, and Air Resources Board), the federal government (including U.S. Forest Service, Bureau of Land Management, U.S. Fish and Wildlife Service, and National Park Service), and representatives of the environmental and business communities. Many of the agencies represented on the Fire Strategy Team also are members of the California Biodiversity Council, which shares the commitment of the Fire Strategy Team to integrated, ecosystem-oriented management of California's natural resources.

Within its evolved approach to fire management, the team has given itself two broad objectives:

1) Advocate appropriate actions and programs that aid in reducing the threat of wildfire (including securing federal, state, and local funds for fire prevention; establishing cooperative partnerships and agreements to facilitate fuel reduction and management programs; and working closely with communities in fire-prone areas that possess valuable fire management experience); and
2) Disseminate for public use information about fire ecology and the long-term wildfire threat that exists in California.

These goals are being pursued collaboratively by the participating agencies in order to augment existing programs and activities, and to effectively fulfill the agencies' responsibilities under law.

Pursuit of these goals - and the overall transition in fire management - are necessitated, in general, by 1) the fact that California's primary relationship to fire in the last century has been one of reaction to its outbreak and of fighting its spread, and 2) the expanding "wildland/urban interface" in the cities and counties of the state.

While fully supportive of the heroic and effective efforts of the thousands of individuals who fight devastating fires seasonally, the Fire Strategy Team advocates minimizing to the greatest extent possible the potential for wildfires before they occur. Smokey Bear's call for personal responsibility in fire prevention must be heeded, but it also must be taken a full step further.

A new era of public/private cooperation - a series of interconnected, preventive actions not previously undertaken fully or in concert with one another - is necessary to achieve enhanced fire prevention. A brief explanation of the major policies and programs being addressed by the Fire Strategy Team follows.

New Funding Needs

Government at all levels must work together to stretch public fire management dollars farther. The federal government must provide new funding for natural fuels management as a component of fire protection. When fire emergencies occur, the need for money to support firefighters, engines, and other activities is visible and immediately apparent, and securing funding from the State Legislature and Congress is comparatively easy. However, additional funding for preventive policies and programs also must be provided. Making it a priority to reduce the fuel load in advance of catastrophic fires is crucial to the health and safety of humans, property, and biodiversity. Similarly, regions that pose the greatest fire risk should be identified and given priority in the allocation of fiscal and human resources for fire prevention.

Last year the federal government spent $950 million on wildfire suppression across the country. It is time for the federal government to commit significant new funding for pre-fire fuels management. It will pay off with healthier forests, safer conditions, and eventually, reduced spending for suppression.

Selective Fuel Removal

The thinning of forests in order to create fuel breaks and to remove dead and dying timber, as well as thick underbrush, can be very effective. This must be done in ways that minimize the impact on remaining trees and sensitive species of the ecosystem.

Wildlands best suited for selective fuel removal (in terms of ownership, topography, etc.) must be identified and prioritized. Fuel removal, when pursued in conjunction with other techniques, can both help to achieve healthy forests and reduce the likelihood of catastrophic fires, but not without significant cost. Abating the fuels crisis in our forests would create a decade of logging jobs for displaced timber workers, and over 10 or 20 years, offset long-term firefighting expenditures.

<u>**Salvaging Dead and Dying Timber**</u>

An aggressive, responsive program of removing dead and dying timber is necessary to reduce fuel and improve forest health. As an added bonus, a stepped-up salvage program would create jobs. The sooner dead and dying trees are removed, the greater their salvage market value, thereby helping to reduce the cost of forest cleanup. As trees die, their values decline, while harvest costs remain the same. For example, a dying tree with a market value of $1,000 today may be worth $500 in six months and zero after a year. Values of trees fluctuate greatly depending on the size, age, speed of deterioration, and market demand.

A prudent salvage program recognizes that a certain number of dead trees known as snags are important to help sustain wildlife, which use them for nesting, shelter, and food provided by insects that inhabit decaying trees. The California Department of Forestry and Fire Protection (CDF) recommends leaving two or three snags per acre. Hundreds of snags per acre create a fire hazard that far outweighs any benefits to wildlife.

A seven-year drought and voracious bark beetle infestation, combined with vigorous fire suppression, have left far too many dead and dying trees standing in California forests. CDF and Forest Service estimates of dead trees in California forests have escalated from 800 million board feet a year before the drought to 8-to-10 billion board feet a year, divided about equally among federal and non-federal ownerships. But in 1993, the Forest Service targeted only 450 million board feet for sale as salvage in Region 5, which includes California, Hawaii, Guam and Pacific Island Trust Territories. This is nowhere near the estimated 4-to-5 billion board feet of dead and dying timber on federal land in California.

Emergency Timber Removal

To encourage and expedite removal of dead and dying timber, the State of California provides for a 60-day emergency notice that allows private landowners to act quickly and aggressively to remove trees damaged by fire, insects, or for emergency road repairs, and avoid the usual delays involved in filing a timber harvest plan. All that's required is certification of a registered professional forester that an emergency exists.

The State of California provided for emergency notice 21 years ago in the original state Forest Practices Act governing management of non-federal forests in California that became law in 1974. After the August 1992 Fountain Fire that burned mostly private land in Shasta County in Northern California, nearly all of the burned timber was salvaged by winter.

The U.S. Forest Service urgently needs the ability to wield the same vital, efficient resource management tool. I believe the Forest Service and the Clinton administration have been negligent in failing to widely implement a more effective salvage program that increases forest health, while capitalizing on the market value of the trees. Trees are wasted at the expense of forest health and federal taxpayers, and all the while, unemployed loggers seek work.

We urge the new Congress to act quickly to ensure that the Forest Service institutes an aggressive program for salvaging dead and dying timber, for the sake of forest health and tree values.

Prescribed Fires

Planned, site-specific burning can reduce the risk of wildfire and protect public safety by largely restoring fire to its natural role in the ecosystem. Prescribed fire can duplicate the type of lower intensity fires (both natural and human-caused) that occurred before fire suppression was widely practiced and that generally did not damage a forest's ability to regenerate itself. Further, when conducted at times other than during the fire season and under controlled conditions, prescribed fire can be achieved with little adverse impact on air quality or biological diversity.

Biomass

The use of wood and agricultural material as fuel to produce energy has become an important component of improving forest health and reducing fire potential. There are currently 45 biomass plants consuming 7.5 million green tons of forestry, agriculture, and urban residues and providing 800 megawatts of power annually in California.

An expansion of this biomass program could have additional - including economic - benefits. Such an increase might entail the hiring of unemployed timber workers to clear dead trees and underbrush and transport it to biomass power plants. Because of the great fiscal constraints on all fire prevention activities, the ability of biomass to offset costs by selling energy makes it an especially attractive alternative to waste disposal that has no saleable end product. The Fire Strategy Team is committed to integrate the biomass industry and the needs of forest health. But there is a cost for gathering and delivering dead and dying trees to biomass facilities that the state alone should not bear.

SOLUTIONS

Devising and implementing a truly effective fire management strategy for California's federal and non-federal forests and wildlands requires a cooperative and coordinated program operating at the local, state, and federal levels. However, the State of California is not asking the federal government to tackle that which we are unwilling to do at home. We have undertaken pre-fire suppression programs at the state and local levels and crafted an ambitious program for fire management. But we cannot fully accomplish these goals without federal cooperation.

The State's Role

California aggressively has begun to organize and integrate the fire management and suppression roles of the federal and local governments with those of the state. We have accomplished the following:

- Established an interagency Fire Strategy Team to reduce the risk of catastrophic wildfire
- Developed plans for a statewide comprehensive hazard map

to help prioritize and reallocate resources more efficiently for pre-fire and fire suppression

- Included wildlife preservation considerations in fire strategies

- Begun to reorganize the CDF's pre-fire management strategies, including prioritizing funding for pre-fire management while carefully maintaining the full effectiveness of our firefighting forces

- Begun a public awareness campaign to encourage local cooperation

- Worked to remove liability and regulatory barriers to more efficient prescribed burning and pre-fire management

- Involved communities in developing solutions at the local level where natural fire disturbance patterns are best known and understood

- Established a communications clearinghouse to help communities, the insurance industry, land-use planners, and others develop more effective local pre-fire and suppression activities

- Kept local governments informed of our Fire Strategy Team plan through the California State Association of Counties. All 58 counties of California have endorsed our plan.

- Ensured the involvement of all stakeholders in pre-fire and fire suppression processes, including environmental, air resources, bioregional, and local community representatives

Local Government's Role

Residents of communities in fire-prone regions of the state are actively participating in preventive fire management, such as:

- Promoting and effecting prudent zoning, residential and small-scale vegetation management, and sound construction practices that limit fire risk
- Establishing bioregional, watershed, landscape and ecosystem groups of community leaders committed to coordinated resource management that incorporates concern for fire ecology
- Working together with government and non-government entities to help the state prioritize pre-fire projects in local areas
- Supporting development of biomass fuel operations and their integration with hazard reduction
- Maintaining a voice on the Fire Strategy Team through Resource Conservation Districts and other local-level resource management programs
- Working to develop communications strategies, such as educational workshops and conferences on fuels management to inform and enlist public support
- Lobbying for funding to support pre-fire programs that include fireproofing, upgrading building standards and land-use policies to accommodate fire prevention strategies, and providing adequate defensible space.

Federal Government's Role

The federal piece of the fire suppression puzzle is the most important for two main reasons: (1) national forests of California are the most at risk to catastrophic fire, and (2) the federal government owns many millions of acres.

We urge the Congress to take the following action:

- Recognize that effective, large-scale fuels treatment and fire management programs must be grounded in ecosystem management, which requires full federal participation and adequate funding

- Appropriate significant amounts of "new" funding for effective pre-fire suppression, recognizing that it will result in savings on firefighting over the next decade

- Recognize that if additional funding is not forthcoming to support pre-fire programs, the federal taxpayers will shoulder a heavier burden in the future for fire suppression, damage, and loss of wildlife and resources

- Integrate wildlife programs with fire strategies so as to avoid planning for one without considering the other. For example, the Forest Service's recently proposed California Spotted Owl program fails to consider substantive provisions for fire suppression. (The report is in draft and could be revised to include this consideration.)

- Devise pre-fire suppression programs that reduce the risk of costly liability for fires that start on federal land and escape to adjoining private property.

- Direct that the Forest Service, including the high-level interagency team recently established by Chief Jack Ward Thomas, work closely in conjunction with the states to develop new pre-fire and fire suppression programs that cut across jurisdictional and programmatic lines

- Remove legal and regulatory barriers to accomplishing these goals

- Direct the federal agencies to thoroughly integrate the entire range of the state's biological diversity -- individual forest watersheds, wildlife, fisheries, native plants, and other resources on federal, state, and private lands -- into fire prevention

- Implement an aggressive salvage policy for green, dead, and dying timber

- Recognize that immediate action is essential because of severe conditions in our forests and the increasing development in communities that abut federal lands

I appreciate having had the opportunity to present this testimony on behalf of the State of California.

- end -